TO VOTE
OR NOT TO VOTE?

To Vote
or Not to Vote?

THE MERITS AND LIMITS
OF RATIONAL CHOICE THEORY

André Blais

University of Pittsburgh Press

Published by the University of Pittsburgh Press, Pittsburgh, Pa. 15261

Copyright © 2000, University of Pittsburgh Press

Manufactured in the United States of America

Printed on acid-free paper

10 9 8 7 6 5 4 3 2 1

Library of Congress Cataloging-in-Publication Data

Blais, André.
   To vote or not to vote? : the merits and limits of rational choice theory / André Blais.
      p. cm.
   Includes bibliographical references and index.
   ISBN 0-8229-4129-5 (cloth : acid-free paper) — ISBN 0-8229-5734-5 (paper : acid-free paper)
   1. Voting. 2. Rational choice theory. I. Title.
   JF1001 .B5 2000

   324.9—dc21   00-009293

CONTENTS

PREFACE AND ACKNOWLEDGMENTS

I like existential questions. Most people may not perceive the decision to vote or not to vote to be of an existential nature. As I show in this book, however, the decision (partly) reflects deep values and conceptions of the rights and duties of individuals in society. And voting is an existential question for political science as a discipline and for the most influential theoretical framework in that discipline, rational choice.

As a social scientist, I think we should give priority to explaining everyday human behavior. Besides filing tax forms, voting is probably the most frequent political act. It is incumbent on political scientists to provide compelling explanations for why people vote or abstain. This book is meant to contribute to our understanding of the simple act of voting.

I do not seek to provide an exhaustive explanation of why people do or do not vote. As I have told my students ad nauseam, any piece of research, even huge endeavors, in the best of circumstances, throws some partial light on the phenomenon under study. I look at the voting decision from one particular perspective, that of rational choice.

My research question is whether it is possible to account for the decision to vote or to abstain from a rational choice perspective. It is, of course, impossible to address that question without understanding the factors that influence voting, and I hope that those who are interested in the act of voting per se will learn from my research. The point remains, however, that I attack the issue from a very specific point of view.

I decided to embark on this project because of my dissatisfaction with the literature on the topic. Rational choice authors admitted that there was a problem. Voting was a paradox. The literature was replete with ingenious attempts to solve the paradox. In my view, these attempts were unsuccessful, mostly because they were purely of a theoretical nature. I was struck by the absence of systematic and empirical tests of the calculus of voting. On the other hand, critics were extremely adept at pointing out the theoretical contradictions of the model but seemed too ready to dismiss it without hearing the case.

I take rational choice seriously. Otherwise I would not have devoted two years to such a project. But I also treat it as I think we should treat any paradigm, with skepticism. I have read the relevant literature, I have thought through the implications of the model, I have assembled all the evidence I could, and I have reached a conclusion on the contribution of rational choice to the understanding of why people do or do not vote. I hope that readers will find my analysis rigorous, my judgment fair, and my final verdict compelling and (why not?) reasonable.

I have incurred many debts from that project. The study would not have been possible without a Killam award provided by the Canada Council and without the support of the Université de Montréal and its Department of Political Science.

I have had the privilege of benefiting from the generosity and insight of numerous colleagues. First, Édouard Cloutier, who, as department chair, enthusiastically supported the project. Second, Robert Young. It was during one visit to Western Ontario, in the midst of free-ranging conversations about politics and political science, that the study was conceived. And it was at the end of lengthy and stimulating exchanges with him that the original survey questionnaires were constructed. Working with Bob has been a great learning and gratifying experience. I have also received extremely helpful comments on preliminary drafts of various chapters from Michael Lewis-Beck, Gary Cox, and Richard Niemi.

I have had the pleasure of working with bright students. They have performed countless analyses of the data sets. More important, I have had valuable conversations with them about the implications of the findings and about the rationality of voting. These students are the main reason why being a university professor is so much fun. I thank Agnieszka Dobrzynska, Miriam Lapp, Martin Turcotte, and Kim Thalheimer for their competent work and thoughtful reflections.

Finally, special thanks to the colleagues at the cafeteria table for sustaining my intellectual curiosity, and to Suzanne, for supporting my struggle with existential questions and for (gently) insisting all the way that it is my civic duty to vote.

INTRODUCTION

Is It Rational to Vote?

This book addresses a simple question: What makes people decide to vote or not to vote? As we shall see, the answer may not be as simple as the question.

I start with a simple model, the rational choice model. According to it, a citizen makes up her mind to vote or not through a simple calculus. She decides to vote if, in her view, the benefits of voting are greater than the costs; if, on the contrary, the costs are greater than the benefits, she decides not to vote.

The "calculus of voting" model was initially developed by Downs (1957) and extended by Riker and Ordeshook (1968). According to this model, the voter must first estimate the expected benefits of voting. In order to do this, she must first determine what she could potentially gain by voting rather than not voting. This means that, in the simple case of a plurality election with only two candidates, she must determine what difference it makes to her whether candidate A or B is elected. If it makes no difference, the potential benefit is nil. The greater the perceived difference, the greater the potential benefit.

In the model, however, it is not the potential benefit but the *expected* benefit that matters. The rational individual must ask what the chances are that her vote will decide whether her preferred candidate wins or loses. If her preferred candidate is sure to win, the expected benefit of voting is nil, since her candidate will win whether she votes or not. If her preferred candidate is sure to lose, the same logic applies; the outcome of the election is the same whatever she does and the expected benefit of voting is nil.

The rational individual must thus determine the probability that her vote will be *decisive,* that is, that it will determine whether her candidate wins or loses. Suppose a plurality election with 100,000 electors and two candidates. If the individual expects that 70,000 electors (besides herself) will vote, she must determine the probability that candidate A and candidate B will each receive 35,000 votes. In that case, it is her vote that will decide which candidate wins.[1]

How high is that probability? It depends on two factors. The first is the number of voters. The probability of a tie vote is much higher if there are only 1,000 voters than if there are 100,000. The second is the closeness of the election. The closer the race between the two candidates, the higher the probability of her casting the decisive vote. But however close the race, the probability of her vote being decisive is very small when the electorate is large. In the above example with 70,000 voters, even in a close race the chance that both candidates will get exactly the same number of votes is extremely small.

In the rational choice model, the expected benefit of voting equals the benefit (B) she would gain from having her preferred candidate win rather than lose, multiplied by the probability (P) of her casting the decisive vote. This expected benefit is necessarily extremely low since P is bound to be extremely small.

Having estimated the expected benefits of voting, the rational individual calculates the costs (C). These costs are essentially opportunity costs. They represent the time it takes to get registered, go to the poll, and mark the ballot, but also the time required to obtain and digest information about the candidates in order to determine which candidate the individual prefers. Since time is a scarce resource, not voting would allow her to do something else (including just relaxing), and it is that something else that she loses when she decides to vote.

The standard conclusion that is reached from the application of such a model is that in an election with a large number of voters the rational citizen decides not to vote. The cost of voting is small, but the expected benefit is bound to be smaller for just about everyone because of the tiny probability of casting a decisive vote.

The Paradox of Voting

Unfortunately for the theory, many people do vote. In fact, a clear majority vote in the most important elections, where the number of voters is extremely large and the probability of casting a decisive vote is minuscule. Hence the paradox of voting.

This paradox is the starting point of my inquiry. The calculus of voting model, in its simplest form, does not seem to work. Does this mean that the model is basically flawed and ought to be dismissed as completely inappropriate? Or does it need to be amended to provide a more compelling explanation of voting behavior? Or is the model, in its simple or more complex form, a valid though partial one that remains useful even though it cannot account for the frequency of voting?

In order to address these questions, I need to review the amendments to the model that have been proposed by rational choice theorists. Seven amendments have been proposed. Citizens may decide to vote: (1) to maintain democracy; (2) out of a sense of duty; (3) because they are risk-averse and wish to avoid the regret of having not voted and seeing their preferred candidate lose by one vote; (4) because they reason that other citizens will not vote and that their own vote could become decisive; (5) because group leaders and politicians make it easy for them to vote; (6) because the cost of voting is practically nil; and (7) because they find it rational not to calculate benefits and costs when both are very small.

The first amendment was proposed by Downs (1957), who argues that the rational individual decides to vote in order to avoid the collapse of democracy. She will reason that everyone else will go through the same cost-benefit calculus and will come to the conclusion that it is rational to abstain. But when no one votes, democracy is threatened, and she benefits from the existence of democracy and has a long-term interest in its maintenance. As a consequence, she is willing to bear the cost of voting in order to insure against the potential breakdown of democracy.

As Barry (1978, 20) has pointed out, such an amendment cannot salvage the theory.[2] The fact is that one ballot cannot make any difference to the maintenance or collapse of democracy any more than a single vote can determine the outcome of an election. The rational citizen should calculate *expected* benefits, which entails multiplying long-term benefits attached to the maintenance of democracy by the probability that her vote will be decisive in whether democracy survives or not. Since that latter probability is practically nil, expected benefits are minuscule and she decides not to vote.

This does not mean that sustaining democracy is not a major inducement for many people to vote. The point is rather that such a motivation is inconsistent with the rational choice approach, which assumes that the individual calculates the benefits and costs of a given action for *herself,* not for the whole community. If we observe that people vote to preserve democracy, we will have to conclude that their behavior does not conform to the predictions of rational choice theory.

The second amendment comes from Riker and Ordeshook (1968). They argue that citizens can also derive psychic gratifications from the act of voting: the satisfaction of "complying with the ethic of voting," of "affirming allegiance to the political system," of "affirming a partisan preference," and of "affirming one's efficacy in the political system," as well as the enjoyment of going to the polls and deciding how to vote. Riker and Ordeshook call such satisfaction D, or citizen duty.

From this perspective, two kinds of benefits are associated with voting: investment (or instrumental) and consumption benefits. The investment benefits are those linked to the outcome of the election: they are the difference in utility the individual attaches to having candidate A win rather than candidate B. These investment benefits are contingent on her casting the decisive vote, and the expected benefit is bound to be exceedingly small. The consumption benefits—the sense of satisfaction one derives from fulfilling her sense of duty—are not contingent: she feels satisfied when she votes, whatever the outcome of the election. She consumes voting for its own sake.

It makes sense to believe that some people vote because they feel it is their duty to do so. The question is whether such an account fits with the rational choice model. It depends on whether one adopts a broad or a narrow notion of rationality.

There are those who adhere to a broad definition of rationality. From that perspective, rationality "is nothing more than an optimal correspondence between ends and means" (Tsebelis 1990, 18). What counts as rational behavior has nothing to do with a person's objectives or motivations (the theory has nothing to say about them); all that is needed is that the individual behaves so as to maximize her utility, whatever that utility happens to be.

This broad perspective has one major advantage and one important drawback. The advantage is one of open-mindedness. Those who use a broad definition of rationality do not have to impute specific goals to individuals; they do not even have to presume that they are egocentric. The drawback is the risk of tautology. It can always be argued that a person chooses to do something because she believes the rewards for performing that act outweigh the costs. At this point, the theory cannot be falsified and loses any predictive power.[3]

Downs was keenly aware of this potential pitfall. He opted for a narrow definition of rationality. In his model, he made a specific assumption about the goal pursued by citizens: "The political function of elections in a democracy . . . is to select a government. Therefore rational behavior in connection with elections is behavior oriented toward this end and no other" (Downs 1957, 7). He made an exception to that rule later on in the book, when he stated that citizens would want to vote in order to maintain democracy. He was consistent, though, in his unwillingness to resort to social or psychological gratifications. Otherwise, "all behavior whatsoever becomes rational because every act is a means to some end the actor values. To avoid this sterile conclusion, we have regarded only actions leading to strictly political or economic ends as rational" (276).

In my view, the risk of tautology is a very serious one, and the theory cannot be saved by merely adding sense of duty as an explanatory variable. The same verdict is reached by most analysts (see, especially, Barry 1978, 16; Mueller 1989, 351; Green and Shapiro 1994, 52). It is more fruitful, I believe, to construe psychic gratifications such as citizen duty as factors that fall outside the rational choice model. In short, the fact that some people vote out of a sense of duty does not support or invalidate the model. The core of rational choice has to be, as Downs has cogently argued, investment benefits, not consumption ones.

There are two possibilities to distinguish. The first is that all the story is in D and that the decision to vote is hardly affected by B, P, and C. Those who adhere to a broad definition of rationality would insist that the theory is confirmed. My response is that sense of duty can be incorporated in alternative schools of thought. It is dubious whether finding that people vote out of a sense of duty corroborates rational choice more than other interpretations. If all the story is in D, we should conclude that the rational choice model is not very helpful.

The second possibility is that people vote on the basis of each of B, P, C, and D. Such findings would confirm the validity of the rational choice model. In other words, rational choice does not rule out the presence of psychic gratifications, but these gratifications should not be used as positive testimony of the model. The crucial test is whether B, P, and C matter.

Ferejohn and Fiorina (1974) provided the third attempt to rescue the model. They argue that we ought to distinguish between decision-making under risk and decision-making under uncertainty. Under the former, probabilities of different outcomes are taken into account; under the latter, such probabilities are unknown or unknowable. Uncertainty calls for different sets of rules. Ferejohn and Fiorina examine one specific procedure, the minimax regret criterion, under which one calculates the loss associated with various outcomes without estimating the probabilities of these outcomes and chooses the option that minimizes regret.

The minimax regretter thus asks herself how much regret she would have if, on the one hand, she voted and her vote was not decisive, and, on the other hand, she did not vote and her preferred candidate lost by one vote. If the latter regret is greater than the former, she decides to vote. This procedure boils down to dropping the P from the calculus of voting. Since P cannot be known, the individual does not take it into account. She votes if B is greater than C and abstains if it is the reverse.

The great advantage of the minimax regret procedure is that it predicts more turnout than the rule of maximizing expected utility. Is it convincing? Two major criticisms have been made about this interpretation. The first concerns its assumption about P. Critics (see especially Beck 1975, 918; Aldrich 1993, 259) point out that even though it may be exceedingly difficult to calculate the exact value of P, it is easy for the rational citizen to figure out that in a large electorate it is minuscule. She is able to give a rough guess of what P is likely to be, and the expected utility model thus applies.

The second criticism is that the minimax regret strategy leads to bizarre behavior. Suppose ten candidates are running in a constituency. According to the minimax regret criterion, the individual should envisage the worst scenario, that the candidate she likes the least wins, without taking into account her probability of winning, and vote if this regret outweighs the cost of voting. Thus the presence of an extremist candidate should substantially increase turnout, whatever the degree of support she enjoys (see Mueller 1989, 353).

The predictions of minimax regret are even more problematic in other contexts. Minimax regretters should not cross the street to buy a newspaper because there is a possibility that they could be killed by a car while doing so (Beck 1975, 918). Ferejohn and Fiorina (1975, 921; 1974, 535) have responded that different decision rules may be used in different contexts (and by different types of individuals). But when it comes to deciding whether to vote or not, should not the minimax regretter consider the possibility that she could get killed by a car going to the polls? Is not the appropriate decision, then, not to vote?

Minimax regret does not appear to be a satisfactory solution to the paradox of voting. Ferejohn and Fiorina, however, raise an important question about what counts as a rational calculus. The standard assumption in the literature is that the rational citizen attempts to maximize expected utility, and thus multiplies B by P. Is it possible that people do not seek to maximize, that they merely attempt to satisfice (Simon 1955)? What should we think of an individual who calculates B and P and gives each some weight in her decision whether to vote or not without multiplying them, as the theory implies? Should such a person count as rational or irrational? Even though minimax regret does not solve the puzzle, perhaps other approaches could.

The fourth potential solution to the paradox of voting is of a game-theoretical nature. The reasoning is the following: "If each rational voter were to decide not to vote because her vote has too small of a chance of affecting the outcome, and all voters were rational, no one would vote. But then any one voter could determine the outcome of the election by voting. . . . The greater the number of other voters I expect will rationally abstain, the more rational it is for me to vote" (Mueller 1989, 351–52).

This raises the possibility that P may not be as minuscule as initially assumed once we take into account the fact that many other citizens will go through the same reasoning. Under some assumptions, some equilibrium solutions entail "substantial" turnout (Palfrey and Rosenthal 1983; Ledyard 1984).

This line of reasoning is not very convincing. As Palfrey and Rosenthal (1985, 73) have demonstrated, "in the presence of a relatively small degree of strategic uncertainty . . . voters with positive net voting costs will abstain." The bottom line is that the rational individual who is not certain that others will abstain, abstains.

Even though the argument is not compelling, it conveys an important message. We should not take for granted that P is perceived to be minuscule by all electors. We should not rule out the possibility that some people vote because they overestimate the probability that their vote could be decisive.

The fifth attempt to salvage rational choice theory is to shift the focus from the individual citizen to politicians and/or group leaders. Politicians attempt to mobilize voters and make it as easy as possible for their supporters to vote and by doing so reduce the cost of voting (see especially Aldrich 1993). A similar line of reasoning is pursued with respect to group leaders. Uhlaner (1986, 1989a, 1989b, 1993) provides the basic model. In the model, politicians and group leaders make bargains in which the latter promise increased support from the group and the former stake issue positions favorable to the group's interests.

The problem with such an approach is that it is not clear why it becomes rational for the individual citizen to vote. True, politicians and group leaders can reduce the cost of voting and can even increase the potential benefit. The point remains, however, that P is bound to be minuscule and that expected benefits do not outweigh the cost. These models must thus rely on other consumption benefits.[4]

Aldrich argues for an expanded notion of D, which makes the model very close to being tautological, notwithstanding his claim to the contrary. Uhlaner resorts to what she calls "relational goods." In her model, group members identify with the group and wish to vote to receive approval from other group members or simply because voting makes them feel truly like members of the group. In this case as well, sense of duty plays a crucial part, though the driving force is a sense of duty toward the group, not toward the whole community. This approach leads to the same problems discussed with respect to the introduction of the D term. There is no inherent contradiction in including consumption benefits, but the real hard test of the rational choice model is whether investment benefits matter.

The sixth amendment boils down to arguing that the cost of voting is practically nil. This argument has been put forward most straightforwardly by Niemi (1976). Niemi makes two points. First, the cost of voting, at least in a national election, is extremely low. It takes very little time to vote, and because it is taken out of leisure time many people must perceive very little opportunity cost.

Though we have no hard evidence on this question, Niemi is probably right in asserting that the opportunity cost of voting, on election day, is very low. He fails to consider, however, the opportunity cost of getting the information to decide how to vote. And, most important, however low the costs are, they are unlikely to be smaller than expected benefits, which are bound to be minuscule. But what if people perceive no cost at all in deciding how to vote and in going to the polling station? It is thus crucial to determine whether citizens feel there are costs involved. I have alluded to the possibility that people vote because they overestimate P. Another possibility is suggested here, that they vote because they underestimate C.

The second point made by Niemi is that we should also consider the cost of not voting. This is "the psychological cost of saying 'no' when asked whether or not you voted" (Niemi 1976, 117). But why should there be a psychological cost in admitting abstention? Perhaps because one feels a moral obligation to vote, in other words, a sense of duty. Niemi wants to distinguish satisfaction from duty, the D term, but the distinction is far from clear. If someone fails to fulfill her duty, should she not feel guilty, in the same way she should feel proud and satisfied if she has voted?

Niemi also raises the issue of social pressure. If someone wants to avoid embarrassment from admitting not voting, it is probably because she perceives voting to be a social norm, which relatives and friends expect her to obey. The presence of social pressure indicates that many people believe it is right to vote and wrong not to vote, and such beliefs presumably flow from the view that it is the duty of every citizen to vote. There is social pressure because most people feel voting is a duty.

It could be, of course, that the individual does not personally think that she has a duty to vote, but that she is aware that most people in her community believe that it is a citizen's duty to vote. She might then reason that her personal reputation would suffer if people knew she did not vote and decide that it is in her best interest to vote.

This is an intriguing hypothesis. Whether people actually engage in such complex reasoning remains to be shown. My point again is not that such psychic gratifications are inconsistent with a rational choice perspective but that they do not suffice to confirm the model. In other words, it must be shown that concerns for one's reputation overcome the initial propensity to abstain because of the expected investment benefits and costs. The voting decision must depend at least partly on B, P, and C.

This leaves one final amendment to the model, which was first proposed by Barry (1978) and is reiterated, in a different fashion, by Aldrich (1993).[5] The argument is simple: "It may well be that both the costs and the (suitably discounted) benefits of voting are so low that it is simply not worth being 'rational' about it" (Barry 1978, 23). Such a position acknowledges the limits of the model: it cannot explain why so many people vote. At the same time, it makes the point that this is no reason to conclude that the rational choice model is of no use; it might be extremely fruitful in accounting for other kinds of behavior, where costs and benefits are higher.

Green and Shapiro (1994, 58–59) criticize this position on two grounds. First, they point to specific cases, such as those "100,000 African-Americans who persevered through the intimidation and poll taxes of the Jim Crow South and voted in the national elections of the 1950s," where the cost of voting could not be construed as low. This is not a very compelling objection, as the phenomenon to be explained is the decision to vote or not to vote in an open democratic system.

The second objection is more serious. The argument is an arbitrary domain restriction because "there is nothing in rational choice theory that specifies the level at which costs or benefits are sufficiently small to render the theory inapplicable." The concern is that it is an easy way to salvage the theory when its predictions do not fit with reality, to decide, ex post, that it does not apply to the particular phenomenon being examined. Yet it is consistent with the basic postulates of the model to argue that, since costs are involved in calculating benefits and costs, it may be rational, when the stakes are low, not to calculate. In other words, we would expect rational choice theory to perform better when the stakes are high than when the stakes are low.

This last amendment salvages the rational choice model but asserts its inapplicability to the simplest political act, voting. A somewhat different position, put forward by Aldrich (1993), argues for differences of degrees. Rational choice would apply to all phenomena, including voting, but it would perform less well for low-stakes behavior.

There have been several attempts, some of them quite imaginative, to solve the paradox of voting. I have discussed the merits but also the limitations of each of these attempts. This discussion leads me to make two general observations. First, most amendments have consisted of adding psychic gratifications to the core model. My position is clear and simple: there is nothing wrong in adding consumption benefits, but there is a great risk of tautology in doing so. The prudent solution is to focus on the core elements of the model and to determine whether they do affect the decision to vote. If people are inclined not to vote because they feel that the expected investment benefits are just too low but psychic gratifications such as sense of duty tend to overcome this inclination, I would conclude that rational choice offers a useful interpretation. If, however, the decision to vote is almost entirely accounted for by the sense that it is a moral obligation to vote, then it seems to me that we should conclude that the model should be discarded.

Second, it must be kept in mind that from the perspective of rational choice, it is individuals' perceptions that matter. Most analysts take for granted that P is minuscule and that C is not. But we have precious little evidence on how people actually perceive the probability that their vote could be decisive and the costs of voting. If P is overestimated and/or if C is perceived to be minuscule, then it might be rational to vote. I present in chapters 3 and 4 new evidence on these perceptions.

Is It Marginally Rational to Vote?

Grofman, in a spirited defense of rational choice, makes two points. First, we should not expect rational choice to explain everything. As he puts it,

> the view that a rational choice model requires that the only element to be allowed in a voter's utility function is the expected short-run instrumental benefit from voting is like saying that the only way we can use rational choice models to predict eating behavior is to limit people's motivations for their food choices to a single parameter—for example, an instrumentally rational choice of a consumption bundle that maximizes expected longevity. (1993, 94)

Rational choice provides partial explanations of human behavior, and the theory should be judged on its ability to account for some aspects of human behavior, neither more nor less.

Grofman's second point is that the theory should be tested for its capacity to predict *changes* in turnout rather than turnout per se. This second point is related to the first. According to Grofman, there are rational and nonrational reasons to vote (and to abstain). Because of this complexity of factors, it is impossible to predict the absolute level of turnout. It is possible, however, to predict that if P or B increases in an election or C decreases, turnout will increase. Conversely, "turnout is lower when the weather is

bad, when the barriers to registration are steep, and in elections whose outcomes few care about" (Grofman 1993, 102). As a consequence, Grofman
claims, the model is quite capable of doing what it is supposed to do: account for change at the margin.

I shall determine in later chapters whether this empirical claim is well
established. For the time being, I am concerned with the epistemological
relevance of the argument. According to Grofman, we should test a theory
according to what it tells us about dynamics. In the case at hand, the prediction of rational choice is that if P or B increases, turnout should increase,
and that if C increases, turnout should decrease. The paradox of voting pertains to the level of turnout and is not really relevant as a test of the theory.

In my judgment, Grofman is partially (marginally?) right and partially
wrong. It must be pointed out that the rational choice model itself is not
couched in terms of marginal change. The model takes the individual as the
basic unit of analysis and identifies the basic parameters of her decision to
vote or not to vote. It is thus consistent with the model to look at the decision that is made at a given point in time by each individual, and by the ag-
gregation of these individuals. I agree with Grofman, however, when he asserts that the mere fact that many individuals vote does not necessarily invalidate the model. It could be that for these individuals nonrational reasons
for voting trump rational reasons for abstaining. I would add, though, that if
we were to observe that an overwhelming majority of people vote, we
would have to conclude that rational reasons for abstaining had a very "marginal" impact. Evidence about the level of turnout may not be conclusive,
but it is nevertheless suggestive.

Furthermore, it is not enough to show that changes in B, P, or C lead to
changes in turnout or that individuals who are different with respect to
these variables have a different propensity to vote. It is also imperative to
take into account the strength of the relationship. If we observe that turnout is reduced when it rains but that it is reduced by only one percentage
point, we may be inclined to conclude that the contribution of rational
choice is indeed very marginal.

Grofman is right in insisting that we should not be looking solely or even
primarily at the level of turnout. The fact that so many people vote does not
require that the rational choice model be discarded. But this suggests that
the model provides, at best, a partial explanation of voting. This opens the
possibility that there are more powerful theories, and that, marginally
speaking, we would be better off exploring alternative avenues.

What Are the Alternatives?

There are four major alternative explanations for why people vote. These are the resource and mobilization models, and what could be called the psychological and sociological interpretations. I will briefly review each of them and indicate how they converge on and diverge from rational choice. It should be kept in mind that these alternative models usually have as their explanandum political participation writ large, and not voting per se.

The first model, laid out most explicitly by Verba, Schlozman, and Brady (1995; see also Brady, Verba, and Schlozman 1995), focuses on *resources*.[6] According to this model, the decision to participate hinges on three main resources: time, money, and civic skills. The more free time, money, and civic skills one has, the more likely one is to participate. Of course, the impact of these various resources varies from one mode of participation to the other. Money, in particular, is less relevant to voting than to other forms of participation.

The fact that time is a crucial resource and that the more free time one has, the more likely one is to vote, is quite consistent with rational choice. Here, the two models clearly converge. The convergence is more ambiguous when it comes to skills. Brady, Verba, and Schlozman (1995, 273) assume that "citizens who can speak or write well or who are comfortable organizing and taking part in meetings are likely to be more effective when they get involved in politics." It is possible to construe these skills as lowering transaction and information costs (290, n. 10), and to infer that the resource model emphasizes costs.

What distinguishes the two models? The resource model assumes that most of the action is in the cost section of the equation, whereas the rational model pays as much attention to expected benefits. In the resource model, people are inclined to vote if the cost is not too high; in the rational model, they weigh benefits and costs and vote only if they perceive the latter to be smaller than the former. The resource model seems to fit better with the facts (it predicts high turnout) but appears unduly partial: it focuses entirely on costs, taking benefits for granted.[7]

The second model, which stresses the role of *mobilization*, has been put forward most forcefully by Rosenstone and Hansen (1993). Their starting point is that the only way to explain political participation is to "move beyond the worlds of individuals to include family, friends, neighbors, and co-workers, plus politicians, parties, activists, and interest groups" (23). These social networks exert pressures on people to behave as members of a group rather than as isolated individuals.

Politicians have an interest in getting out the vote. They mobilize individuals, especially through social networks, and induce them to vote. They do so by reducing the cost of voting: they drive people to the polls on election day and provide cheap information about the issues.

This second model, with its emphasis on social networks, overlaps to some extent with the sociological interpretation discussed below. It also has some obvious connections with the resource model, since both pay particular attention to how the cost of voting can be reduced. The two models seem complementary, as the resource model may better explain who participates, while mobilization may do a better job of explaining when (Rosenstone and Hansen 1993, 20).[8]

The problem is that, from the perspective of rational choice, the paradox of voting lies with the expected benefit, not with the cost. Even if a party drives an individual to the poll, it will take her some time to vote and it is difficult to imagine that this "waste" of time is worth less than the minuscule probability of casting a decisive vote.

Rosenstone and Hansen argue that social networks help to overcome the paradox of participation because they "create solidary rewards and bestow them, selectively, on those who act in the public interest." How do they do so? Basically through social pressure. Rosenstone and Hansen assume that "people want to be accepted, valued, and liked" and that they accept being mobilized (that is, participating) in order to be well esteemed. The mobilization model, then, pays particular attention to the impact of social pressure, a factor that has also been mentioned by some rational choice authors (1993, 23).

The third model, or explanatory mode, looks at *psychological involvement*. Bluntly put, it asserts that the more interested a person is in politics, the more likely she is to participate in general and to vote. The main problem with this line of explanation is that it appears trivial. The hypothesis is eminently plausible, but it is not clear what it tells us.

Despite its apparent superficiality, the psychological involvement interpretation should not be discarded too hastily. From the perspective of rational choice, the relationship between political interest and voting is not straightforward. If someone is highly interested in politics, she is likely to perceive the stakes of an election to be great: her B will be high. Her information costs might also be lower, but not her P. The bottom line is that from a rational choice perspective, the relationship between interest and voting should be only modest.

This indicates that when we want to explain why some people vote and others don't, it is imperative to take into account individuals' overall level of political interest. For the same reason that people are unlikely to watch basketball if they don't like the game, they are less likely to vote if they hardly follow politics.

The last approach to be considered is what I would call the *sociological* interpretation, which most directly challenges the rational choice model. It challenges the basic assumption that the individual acts in her own (narrowly defined) self-interest. According to the sociological interpretation, individuals behave as members of a collectivity.

We should distinguish two strands within this school. The first strand stresses the role of social pressure: people vote because their friends or relatives tell them to vote. The second strand assumes that citizens are concerned with the well-being of their community as much as with their own self-interest. The concept of *sense of duty* encapsulates such a view. People vote because they feel it is a moral obligation for citizens in a democracy to vote. The reference point is not the self but the whole community. The individual feels she owes it to society to perform the act of voting, whatever the personal benefits and costs.

This review of other theoretical explanations for why people do or do not vote leads to three main conclusions. First, there is some overlap between the various theories. Rational choice, resource, and mobilization theories all insist on the costs of participation and they converge on the conceptualization of these costs. Second, the trademark of rational choice is in the P term. It is the sole theory to include it as a key variable. This is why the paradox of voting emerges only within a rational choice perspective. Consequently, determining whether P matters should be a priority when it comes to assessing the fruitfulness of the model. Third, the concept of sense of duty, which is often added in rational choice models, is also quite consistent with a sociological interpretation. Finding that people vote out of a sense of duty should not be construed as supporting a rational choice perspective.

Outline of the Book

The objective of my inquiry is to come to a comprehensive understanding of why people do or do not vote and to assess the capacity of the rational choice model to account for the simple act of voting. At first sight, rational choice seems to be on shaky ground in explaining voting behavior. As we have seen, the various attempts to solve the paradox of voting are not completely satisfactory. All these attempts, however, have been made at the theoretical level. We need to look more closely at the empirical evidence and determine whether there is at least partial support for the model.

I start with the presumption that rational choice is unlikely to provide a fully satisfactory theory of turnout. Perhaps, though, the theory provides some helpful insights into why some people are more likely to vote than others and why turnout is higher or lower in certain places and times.

The inquiry proceeds in the following fashion. In the first two chapters, I leave aside rational choice theory to focus on the "facts" of turnout. I address two questions. First, *where* and *when* is turnout higher and lower? I look at cross-national variations in turnout and identify the factors that seem to explain why it is higher in certain countries than in others. Second, *who* votes and who does not? To answer this question, I look at the socioeconomic variables that are most closely associated with turnout at the individual level.

I start with empirical observations because rational choice theory has been sharply criticized for its lack of empirical rigor (Green and Shapiro 1994). It is a useful antidote to forget about the theory temporarily and to immerse ourselves in the data, to assemble as much information as possible about the patterns of voting at the micro and macro levels, and to digest that information before returning to the big theoretical questions.

In chapters 3 to 5, I proceed to a full empirical assessment of the rational choice model. As already indicated, the core elements of the model are B, P, and C. I also include D, sense of duty, that is often incorporated into rational choice models but whose status is ambiguous since it is consistent with a sociological interpretation, and level of political interest, an extraneous taste factor that should be taken into account as a control variable. The test of the theory is whether each of B, P, and C has an independent effect on the decision to vote.[9]

I start with P, in chapter 3. As just mentioned, P represents the most interesting and problematic contribution of rational choice model. It is thus crucial to determine whether people believe that their vote could be decisive and whether perceptions of P affect the propensity to vote. I review the empirical literature on this question and provide new evidence.

I address the cost term in chapter 4. In the extreme, if the cost of voting is perceived to be nil, it could become rational to vote. Do citizens perceive any cost at all in the act of voting and/or in the process of finding out which candidate they should support? How much impact do these perceptions have on the decision to vote or not to vote?

Chapter 5 deals with sense of duty. Do people feel they have a moral obligation to vote? How strong is that feeling? Where does it come from? And are people who believe it is their duty to vote insensitive to expected benefits and costs?

Chapter 6 goes beyond the simple act of voting and considers the broad issue of rationality and participation. Not voting is part of a larger social phenomenon, the propensity to "free ride." While turnout and the capacity of rational choice to explain it are the central focus of this book, it is imperative, at the end of our journey, to adopt a broader perspective. We need, especially, to determine whether rational choice does a better job of explaining other kinds of behavior, especially those with higher stakes. When the costs of participation are higher, is the propensity to free ride higher? Could it be that, as Barry has argued, rational choice does not perform well for voting because people do not make cost-benefit calculations when the stakes are too low?

In the conclusion, I render my verdict on why people do or do not vote, and on the capacity or incapacity of rational choice to provide a compelling explanation of turnout.

CHAPTER 1

When and Where Are People More Likely to Vote?

My empirical inquiry starts with a macroscopic perspective. My first question is: how many people vote in a typical election? The higher the turnout, the more acute the paradox of voting. But there may be few typical elections. We need to know in which elections turnout is highest and lowest, and why. I examine cross-country variations in turnout for national elections, identify countries with particularly high and low levels of turnout, and test a number of hypotheses about the sources of variations.

I then look at over-time variations, first determining whether turnout in a given country remains relatively stable or changes substantially over time. I also check whether there has been an overall trend for turnout in national elections to increase or decrease in the recent past. Finally I look at contextual factors that could account for the ebb and flow of turnout in a given country.

The focus of my analysis, and of the literature on the topic, deals with variations in turnout in national elections. In the last section of the chapter, I consider variations in turnout for different types of elections and make three kinds of comparisons. First, is turnout higher or lower in subnational elections for local, regional, or provincial governments? I then look at presidential systems and inquire whether people are more inclined to vote in presidential or legislative elections. Finally, I compare turnout for elections and for referenda, and indicate what this suggests about the factors that induce people to vote or to abstain.

Cross-National Variations

In which countries is turnout highest and lowest and why? Powell (1980, 1982, 1986) was the first to address the question directly. Powell analyzed voting turnout in twenty-nine democratic countries.[1] He considered average turnout in national legislative elections between 1958 and 1976:[2] "turnout" is defined as the percentage of citizens of eligible age who vote. Median turnout among these twenty-nine countries is 77 percent. In a national election, typically, three out of four citizens vote. Most people vote in most elections, so that the paradox of voting holds not only for many people but for the great majority of them.

Powell finds two major direct determinants of cross-national variations in turnout. The first is what he calls "mobilizing voting laws." Turnout tends to be higher in those countries where the government assumes responsibility for voter registration than in those where it is up to citizens to get registered on the electoral list. Turnout is also higher in those countries where voting is made compulsory by law. The second factor is the existence of a party system with strong party-group alignments. The stronger these attachments, the higher the turnout. Powell (1982, 116) suggests two reasons for such a relationship. First, when parties are clearly linked to social groups, it is easier for citizens to sort out the major issues of the election. Second, the groups themselves can play an important role in mobilizing voters.

Powell identifies two more distant factors that affect voting. He finds that turnout is higher in more economically developed countries. Economic development facilitates turnout only indirectly, because it sustains a strong party system. The same pattern holds for what Powell calls "representational constitution." Turnout is lower among countries with a presidential executive and with majoritarian electoral laws. This is so only because such countries are less likely to have a strong party system and to have mobilizing voting laws.

In his analysis of the determinants of turnout Powell excludes Switzerland, which has the lowest average turnout among all the countries examined.[3] Powell argues that Switzerland is a very special case of deliberate demobilization of party competition by the four major parties, which have agreed to share among themselves the collective executive, thus making electoral outcomes virtually meaningless. He also refers to the frequent use of referenda and to the strong role of cantonal governments as additional reasons for the low turnout.

At almost the same time as Powell, Crewe (1981) also searched for explanations of variations in national turnout. Crewe examines mean turnout between 1945 and 1980 in twenty-seven countries. The measure of turnout is the percentage of those registered who vote. Average turnout in those countries is 79 percent.

Crewe explores the sources of cross-national variations. He does not present a multivariate analysis of the determinants of turnout but rather confines himself to bivariate correlations. He distinguishes four types of factors: legal, organizational, electoral systems, and micropersonal.

With respect to legal factors, Crewe notes, as does Powell, that turnout is higher when voting is compulsory. He also looks at various procedures used in a number of countries to facilitate voting, such as advance voting, postal voting, and proxy voting, but notes that they are unlikely to make a noticeable difference. There is an exception: the United States is the only country where citizens must take the initiative to become registered, which has to be an important reason for the low turnout in that country.

Crewe then turns to organizational factors. He focuses, as Powell does, on the party system and finds a strong correlation between turnout and close party-group alignments. He also observes that turnout is slightly higher in proportional representation (PR) systems but notes that this may be because PR produces stronger party-group alignments. On this, he is, of course, in close agreement with Powell. He finally looks at personal factors. He reports no correlation between mean turnout and enrollment in postsecondary education or GNP per capita. The latter result contradicts Powell's finding that economic development (indirectly) increases turnout.

Jackman (1987) also examines the sources of cross-national variations in turnout. His analysis covers nineteen industrial democracies and deals with average turnout, expressed as a percentage of the total population, in the 1960s and 1970s. Average turnout in his sample is 78 percent.

Jackman finds turnout to be related to five variables: compulsory voting, nationally competitive districts, electoral disproportionality, multipartyism, and unicameralism. The findings concerning compulsory voting and national districts replicate those of Powell.[4] The other results are new. Turnout emerges as higher in unicameral countries and more proportional systems, and declines as the number of parties increases. Jackman interprets these findings as indicating that the decisiveness of elections and of the government that ensues matters. When there is a second house, the lower house has less power and there is less at stake in the election. Similarly, minor parties find it difficult to get their candidates elected in highly disproportional systems: their supporters may feel that their votes will be wasted, and, as a result, may be inclined to abstain. Finally, the more parties there are, the greater the probability of a coalition government, in which case elections play a less decisive role in the formation of government, and citizens have less incentive to vote.

Jackman notes that turnout is atypically low in two countries, Switzerland and the United States, and creates dummy variables for these two countries, as Powell had done in his 1986 piece. He reports the results with and without these two dummy country variables. He shows that the relationships hold even without these dummies, except for electoral disproportionality. Finally, what was perhaps Powell's most important finding, the impact of party-group alignments, is not replicated by Jackman. He points out two problems with this variable—it refers to different groups in different countries and it does not include all relevant groups—and indicates that it did not come out significant in his analysis.

Jackman and Miller (1995) expanded the initial analysis in two different ways. First, they apply the same model to voter turnout in the 1980s, adding three more countries—Greece, Portugal, and Spain—and show very similar results. Second, they argue that cross-national variations in turnout cannot be explained by cultural factors. As they point out, the cultural interpretation would predict that turnout would be lower in new democracies. They indicate that turnout in these countries is about what the institutional model would have predicted. Furthermore, they find no significant relationship, at the macro level, between turnout and such aspects of political culture as life satisfaction, trust in people, or political discussion rates.

The next piece of research to be considered is Blais and Carty (1990). Their data cover twenty countries and include the 509 elections held in those countries up to 1985.[5] Average turnout (measured as the percentage of those registered who voted) in these elections is 78 percent. They find turnout to be higher with compulsory voting, when the population is smaller, and in PR systems. The result concerning size of population is at odds with that of Powell, who found no relationship.

But the most important finding concerns the impact of electoral systems. Blais and Carty conclude that, everything else being equal, turnout is seven percentage points lower in a plurality election, and five points lower in a majority one than under PR. This result is consistent with those of Powell and Jackman, who both stress the role of electoral laws. That consistency, however, may be more apparent than real.

First, Blais and Carty operationalize electoral laws in a different way. They look at electoral formulas and compare plurality, majority, and PR systems. Powell and Jackman resort to a variable called "nationally competitive districts," which encapsulates the effects of the electoral formula and of district magnitude. Blais and Carty argue that these two effects should be distinguished.

Second, although Blais and Carty find PR to foster turnout, they are unable to explain why. Most important, they report that electoral disproportionality is not related to turnout, contrary to Jackman's finding.[6]

Third, they include dummy variables for one country (New Zealand) where turnout is particularly high and for three countries (Switzerland, Sweden, and Norway) where it is substantially lower than expected. Reanalysis of the data indicates that if these dummy variables are dropped, differences among electoral formulas are no longer significant.

For his part, Black (1991) examines the determinants of cross-national variations in turnout (as a percentage of registered) among eighteen countries in the 1980s. As in the other studies, he uses a dummy variable for Switzerland,[7] and compulsory voting comes up as the most significant variable. The other results, however, tend to be weak. Most important, turnout is not statistically associated with electoral systems, degree of disproportionality, or unicameralism.[8]

Finally, Franklin (1996) looks at average turnout (as a percentage of registered) in twenty-nine countries over the 1960-95 period. He finds that turnout is affected positively by the degree of proportionality of electoral outcomes and by the presence of compulsory voting, postal voting, and Sunday voting, and negatively by the number of polling days.

What is to be concluded from this review of previous studies? The main conclusion is that there are few robust findings, and that the existing literature does not provide us with a solid explanation of why turnout is higher in some countries than in others. There is one consistent result: turnout is substantially higher in countries with compulsory voting. Apart from that, the results vary from one study to the other. Powell reports that turnout is higher in countries with strong party-group alignments; Jackman finds no relationship. Powell indicates that turnout is higher in more economically advanced democracies; Crewe finds no relationship. Jackman concludes that turnout is higher in countries with nationally competitive districts and low degree of disproportionality; Blais and Carty seem to converge when they report that turnout is higher in PR systems, but the convergence is only apparent since they are unable to sort out the intervening variables through which this occurs, and, most important, the relationship depends entirely on the treatment of New Zealand as a deviant case; and Black finds no significant relationship between electoral systems and turnout.

I present below a new analysis of the determinants of cross-national variations in turnout that builds on previous studies.[9] I will examine those factors that these studies suggest are potentially important. The analysis, however, departs from previous ones in a number of ways, the most important being the sample of countries.

The literature has been weak in its justification of which countries to include or exclude. I assume that we are interested in turnout in *democratic* elections. This raises the question of how to assess which elections are democratic and which are not. Powell (1982) pays close attention to the question. He defines five criteria that ought to be met for a country to be deemed to be democratic, reviews the work of other scholars, and comes up with a list of twenty-nine countries that in his view meet his criteria. The approach is interesting. It is not entirely satisfactory, however, because Powell relies on the work of others who did not have exactly the same criteria and because there is disagreement among authors about a number of cases, the inclusion or exclusion of which appears somewhat arbitrary.

Crewe (1981), like his coauthors in *Democracy at the Polls,* examines those countries that are classified by Freedom House as "free" or "partly free" and that have a population of more than three million. Size is not a meaningful criterion; the editors of *Democracy at the Polls* themselves acknowledge that they eliminated small countries only to keep the number manageable.

Jackman, for his part, chose to confine his analysis to nineteen industrial democracies (twenty-three in the 1995 article with Miller), but it is not clear why nonindustrial democracies are excluded. The reason could be that he wanted to compare countries as similar as possible in socioeconomic characteristics in order to better isolate the impact of political institutions. The downside is that the number of cases is small, and that the results may be sensitive to the inclusion or exclusion of cases[10] and may not be generalized to the universe of democracies. Moreover, this approach does not permit for the measurement of the potential effect of social factors, such as economic development, on turnout. Clearly, if we wish to arrive at a comprehensive understanding of the sources of cross-national variations in turnout, we should look at as many cases as possible (see King, Keohane, and Verba 1994) and exploit the richness of data provided by the process of democratization.[11]

The analysis to be presented below includes all democratic countries. Like Crewe, I rely on Freedom House to characterize a country as democratic or not. Freedom House has been rating "political rights" and "civil liberties" in each country of the world for every year since 1972. It is the most systematic evaluation of the degree of democracy, an evaluation whose validity is judged to be quite acceptable (Bollen 1993). Its index of democracy is now widely used in cross-national research (see, especially, Burkhart and Lewis-Beck 1994; Helliwell 1994).

Freedom House gives every country a rating ranging from 1 to 7 on political rights and on civil liberties, a rating of 1 corresponding to maximum degree of freedom, and a rating of 7 to the minimum degree. I use only the "political rights" scale, which focuses on the fairness of elections. I construe ratings of 1 and 2 as reflecting a "satisfactory" level of democracy; Freedom House itself collapses ratings of 1 and 2 as indicating a "free" country (Gastil 1979, 24).

The second major methodological issue concerns the measure of turnout. My measure of turnout is the percentage of those registered on the electoral list who cast a vote. This is the measure reported in official documents and used by Crewe (1981), Blais and Carty (1990), Black (1991), and Franklin (1996). Powell (1980, 1982, 1986) and Jackman (1987) rely on a different measure, the percentage of the eligible population who cast a vote.

The latter measure has one major shortcoming, which has to do with the procedure for estimating the size of the eligible population. The eligible population is assumed to be the voting-age population. As Powell acknowledges, however,

> [I]n most democracies voting eligibility is limited to citizens. Population figures . . . usually include noncitizens resident for a year or more. Countries vary substantially in the percentage of such aliens. . . . Unfortunately, we do not have good data on percentage of residents . . . who are aliens of voting age, and cannot systematically adjust our turnout data to remove them. (1986, 40)

Likewise, Black (1991, 71) reports that "the entire exercise required drawing some overly simplified assumptions."

I believe it is more prudent to use the percentage of those registered on the electoral list who cast a vote. This measure raises a serious problem only in the United States. The appropriate solution, it seems to me, is to treat the United States as a special case. The analysis presented below excludes the United States.

I distinguish three kinds of factors that may affect turnout: the socioeconomic environment, the institutional setting, and the party system (for a similar approach, see Powell 1982). I start with the first bloc and examine which socioeconomic variables influence electoral participation. I then look at the impact of various institutions, controlling for the socioeconomic environment. I finally assess whether the party system has an additional independent effect.

I have been able to obtain data on turnout in 324 democratic elections for the national lower house held in 91 different countries, between 1972 and 1995 (see appendix A, Democratic Elections, 1972–95, and Participation Rate).[12] Mean turnout in these elections is 77 percent.

The Socioeconomic Environment

I first consider six socioeconomic variables: *GNP per capita, growth of GNP per capita, average life expectancy, degree of illiteracy, size* and *density of population* (see appendix B for a detailed description of the variables). Perhaps the most important hypothesis to be tested is that economic development fosters turnout. The reasoning underlying this hypothesis is that economic development makes people more informed and engaged in the political process (Powell 1982, 37). Powell does find a positive correlation between economic development and turnout but Crewe (1981) and Jackman (1987) report no such correlation. The discrepancy could stem from the fact that these authors have examined different samples of countries. There is also the possibility that the relationship is nonlinear, that what is required for a good turnout is a modest level of economic development but that above a certain threshold more development does not have any additional effect on turnout. I use the standard and most simplest measure of economic development, *GNP per capita.*[13]

It may be not only the level of economic development that matters but also the economic conjuncture at the time of the election. Rosenstone (1982), in particular, argues that economic adversity depresses turnout, because it disrupts the kind of social relationships that nurture political participation and induces people to withdraw from politics and focus on their personal concerns.[14] The indicator of economic conjuncture is the *increase or decrease in GNP per capita* in the election year, compared to the previous year.

The larger social environment must also be taken into account. It is possible that the most important condition for people to get engaged in political life is that their basic needs be met (see, especially, Moon 1991). I have included one standard indicator of quality of life, *average life expectancy.*

As Verba, Schlozman, and Brady (1995) show, voting is the least demanding form of political activity, and the one that is least dependent on the possession of civic skills. Still, some minimum of skill may be required, and they note that those with little linguistic skill are less likely to vote. It seems reasonable to predict that high *levels of illiteracy* tend to depress turnout.

I also consider *size of population.* The relationship between community size and turnout is far from being unambiguous (see Dahl and Tufte 1973). Verba, Nie, and Kim (1978) show, however, that once individual socioeconomic characteristics are controlled for, communal activity is more prevalent in smaller settings,[15] in good part because social and political life tends to be more impersonal and distant in larger communities (Verba and Nie 1972). I expect to replicate the finding of Blais and Carty (1990) that turnout tends to be higher in smaller countries.[16]

The last variable is *population density*. I assume that turnout tends to be lower in less densely populated countries, because people who are dispersed over a wide territory are less likely to be exposed to group pressure to vote (Lipset 1981) and are more difficult to mobilize.

The analysis includes dummy variables for each of the continents (Europe is the reference category). These variables reflect the impact of other unmeasured factors that may be specific to a given geographic area. Lijphart (1992, 940), especially, has highlighted "the remarkable clustering of the four basic forms of democracy in four geographical-cultural world regions." This raises the possibility that political culture differences, regarding whether voting should be construed as a civic duty, for instance, lead to variations in turnout in different regions of the world. I also have a dummy for Switzerland, a clearly deviant case that has been treated as such in all previous studies.

Table 1.1 presents the findings. Three variables emerge as significant. First, GNP per capita. This finding confirms that of Powell: economic development does seem to facilitate turnout. It is the economic structure, however, and not the economic conjuncture, that seems to matter, as higher economic growth does not appear to foster turnout.

Table 1.1. The Determinants of Electoral Participation: Socioeconomic Environment (OLS Regression)

Variables	OLS Coefficient	(SE)
North America	−8.85***	(2.09)
South America	−0.69	(2.63)
Africa	−6.59**	(3.31)
Asia	−2.89	(2.50)
Oceania	9.69***	(2.48)
Average life expectancy	−0.13	(0.21)
Density	6.69*	(4.02)
GNP per capita (log)	3.32***	(0.97)
Growth of GNP per capita	0.03	(0.09)
Illiteracy rate (squared)	−0.002**	(0.001)
Size of population (log)	−2.72***	(0.88)
Switzerland	−36.81***	(4.82)
Constant	71.62	(13.76)
N	298	
Adjusted R^2	0.40	

* Significant at the .10 level
** Significant at the .05 level
*** Significant at the .01 level

Economic development is not all that matters. Even at a given level of economic development, turnout is affected by the degree of illiteracy.[17] This confirms that a minimum degree of literacy is almost a prerequisite to a good turnout. Turnout is also higher in smaller countries. This confirms the view that smaller countries are able to arouse a greater sense of community, which itself fosters a higher turnout. The results also indicate that turnout is somewhat higher in more densely populated countries. The relationship, however, is not very strong.

Finally, turnout varies substantially across continents, even when other socioeconomic factors are controlled for. It is particularly high in Oceania and particularly low in Africa and North America. It would seem that un-measured factors that are specific to the political culture of these continents affect voting participation.

The Institutional Setting

Voting is a political act, and turnout depends not only on social and economic factors but also on how elections and politics more broadly are structured. The second stage of the analysis looks at the effect of political institutions.

Five institutional features appear particularly worthy of examination. Three have to do with the *electoral law*. First, in a number of countries the law makes it compulsory to vote. As previous studies have shown (Powell 1982: Jackman 1987; Blais and Carty 1991; Black 1991; Franklin 1996), I expect *turnout to be substantially higher in countries where voting is compulsory*. Second, the voting age varies from one country to another. As young voters are less inclined to vote, in good part because they have been less exposed to politics (see, especially, Wolfinger and Rosenstone 1980), the hypothesis is that the *lower the voting age, the lower the turnout*.

Finally, the electoral system. The standard assumption is that *turnout tends to be higher in PR systems*, for any (combination) of the following three reasons (see Blais and Carty 1990). First, PR is a fairer system, and because it is fair people feel less alienated and are thus more inclined to vote. Second, PR increases the number of parties and the variety of options among which people can choose. Third, PR makes elections more competitive: as there are many members to be elected in each district, most parties have a chance to win at least one seat, and as a consequence they attempt to mobilize electors throughout the country. I have created dummy variables for *PR, plurality, majority,* and *mixed* systems.

The next institutional characteristic pertains to the decisiveness of elections. As Jackman (1987) has argued, we would expect turnout to be higher, the more important the election, that is, the greater the power that is bestowed on those elected. The data pertain to the election of the national lower house. The more powerful the national lower house, the more decisive the election, and the higher the expected turnout.

The lower house may have to share power with other institutions, specifically with an upper house, a president, or other subnational institutions. Unfortunately, we do not have standardized data on the relative power of these institutions. We may assume, however, that they are more likely to be powerful if they are directly elected.

We may thus predict that turnout will be lower if there is an elected upper house or president or if the country is a federation. This prediction holds only if subnational, presidential, or upper house elections are not held at the same time. The presence of an elected upper house, for instance, matters only if the lower and upper house elections are *not* held at the same time: in such a context, the lower house election can be construed as being less decisive, and turnout could be lower. If the two elections are held at the same time, the situation is equivalent to there being one house.

I constructed a variable that takes into account the presence and the timing of subnational, upper house, and / or presidential elections. The variable takes the value of 1 if there are no such elections or if the elections are simultaneous (the lower house election in both cases is decisive), of 0.5 if there is one other election (subnational, upper house, or presidential) that is held nonsimultaneously, and of 0 if there are two (the election can then be construed as being less decisive).[18] The prediction is that *turnout is higher when the election is more decisive*.

Finally, I have included *degree of democracy* as an additional institutional variable. All elections included here are considered to be democratic but the degree of democracy may vary from one case to another. More specifically, some countries obtained a score of 1 on political rights, and others a score of 2. In the latter case, elections can be construed as somewhat less democratic, and possibly less decisive, thus yielding a somewhat lower turnout.

The findings are reported in table 1.2. Compulsory voting seems to boost turnout by 11 points. This is consistent with the results of previous studies. Likewise, the lower the voting age, the lower the turnout: everything else being equal, turnout is reduced by almost two points when the voting age is lowered one year. This is not surprising given the lower propensity of younger electors to vote.

The results also indicate that turnout is affected by the decisiveness of elections: everything else being equal, turnout is reduced by six points when lower house elections are least decisive. These findings are consistent with those reported by Jackman.

The results concerning electoral systems are interesting. Column 1

Table 1.2. The Determinants of Electoral Participation: Socioeconomic Environment and Institutional Setting (OLS Regressions)

					B (SE)					
	Column 1		Column 2		Column 3		Column 4		Column 5	
Variables										
North America	-8.74***	(2.40)	-9.13***	(2.41)	-7.61***	(2.21)	-8.28***	(2.07)	-7.94***	(2.41)
South America	-5.70**	(2.40)	-4.82**	(2.36)	-4.35*	(2.34)	-7.63***	(2.46)	-8.34***	(2.63)
Africa	-3.88	(3.13)	-4.38	(3.14)	-3.20	(2.99)	-10.10***	(3.43)	-9.12**	(3.70)
Asia	-2.80	(2.54)	-3.14	(2.53)	-1.88	(2.44)	-4.53*	(2.40)	-3.77	(2.48)
Oceania	9.97***	(2.99)	9.74***	(2.99)	9.79***	(2.73)	8.27***	(2.33)	9.28***	(2.87)
Density	7.49**	(3.60)	7.51**	(3.58)	8.13**	(3.55)	4.51	(3.67)	3.68	(3.78)
GNP per capita (log)	3.51***	(0.81)	3.36***	(0.82)	3.37***	(0.81)	2.99***	(0.90)	2.79***	(0.92)
Illiteracy rate (squared)	-0.001*	(0.001)	-0.002**	(0.001)	-0.002**	(0.001)	-0.0004	(0.001)	-0.001	(0.001)
Size of population (log)	-2.98***	(0.83)	-2.98***	(0.82)	-3.02***	(0.81)	-3.08***	(0.83)	-2.82***	(0.84)
Switzerland	-35.17***	(4.32)	-35.22***	(4.31)	-35.19***	(4.31)	-35.50***	(4.25)	-35.53***	(4.25)
Compulsory voting	11.72***	(1.58)	11.73***	(1.58)	10.59***	(1.46)	10.55***	(1.43)	10.82***	(1.51)
Degree of democracy	-0.13	(1.52)	-0.24	(1.52)	-0.21	(1.52)	-0.47	(1.59)	-0.86	(1.59)
Decisiveness	4.71**	(2.14)	4.84**	(2.13)	5.93***	(2.04)	5.80***	(2.13)	5.65***	(2.12)
Voting age	1.28**	(0.55)	1.25**	(0.55)	1.33**	(0.55)	1.69***	(0.57)	1.84***	(0.57)
Plurality	-0.52	(1.93)	-0.62	(1.92)						
Majority	-6.19*	(3.14)	-6.18**	(3.12)						
Mixed	1.62	(2.20)								
Mixed 2			-4.91	(3.35)						
PR					2.66*	(1.59)			5.88**	(2.87)
Disproportionality							-0.19**	(0.08)	0.05	(0.14)
Disproportionality × PR									-0.46**	(0.21)
Constant	31.33	(13.61)	33.54	(13.65)	28.63	(13.75)	30.41	(14.08)	24.47	(15.12)
N	298		298		298		271		271	
Adjusted R²	.54		.54		.54		.54		.54	

* Significant at the .10 level
** Significant at the .05 level
*** Significant at the .01 level

shows that turnout is slightly higher in PR than in plurality, majority, or mixed systems: the differences, however, are small and not significant, except in the case of majority systems. Among mixed systems, we may distinguish those that are corrective (such as Germany), where PR seats are distributed so as to compensate weaker parties that do poorly in single-member seats, and those where PR and plurality or majority are simply combined without any corrective (Blais and Massicotte 1996). It could be argued that the former are basically PR systems. When they are coded as such, the differences between PR and mixed systems become somewhat larger, though still not statistically significant (column 2).

The main difference, then, is between PR (including corrective mixed systems), on the one hand, and all other systems, on the other hand. Column 3 establishes that, everything else being equal, turnout is three points higher in PR systems. The difference is small but statistically significant.

It could be argued that what really matters is not the type of electoral system as such but the overall degree of disproportionality it produces. There are a great variety of PR systems (Blais and Massicotte 1999), which diverge substantially in the degree to which they represent smaller parties. In column 4, I substitute the degree of disproportionality for the dummy PR system. It can be seen that the variable is statistically significant.

Column 5 combines the electoral system and the degree of disproportionality. It shows that a fully proportional system, in which seat shares correspond exactly to vote shares, yields a turnout that is six points higher than a non-PR system. The impact is reduced, however, as the degree of disproportionality increases: for a deviation index of 13, the difference vanishes entirely.[19] And disproportionality does not have any independent impact in non-PR systems, which is what we would expect since the degree of disproportionality observed within non-PR systems is likely to depend more on the distribution of the vote than on the mechanics of the electoral law.

Finally, turnout does not appear to be lower in countries where political rights are not as well protected. This may not be surprising. Most of these cases are new democracies and the stakes in these countries are probably as high as in well-established democracies.

It is also interesting to note that economic development and size of population still affect turnout, even after institutional variables are included. Turnout is lower in countries with a lower GNP per capita and a larger population for reasons that have little to do with institutional factors. The same pattern holds for continental variations.

The Party System

In a legislative election, electors are offered to make a choice among parties and candidates. We would expect turnout to depend to a good extent on the kind of choice people are offered, and that choice is very much structured by the party system. The party system stems in part from the socioeconomic environment and the institutional setting, but we may suppose that it has a life of its own.

I consider two aspects of the party system. First, the number of parties. It can be predicted that *the greater the number of parties, the more choice electors are offered, and the higher the turnout* (Blais and Carty 1990). Counterarguments, however, have to be considered: the greater the number of parties, the more complex the system, and the more difficult it can be for electors to make up their mind. Moreover, the greater the number of parties, the less likely it is that there will be a one-party majority government. Elections that produce coalition governments can be construed as being less decisive, because the composition of the government is the product of backroom deals among the parties as much as of the electoral outcome per se (Jackman 1987). This suggests the opposite hypothesis that *the greater the number of parties, the smaller the probability of a one-party majority government and the lower the turnout.*

There are conflicting results on these dimensions. Jackman (1987) finds that multipartyism depresses turnout and infers that this is because multipartyism produces coalition governments. Blais and Carty (1990) report a similar pattern though the relationship is curvilinear, but they do not find that turnout is increased when there is a one-party majority government. Finally Black (1991) observes no link between number of parties and turnout.

I use three measures of the number of parties: the number of parties running in the election, and the effective number of electoral and legislative parties (see Laasko and Taagepera 1979). I also include a dummy variable that equals 1 for all those elections when one party wins a majority of the seats.

The second dimension of the party system is competitiveness. The expectation is that *the closer the election, the higher the turnout.* The measure of closeness is the gap (in vote shares) between the leading and the second parties.

Table 1.3 presents the findings. It can be seen that closeness does matter. When there is a gap of 10 points between the leading and the second parties, turnout is reduced by 1.4 points. It should be stressed that I am measuring only the impact of overall systemic competitiveness. An election may be

Table 1.3. The Determinants of Electoral Participation: Socioeconomic Environment, Institutional Setting, and Party System (OLS Regression)

Variables	OLS Coefficient	(SE)
North America	-9.47***	(2.29)
South America	-8.22***	(2.35)
Africa	-8.35**	(3.41)
Asia	-2.44	(2.26)
Oceania	6.55**	(2.71)
GDP per capita (log)	2.85***	(0.68)
Size of population (log)	-2.58***	(0.80)
Switzerland	-34.71***	(4.23)
Compulsory voting	10.39***	(1.48)
Decisiveness	7.44***	(2.06)
Voting age	1.80***	(0.56)
PR	4.87***	(1.79)
Disproportionality × PR	-0.34**	(0.14)
Closeness	-0.14**	(0.06)
Number of parties (log)	-9.02**	(3.66)
One-party majority government	-0.26	(1.96)
Constant	31.88	(13.39)
N	276	
Adjusted R^2	0.57	

** Significant at the .05 level
*** Significant at the .01 level

very close at the national level but not close at all in a number of districts, or vice-versa.[20] These results underestimate the true impact of closeness.

As for the number of parties, the results confirm Jackman's finding that turnout tends to be reduced when the number of parties increases.[21] Some have suggested that a greater number of parties makes it less likely that a one-party majority government will be formed after the election, and that this makes elections less decisive. If such a view is valid, it should follow that elections in which one party gets a majority of seats tend to produce a higher turnout. The "majority government" variable does not become significant. Not too much should be made of this null finding, however. That variable is strongly correlated with the number of parties and electoral systems, and this collinearity may make it impossible to sort out its specific impact.

It seems difficult to make sense of the results concerning the negative effect of the number of parties without the "majority government" hypothesis. The only alternative interpretation would be that complexity increases with the number of parties. If it were so, however, turnout should decline substantially when the number of parties gets very high. But turnout is only slightly reduced when the number of parties moves from ten to fifteen. The important difference is between a system with very few parties, two or three, and one with six or seven. The most plausible explanation for that difference is that in the former case people are more likely to feel they are electing the party that will form the government.

It is interesting to note, finally, that the introduction of these party system variables does not substantially affect the coefficients of the other variables. The fuller equation does help, however, to account for the slightly higher turnout observed in PR systems. Three reasons have been adduced to predict a higher turnout in PR systems: a fairer system, more competitive elections, and more parties. The data indicate that fairness and competitiveness do foster turnout. As for the number of parties, the relationship is negative: PR rarely produces one-party majority governments, thus slightly reducing turnout. PR thus has both positive and negative effects, with the overall impact being a slightly positive one.

These new results are more satisfactory than those obtained by Blais and Carty (1990). They indicate that, everything else being equal, turnout is three points higher in PR than in non-PR systems. This estimate is lower than that of Blais and Carty, but in this study I am able to explain why PR modestly increases turnout.

Finally, dummy variables for the continents remain significant. It would seem that even taking into account the socioeconomic environment, the institutional setting, and the party system, turnout is particularly high in Oceania and particularly low in America and Africa. Further analysis would be required to determine if these variations reflect, as I suspect, differences in political culture.

Turnout in the national lower house election is thus affected by a great number of factors: economic development, degree of illiteracy, population size and density, the presence or absence of compulsory voting, voting age, the electoral system, the closeness of the electoral outcome, and the number of parties.

Fluctuations within Countries

Does turnout fluctuate substantially over time in a given country? The simplest way to answer that question is to calculate how much turnout in a given election differs from turnout in the previous election in the same country. Among my sample of democratic elections, I have 228 elections for which it is possible to compute such a difference.[22] The average absolute difference is four percentage points. Typically, turnout increases or decreases by four points from one election to the next. Fluctuations are relatively small, especially compared to cross-national variations. The overall standard deviation in our sample of democratic elections, for instance, is 14 percentage points. Turnout varies much more over space than over time.

Even though turnout does not fluctuate wildly over time, it could be going down or up slowly but consistently. The data indicate that there is a trend: on average, turnout at a given election is 1.35 points lower than turnout at the previous election. That trend, however, is not consistent over the whole period: the mean decrease in turnout is 0.3 point in the 1970s, 0.7 point in the 1980s, and 3 points in the 1990s. It is only in the last decade that turnout seems to be dropping substantially in most countries.

Short-term fluctuations in turnout may not be large, but they are not negligible either. How can we account for them? Only a few studies have looked at the factors that make turnout increase or decrease over time. With one exception, all these studies have dealt with the American case.

The first study to be published is by Arcelus and Meltzer (1975). They examine turnout in U.S. congressional elections from 1896 to 1970 and focus on the impact of economic variables. They find unemployment, inflation, and income not related to turnout. Their study, however, suffers from a number of weaknesses. Most important, they do not control for the low turnout observed in war years nor do they include turnout in the previous election.[23]

Settle and Abrams (1976), for their part, look at turnout in presidential elections from 1868 to 1972. They report that turnout is positively related with campaign and government spending as well as with media use, and negatively correlated with per capita GNP, the winning majority, and the presence of a third-party candidate. The results are suspect for the same problems noted in the Arcelus/Meltzer study: no control for turnout in the previous election or for the war years.

Rosenstone (1982) provides the first systematic analysis of changes in turnout in American elections. He focuses on the impact of the economy but is careful to include the lagged dependent variable, changes in the legal environment, and the war periods. He performs two separate analyses, one for the 1948–80 period and one for the 1896–1980 period. He shows that economic adversity depresses turnout.

The most recent study is by Radcliff (1992), who also considers the impact of the economy on turnout but argues that this impact depends on the extensiveness of security programs designed to protect citizens against economic downturns. He first examines national elections for twenty-nine countries from 1960 to 1987. He finds social security to increase turnout and to interact with economic growth: economic downturns increase turnout at low and high levels of welfare spending but depress it at intermediate levels. The same pattern emerges in a longitudinal analysis of turnout in the United States from 1896 to 1988.

This is an impressive study, with intriguing results. However, some of the findings, especially those concerning the effect of previous elections, are perplexing. In the twenty-nine-country analysis, the moving average of the two previous elections does not come out significant, which is surprising given what we know about the relative stability of turnout. Furthermore, Jackman and Miller (1995, appendix B, n. 3) have failed to replicate his findings for industrialized countries, which casts some doubt on the robustness of the results.

In short, we know very little about the determinants of short-term fluctuations in turnout. I propose the following study. As the objective is to understand why turnout fluctuates from one election to another within a country, it is appropriate to confine the analysis to a set of countries where there have been a good number of democratic elections. For that purpose I have selected those countries that have been deemed to be democratic (a rating of 1 or 2) every year on the Freedom House political rights scale. Twenty-seven countries meet this criterion. I have been able to assemble data on nineteen of them.[24] In each country, I examine turnout for all elections held since 1960. I focus on two independent variables: the impact of the economy—the variable that has been the most extensively studied in the literature—and competitiveness.

The dependent variable is the change in turnout in a given election, compared to the previous election. I have a total of 201 elections[25] in the nineteen countries, and the mean change in turnout is −0.7 percent. The implication is that over a period of thirty years (and about ten elections), turnout has decreased by about seven percentage points overall.

I have nine independent variables. The first two have already been mentioned: the economic conjuncture and closeness.[26] The next four are changes in the institutional setting. I created dummy variables for the 1971 Swiss election, the first election in which women had the right to vote in that country, for all those elections in which the voting age was reduced (Age);[27] for the Dutch 1971 election, in which voting was no longer compulsory (Not compulsory); and for the 1986 and 1988 French elections, in which the electoral system went from majority to PR and back to majority (Electoral system).[28]

The seventh variable is meant to capture the overall downward trend that has taken place during the period. Close inspection of the data suggests that the trend is recent: turnout started to decline only in the 1980s. I created a variable (Trend [1980]) that equals 0 until 1980 and 1 to 15 from 1981 to 1995.

The last two variables concern special cases. Turnout declined by seven points in the Finnish 1975 election, because for the first time residents outside Finland had the right to vote. As most of them did not vote, this depressed turnout.[29] Finally, turnout was particularly low in France in 1962, 1981, and 1988: the 1962 legislative election had been preceded by two referenda, while the 1981 and 1988 legislative elections came only one month after the presidential election. I created a variable (France/Other) to take account of these exceptional circumstances.[30]

Table 1.4 presents the findings. The results confirm that turnout is affected by the economic conjuncture. Electoral participation declines when there is a slowdown of the economy. The relationship is modest, and it emerges only in the longitudinal analysis, based on more reliable measures of economic performance.

The results also confirm that turnout increases slightly when the election is close. The coefficient is weaker than the one produced in the cross-sectional design, probably because this is a tougher test, where country-specific factors are better controlled for. The bottom line, however, is that in both tests closeness fosters turnout.

The other findings confirm that changes in the electoral law can affect

Table 1.4. The Determinants of Short-Term Fluctuations in Turnout (OLS Regression)

Variables	OLS Coefficient	(SE)
Per capita GDP	0.22**	(0.08)
Closeness	0.50	(0.34)
Switzerland 1971	-7.19**	(2.89)
Age	-0.19	(0.29)
Not compulsory	-15.93***	(2.89)
Electoral system	0.86	(2.50)
Trend (1980)	-0.09*	(0.05)
Finland 1975	-7.29**	(2.93)
France/Other	-8.54***	(1.47)
Constant	-0.83**	(0.39)
N	197	
Adjusted R^2	0.36	

* Significant at the .10 level
** Significant at the .05 level
*** Significant at the .01 level
Note: For a description of variables, see text.

turnout. Abolishing the obligation to vote seems to reduce turnout by 16 points. In France, the introduction of PR in 1986 appears to have slightly increased turnout.[31] In Switzerland, turnout declined substantially in the first election where women had the right to vote. Finally, there is some suggestion that lowering the voting age may slightly reduce turnout. Readers will note that the relationship here is weak, much weaker than in the cross-sectional design. Again, the longitudinal test is a more stringent one, and I am inclined to have greater confidence in its results. It would seem that lowering the voting age has only a minor impact on electoral participation.

I noted earlier that turnout had dropped since 1980. Table 1.4 shows that this drop cannot be accounted by the other variables included in the model. It seems that most recent elections have produced lower turnouts. The difference is not huge but is not negligible either. The implication is that by the 1990s turnout typically declined by one point in every election. If that trend were to persist, average turnout could decline from 77 percent to 67 percent over the next thirty years (assuming an election every three years).

Turnout in Different Types of Elections

Until now, the analysis has centered on national legislative elections. There are different types of elections, and it is interesting to know in what kind of election turnout tends to be lowest and highest, and why.

The first obvious comparison to be made is between national and local elections.[32] Rational choice theory would predict that turnout will be higher in elections where the stakes and the probability of casting a decisive vote are the greatest. We will see to what extent variations in turnout between national and local elections can be explained in those terms.

The second comparison is between legislative and presidential elections. In many democracies the head of the state is directly elected by the people. It is useful to know whether turnout in presidential elections tends to be lower or higher than turnout in legislative elections. Is it the case, in particular, that turnout is higher for the institution that has more power?

Finally, I look at turnout in referenda, which can be construed as quasi-elections. They resemble elections in the sense that people are invited to express their preferences. They are different in a number of ways, perhaps the most important being that they focus on one or a small set of issues. Do these differences affect turnout in a systematic way?

Variations Across Levels of Governments

Is turnout higher or lower for local elections? The evidence shows that it is lower. There is no systematic data set that would allow us to compare turnout in local and national elections in all democratic countries over a given period of time. Table 1.5 summarizes all the evidence I have been able to assemble from many different sources in as many countries as I could.[33]

Table 1.5 shows that the median difference in turnout for local and national elections is 13 percentage points. We can surmise that if turnout in a typical national election is 77 percent, it is 64 percent in a local election. It amounts to a relative difference of 17 percent.

Why is this so? Two main interpretations are usually provided (see, especially, Morlan 1984 and Hoffmann-Martinot 1992). The first is that national governments are deemed to be more important than local ones. The only piece of evidence I have been able to obtain on this comes from *The Civic Culture* (Almond and Verba 1965). Table 1.6 presents the distribution of re-

Table 1.5. Comparing Turnout in Local and National Elections

Country	Period	Average Turnout		Difference
		Local	National	
Denmark[a]	1970–79	72.8	87.1	-14.3
Finland[a]	1956–79	75.3	79.7	-4.4
Ireland[a]	1956–79	59.8	74.5	-14.7
Netherlands[a]	1970–79	70.0	83.5	-13.5
Norway[a]	1956–79	74.5	81.6	-7.1
United States[a]	1956–79	31.0	50.0	-19.0
West Germany[a]	1956–79	76.9	88.4	-11.5
Britain[b]	1973–92	41.8	75.6	-33.8
Japan[c]	1952–63	86.0	74.6	+11.4
Belgium[d]	1976–91	94.2	93.8	+0.4
France[e]	1945–95	75.5	77.2	-1.7
Israel[f]	1977–93	58.1	78.7	-20.6
Iceland[f]	1982–94	84.5	88.7	-4.2
New Zealand[g]	1962–93	48.9	87.2	-38.3

[a]*Source:* Morlan (1984), table 1. For Germany, the figure is the median turnout among nine of the ten Länder (excluding West Berlin).
[b]*Source:* Rallings and Thrasher (1993). The figure for local elections corresponds to the median turnout for London boroughs, Greater London Council, metropolitan counties and boroughs, and English shire counties and districts.
[c]*Source:* Richardson (1973). The figure for local elections corresponds to the median turnout for local (mayor) elections.
[d]*Source:* Ackaert, de Winter, Aish, and Frognier (1992).
[e]*Source:* Quid 1995 (I thank Jean-Dominique Laffay for providing the information).
[f]Information provided by Henry Milner.
[g]*Source:* New Zealand, *Local Authority Election Statistics* (I thank Jack Vowles for providing the information).

Table 1.6. The Relative Importance of National and Local Governments

	Great effect	Some effect	No effect	Mean effect
United States				
National	43%	46%	11%	0.69
Local	36	54	10	0.63
Great Britain				
National	34	42	24	0.55
Local	24	53	24	0.51
Germany				
National	43	36	19	0.61
Local	36	45	20	0.59
Italy				
National	32	42	26	0.53
Local	24	49	28	0.49

Source: Almond and Verba (1965, 46–47).
Note: Mexico, which was not democratic at the time of the study, is dropped. "Other" and "Don't Know" responses are excluded from computations. The mean effect is obtained by giving a score of 1 to "great effect," of 0.5 to "some effect," and of 0 to "no effect."

Question wording:
"Thinking now about the national (local) government in _____, about how much effect do you think its activities, the laws passed, and so on, have on your day-to-day life? Do you think they have a great effect, some effect, or no effect?"

sponses obtained in the United States, Great Britain, Germany, and Italy in the late 1950s, when people were asked how much impact they perceived national and local governments to have on their lives.[34]

Table 1.6 shows that in every country the national government is indeed seen as having a greater effect on day-to-day life. The differences, however, are not large. While a greater percentage imputed a great effect to the national government in each country, the percentages indicating no effect are almost identical for the two levels of government in each instance. The perceived lower stakes of local elections could thus account for some of the gap in turnout, but the data suggest that the perceived importance of the level of government is only one part of the story.

The second factor that is often referred to as an explanation of lower turnout in local elections is the lesser degree of "politicization." As Morlan (1984, 463) put it, "it appears that the countries in which the highest municipal turnout occurs are those in which local elections are the most nationally politicized, in terms of both issues and party activity."

This would seem to account for the lower turnout observed in North America, compared with Europe. Many municipal elections in Canada and the United States are held on a nonpartisan basis, whereas local elections in

Europe are systematically partisan. This is buttressed by studies that have shown that turnout in the United States is higher in cities with partisan elections (Alford and Lee 1968; Karnig and Walter 1983).

The argument is compelling. The decision to vote or not to vote depends in part on whether the individual is being asked to vote. The extent of mobilization is thus an important factor, and there are good reasons to believe that there is much greater mobilization in national elections than in local ones.

This interpretation is not entirely satisfactory, however. We do not have much information on the extent of mobilization that goes on in different types of elections. Why local candidates are less able to mobilize than parties is not clear. Furthermore, wide variations in the gap between local and national turnout remain: the gap is very small in Scandinavian countries and in France, but very substantial in Great Britain. Why?

Unfortunately, this is one of the questions that I am unable to answer satisfactorily. I would like to propose a hypothesis that cannot be tested systematically here: the gap is greater in more urban societies. Turnout in municipal elections decreases as the size of the city increases (Morlan 1984). I suspect the same pattern holds in national elections, but to a lesser degree. As a consequence, it would be only in urban settings that turnout is substantially lower for national elections.[35] This could account for the particularly low turnout in British local elections.

Finally, another reason why turnout is higher in national elections could be that they are more widely covered in the media. Citizens are much more likely to hear on the news about a national campaign than about a local one, to see the main candidates, and to be exposed to the major issues on the news.[36] Unfortunately, the data to test this hypothesis are not available.

Turnout in Legislative and Presidential Elections

The second kind of comparison concerns turnout in legislative and presidential elections. Does one type of election arouse greater turnout than the other? In principle, turnout should be higher for the most important election, which in some countries should be the legislative election and in others the presidential one. But does turnout really hinge on the relative power of the legislature and of the president?

Table 1.7 presents turnout for both sets of elections. I consider only those cases where the two elections are not held together. I compare median turnout in these two kinds of elections, for each country and decade since 1960.[37] Turnout tends to be slightly higher in presidential elections, the median difference being two percentage points.

The results are particularly striking for three countries where the presi-

Table 1.7. Comparing Turnout in Presidential and Legislative Elections

Country	Decade	Median Turnout Presidential	Legislative	Difference
Austria	1960s	95.8	93.8	+2.0
	1970s	94.7	92.3	+2.4
	1980s	89.5	91.5	-2.0
	1990s	83.8	82.1	+1.7
Colombia	1970s	40.3	33.0	+7.3
Finland	1960s	75.7	85.0	-9.3
	1970s	64.3	78.4	-14.1
	1980s	79.5	73.9	+5.6
	1990s	82.3	68.4	+13.9
France	1960s	81.2	80.0	+1.2
	1970s	84.2	82.3	+1.9
	1980s	85.0	70.9	+14.1
	1990s	79.7	67.5	+12.2
Ireland	1960s	65.4	75.1	-9.7
	1970s	62.3	76.5	-14.2
	1990s	64.1	68.5	-4.4
Iceland	1960s	92.1	91.3	+0.8
	1980s	81.7	89.4	-7.7
Portugal	1980s	81.2	77.0	+4.2
	1990s	62.0	67.5	-5.5
Korea	1990s	81.0	71.9	+8.1
Poland	1990s	55.0	48.0	+7.0

dent has very little power: Austria, Ireland, and Iceland. In these three countries, median turnout in presidential elections is only two points lower than
in legislative elections. This is another indication that the "objective" importance of the election may not be as determinant as many are inclined to believe. Presidential elections are more personalized than legislative ones, and
this may make them more appealing to voters. It is probably easier to make
judgments on individual characters than on parties. For the same reason, the
media may pay as much attention to presidential elections, even when they
do not matter much in terms of real political influence.

Turnout in Referenda

We may finally compare turnout in nationwide referenda and elections.
Table 1.8 presents the evidence. For each country and each decade, I compare median turnout in these two types of popular consultations.

Table 1.8 indicates that the median difference in turnout in referenda

Table 1.8. Comparing Turnout in Referenda and Legislative Elections

		Median Turnout		
Country	Decade	Presidential	Legislative	Difference
Austria	1970s	64.1	92.3	-28.2
Denmark	1960s	63.6	87.2	-23.6
	1970s	76.8	88.0	-11.2
	1980s	74.8	86.2	-11.4
	1990s	77.4	83.4	-6.0
France	1960s	76.9	80.0	-3.1
	1970s	60.7	82.3	-21.6
	1980s	37.0	70.9	-33.9
	1990s	69.7	67.5	+2.2
Ireland	1960s	63.0	75.1	-12.1
	1970s	60.8	76.5	-15.7
	1980s	54.3	73.3	-19.0
	1990s	68.7	68.5	+0.2
Italy	1970s	84.8	93.2	-8.4
	1980s	78.0	89.8	-11.8
	1990s	62.5	86.7	-24.2
Norway	1970s	77.6	81.6	-4.0
Britain	1970s	64.5	74.6	-10.1
Canada	1990s	74.7	69.7	+5.0
New Zealand	1960s	71.2	89.3	-18.1
	1990s	55.2	85.2	-30.0
Switzerland	1960s	41.8	64.2	-22.4
	1970s	40.3	52.4	-12.1
	1980s	38.0	47.5	-9.5
	1990s	40.5	46.0	-5.5
Australia	1960s	93.8	95.2	-1.4
	1970s	93.4	95.4	-2.0
	1980s	92.1	94.3	-2.2

Source: Butler and Ranney 1994 (appendix A, tables 4-1 and 5-1). Referenda that were held at the same time as a legislative election are excluded.

and national elections is 11 percentage points. The typical turnout in a referendum would thus be around 66 percent, basically the same as in local elections.

Elections differ from referenda in two ways. In a referendum, voters are asked their opinion on a specific issue. In an election, voters are asked to choose the party that best represents their opinions on a whole range of issues. Turnout in elections may tend to be higher because more is at stake and/or because the campaign itself is more personalized.

I suspect, though I cannot offer any proof, that both factors are at play. The fact that in a presidential system where power is equally shared by the presidency and the legislature turnout is higher for presidential elections suggests that the lesser personalization of politics in referenda hinders turnout. Elections make for more lively campaigns, and they tend to be more widely covered by the media.

Voters may often see the stakes of a referendum to be lower. That, however, is bound to vary a great deal from one referendum to another. And there must be some referenda where the stakes are perceived to be extremely important. In those circumstances, should we get a higher turnout than in an election?

It is extremely difficult to answer that question because the importance of an election or of a referendum is a highly subjective matter. I propose, however, the following test. Rather than comparing turnout in typical elections and referenda, let us look at the highest turnout ever obtained in a given country in an election and in a referendum (see table 1.9).[38]

The difference between the most stimulating referendum and the most stimulating election is quite small: the median difference is only two points. The fact that even here elections slightly outperform referenda suggests that the personalization of politics that is more likely to be found in elections does foster turnout. Turnout in referenda tends to be lower than in legislative elections for the same reason that turnout in legislative elections is lower than in presidential elections. It is important to note, however, that in Ireland and Switzerland, where turnout in legislative elections is below average, the most stimulating referenda greatly outperform the most stimulating elections.

Table 1.9. Highest Turnout in Referenda and Legislative Elections

	Highest Turnout		
Country	Referenda	Legislative Elections	Difference
Denmark	90.1	89.3	+0.8
France	80.6	83.2	-2.6
Ireland	88.1	76.9	+11.2
Italy	88.1	93.4	-5.3
New Zealand	85.2	91.7	-6.5
Switzerland	78.3	63.8	+14.5
Australia	93.8	95.7	-1.9

Conclusions

This first chapter was intended to assemble as much evidence as possible on the level of turnout in democracies. We have seen that the typical level of turnout in a democratic national legislative election is 77 percent, that it is slightly higher for presidential elections and about 10 points lower for local elections. As for referenda, the typical turnout is about the same as for local elections, but the most important of them attract almost as many voters as the most important national elections. We have also seen that turnout in a given country does not fluctuate much from one election to the next. Notwithstanding this stability, we have observed that turnout has declined recently.

Variations in turnout, both across nations and over time, are linked to a great number of factors: economic development and conjuncture, degree of illiteracy, population size and density, the presence or absence of compulsory voting, voting age, the electoral system, the closeness of the election, and the number of parties.

Most of these factors affect turnout only at the margin but when combined together they can make a substantial difference. Turnout for national legislative elections is likely to be highest in a small, industrialized, densely populated country, where the national lower house election is decisive, voting is compulsory and the voting age is 21, having a PR system with relatively few parties and a close electoral outcome, and in a period of economic growth. When most of these conditions are met, turnout can exceed 90 percent; when most conditions are not met, turnout can easily be under 60 percent.

Some of these findings are particularly interesting with regard to the merits and limits of rational choice theory. There is some support for each of the three components of the rational choice model.

First, with regard to B. More important elections attract more voters. The more powerful the legislature, the higher the turnout in legislative elections. Likewise, turnout is lower for local elections in part because the stakes are perceived to be smaller. Some other pieces of evidence, however, are less supportive of the model. The turnout gap between national and local elections is much higher than the gap in the perceived importance of the two levels of government. And turnout in presidential elections in those countries where the president has very little actual power is amazingly high.

With regard to P, the evidence is also partly supportive and partly negative. On the positive side, turnout is higher when the election is close. This is consistent with rational choice, since the probability of casting a decisive vote increases with the closeness of the election. On the negative side, there is little support for the view that turnout is affected by the interaction of B and P. From the perspective of rational choice, it is not clear at all that turnout should be lower in local elections. The latter may be less important but this is compensated by the fact that the electorate is smaller, which means that P is greater. If a national election is perceived to be ten times more important than a local election, but the probability of casting a decisive vote is ten times smaller, turnout should be about the same, according to the model. The evidence presented in this chapter indicates that this is not so. This suggests that B matters more than P.

Finally, with respect to C, it is interesting to note that when voting is made compulsory, turnout is much higher. Clearly, in such circumstances, the cost of not voting is higher. There is also circumstantial evidence that administrative procedures that facilitate absentee voting (and reduce the cost of voting) increase turnout (Black 1991). But we should keep in mind that even when people are free to vote or not to vote and when absentee voting is difficult, most people do vote, in spite of the costs entailed.

CHAPTER 2

Who Votes?

It is revealing to know in which countries and for what types of elections turnout tends to be highest or lowest. In the same vein, it is important to understand what kinds of individuals tend to vote and what kinds of individuals tend to abstain. This chapter focuses on who votes and who does not. It addresses two questions: First, are the same people voting or abstaining in every election or do people move back and forth between voting and abstaining? Second, what are the main socioeconomic characteristics of those who vote?

Regular and Irregular Voters

We may distinguish two polar images of voters and abstainers. The first image is one of constancy. In this view, there are basically two types of people: those who vote in every election and those who abstain in every election. Very few people vote in one election and abstain in the next. The assumption underlying such a view is that the motivations for voting or not voting are deeply rooted in individuals' psychology and do not vary much from one election to another.

The second image is one of change. In this view, many people move back and forth between voting and abstaining. The assumption here is that the decision to vote is made at the margin and is related to election-specific factors.

The latter view has been put forward most forcefully by Aldrich (1993). Aldrich argues that voting is a low-cost, low-benefit, decision-making problem, and that small changes in costs or benefits can make a big difference. According to Aldrich, since both benefits and costs are so small, it is a close call for many citizens to vote or not to vote, so that the decision has a major random component and is strongly affected by election-specific factors.

I have shown in chapter 1 that there is little fluctuation in turnout from one national legislative election to another. Such stability would seem to support the constant voter model. This overall stability could be misleading, however. We cannot dismiss the possibility that, even though turnout remains about the same from one election to another, there is a lot of individual movement in and out of voting, which cancels out at the aggregate level.

What are the facts? We know very little about this simple but important question. To my knowledge, the only piece that has directly tackled this issue is the study by Sigelman, Roeder, Jewell, and Baer (1985). These authors rely on data from one American state, Kentucky, which "maintains a computerized voter registration system in which each registrant's voting history is recorded over a running five-year (10-election) period." Among those registered, 14 percent did not vote in any election, and another 28 percent voted in only one or two; at the other end of the scale, 18 percent voted seven times or more. In between, a good 40 percent voted in three to seven elections. They conclude that "there was no hard-and fast distinction between voters and non-voters . . . there were only degrees of electoral participation that shaded into one another . . . electoral participation should not be conceived in binary terms" (751–52).

Such findings support the image of the changing marginal voter. The setting, however, is quite peculiar. What makes it peculiar is the fact that it is in the United States, where the level of turnout, as we have seen, is exceptionally low. Nor is it typical for a citizen in a democracy to be faced with ten elections in a five-year period.

What is the situation in countries with more typical levels of turnout? I focus on two countries—Great Britain and Canada—whose levels of turnout are about average and whose election studies have produced data that throw light on the regularity or irregularity of voting.

In these two countries, researchers have constructed flow-of-the-vote tables that indicate how voting behavior at a given election is related to voting behavior at a previous election. The starting point for the construction of these tables is survey data on voting behavior in both elections.[1] The reported vote, however, differs from the official results, especially in the underreport of abstention. To correct for this, survey marginals are replaced with data from official results, and supplemented with demographic data on the entering and leaving electorates. Cell percentages are then adjusted by successive row and column multiplications that reconcile the new margins with the initial association observed in the survey data. This procedure is commonly referred to as "Mostellarization," after Mosteller (1968).[2]

On the basis of these flow-of-the-vote tables, we can estimate, for a pair of elections, the proportion, among those who were eligible to vote in both elections, who voted in both—I will call them the regular voters; who abstained in both—the regular abstainers; and who voted in one but not the other—the irregular voters.

Table 2.1 reports the proportion of these three groups of electors for each pair of elections for which a flow-of-the-vote table is available. The typical situation is to have 63 percent regular voters, 24 percent irregular voters, and 14 percent regular abstainers. The great majority of voters are regular voters. According to these flow-of-the-vote tables, in a typical election 84 percent of those who vote in a given election also voted in the previous one.[3]

It may be too easy to infer that someone who has voted in two elections is a regular voter. But there is little doubt that the great majority of voters are regular ones. If the probability of voting in a given election for someone who voted in the previous *one* is 84 percent, the probability that someone who voted in the previous *two* elections should be in the vicinity of 90 per-

Table 2.1. The Consistency of Voting in Elections: Britain and Canada

| Election | Voters | | Regular Abstainers |
	Regular	Irregular	
Britain			
1959–64	65	25	19
1964–66	67	18	15
1959–66	65	25	10
1970–74 (Feb.)	62	27	11
1970–74 (Oct.)	58	29	13
1974 (Feb.–Oct.)	66	19	14
1974 (Oct.)–1979	65	23	13
Canada			
1988–93	63	22	16
1993–97	57	26	17
Average	63	24	14

Sources: Butler and Stokes (1969); Särlvik and Crewe (1983); Johnston, Blais, Brady, Gidengil, and Nevitte (1996).

Note: Regular voters voted in both elections, irregular voters voted in one but not the other, and regular abstainers did not vote in either.

cent. If we were to classify as regular voters those who vote in each of three elections, regular voters would constitute three-fourths of those who vote in an election (again confining ourselves to those who are eligible to vote in the three elections).

The verdict must therefore be that in countries where turnout is not exceptionally low, the image of the constant voter is a compelling one. The point should not be overstated: a number of people vote only from time to time, depending on how they feel about particular elections. The fact is, however, that the great majority of those who vote tend to vote in about every election.[4]

If the bulk of those who vote in a given election are regular voters, it should follow that the decision to vote is made at the very beginning of the election campaign. Unfortunately, most election surveys are conducted after the election and do not allow us to test that hypothesis. Recent Canadian election studies, however, have included a campaign rolling cross-section component, in which mini subsamples are interviewed every day of the campaign. In the 1993 election study the questionnaire included the following question: "How likely is it that you will vote on election day? Would you say very likely, somewhat likely, somewhat unlikely, or very unlikely?" Among those interviewed in the first two weeks of the campaign, 79 percent said they were very likely to vote, and 94 percent of those went on to report in the post-election survey that they had voted.

During that same election, Robert Young and I conducted a study among students at two Canadian universities, the Université de Montréal and the University of Western Ontario (see appendixes C and D). Five classes were administered three questionnaires—two prior to the election and one following it. Respondents were asked to indicate the likelihood they would vote on a scale from 0 to 10, where 0 meant it was certain they would not vote and 10 meant it was certain they would. In the first questionnaire, administered in the second week of the campaign, 62 percent gave a response of 10, indicating they were certain to vote. Among those, 84 percent gave exactly the same response two weeks before the election (an additional 7 percent chose a score of 9), and 89 percent said they had voted in the post-election questionnaire.[5]

Not only, then, do most people vote regularly in just about every election, but they also decide early on in an election campaign that they will vote. This constancy is an important fact that has to be taken into account when it comes to making sense of why people vote.

Who Votes?

There remains the fact that in a given election some people vote and others do not. Which socioeconomic characteristics distinguish voters and abstainers? The starting point of the analysis is the seminal study by Wolfinger and Rosenstone (1980), *Who Votes?*, which systematically examines the relative impact of various socioeconomic characteristics on turnout in the United States.

This study constitutes an important breakthrough for at least three reasons. First, it is based on a huge survey, the 1972 Current Population Survey (CPS) of the Bureau of the Census. Wolfinger and Rosenstone were able to rely on data obtained from 88,105 respondents.[6]

Second, the CPS overestimation of turnout is smaller than usual. Surveys systematically overestimate turnout for several reasons. One is that most survey samples exclude categories of people, such as residents of institutions for the elderly, who are unlikely to vote. Moreover, those who accept to answer an election survey tend to be more interested in politics and are thus more likely to vote. Finally, there is some misreporting, as some people who did not vote told interviewers that they had done so (Clausen 1968; Traugott and Katosh 1979). The main virtue of the CPS is that it had a very high completion rate (94 percent) and was thus less likely to exclude the least politicized. Turnout is still overestimated, at 67 percent compared with an actual turnout of 57 percent, but the bias is smaller than in the National Election Study, which had a reported turnout of 73 percent for the same election.

Finally, Wolfinger and Rosenstone present a full-fledged multivariate analysis that allows them to assess the specific effect of each socioeconomic characteristic, controlling for the impact of all others.

What do they find? Their main conclusion is that education is the socioeconomic characteristic that is most closely associated with voting. Everything else being equal, citizens with a college degree are 38 percent more likely to vote than are those with less than five years of schooling. Income has a much smaller effect, and the only significant difference is between the poor and all other citizens; there is no difference between middle- and high-income respondents. The impact of occupation is also relatively small. More specifically, there is no systematic difference between higher- and lower-status occupations; the occupational group most likely to vote, controlling for other variables, are farm owners.

Wolfinger and Rosenstone found that the second most important characteristic affecting turnout, after education, is age. They show that the propensity to vote increases substantially as one gets older. The rate of increase levels off at around age 55 but turnout continues to rise through the seventies. They also report that it is only among the elderly that there is a slight gender gap, with men voting more than women.

At least three other socioeconomic characteristics were found to have a nonnegligible impact on turnout. Government employees, the less mobile, and married people are more likely to vote.[7] It would seem, though, that marriage increases turnout only in the long run, as its initial short-term impact is negative (Stoker and Jennings 1995).

In short, Wolfinger and Rosenstone conclude that among all socioeconomic characteristics, education is of "transcendent" importance, while age comes second. They are not as clear with respect to the rest of the pecking order but my reading of their evidence would lead me to choose mobility and marriage as third and fourth factors. In the United States, then, the person with the greatest likelihood of voting has the following characteristics: he/she is highly educated, old, married, and has stayed at the same residence for many years. Conversely, the person who is least likely to vote has little education, is young, unmarried, and has moved recently to a new residence.

The major limitation of Wolfinger and Rosenstone's study is that it deals with only one country, one with an exceptionally low turnout. What is the situation in more typical democracies? Do the same patterns hold?

There has been no systematic comparative analysis of who votes in national elections. There have been a few comparative analyses of voting, but none has focused on sorting out the relative impact of various socioeconomic characteristics.

Perhaps the most ambitious study is the one by Verba, Nie, and Kim (1978). They examine political participation in seven countries: Austria, India, Japan, the Netherlands, Nigeria, the United States, and Yugoslavia. They are interested in many modes of political activity, voting being only one of them. They look at the correlation between a voting scale and a socioeconomic resource scale, the latter being based on education and income. They find a relatively strong correlation in the United States and Yugoslavia but much weaker relationships in the other five countries.

These results confirm that the patterns observed by Wolfinger and Rosenstone cannot be generalized outside the United States. The strong correlation between education and voting may not hold in most countries. However, Verba, Nie, and Kim do not provide us with an overall picture of who votes and who does not in these countries. We are told that socioeconomic advantage plays a greater role in the United States than in other countries, but the study fails to indicate which socioeconomic characteristics are most closely linked to turnout in the various countries.

Other researchers have looked at voting and nonvoting among European countries. Lewis-Beck and Lockerbie (1989) look at the impact of economic factors on the propensity to vote in Great Britain, France, Germany, and Italy. They find that personal finances do not matter but that perceptions that the economy will improve increase turnout. They include other socioeconomic variables as control variables but they do not attempt to disentangle their impact.

Schmitt and Mannheimer (1991; see also Eijk and Oppenhuis 1990), for their part, examine the factors leading to voting and nonvoting in European elections. They report that voting is weakly correlated with age, sex, and education. They focus, however, on the role of attitudinal variables, and they do not present a profile of voters' and abstainers' socioeconomic characteristics.

Franklin (1996), finally, pools data from twenty-two different countries and relates turnout to a number of individual-level characteristics. With respect to West European countries (which form the majority of the twenty-two countries included), however, the data pertain to European elections, in which turnout is particularly low. Furthermore, Franklin's multivariate regression does not allow us to assess the full impact of socioeconomic characteristics, as intervening variables such as party identification and political discussion are included. It is interesting to note, though, that age comes out as the most important socioeconomic variable in his analysis.

We are thus faced with the following situation. Wolfinger and Rosenstone provide us with a telling description of who votes in the United States, but we do not have similar thorough descriptions for other countries, even though there are good reasons to believe that the correlates of voting are substantially different outside the United States.

I offer below a comparative analysis of who votes and who does not. I use the Comparative Study of Electoral Systems (CSES) survey, which was conducted in nine different countries (Australia, Britain, Czech Republic, Israel, Poland, Romania, Spain, Taiwan, and the United States) in 1996–97.[8] This survey offers three major advantages. First, it covers nine countries with varying levels of turnout. Average turnout in the nine elections covered by the survey is 72 percent, just slightly lower than mean turnout in democracies (see chapter 1). Second, the survey contains a question about whether the respondent voted in the last national election. Eurobarometer surveys either ask about voting in European elections, which are untypical because they do not mean much and have low turnout rates, or about the likelihood of voting in the next election. It is more prudent to study voting than the intention to vote.[9] Third, the questionnaire includes a number of questions about socioeconomic characteristics, which will allow me to sort out the specific effect (or noneffect) of all the major variables that need to be examined.

The total sample for the nine countries combined is more than 11,000 respondents. In the sample, 83 percent said they had voted in the last national election and 17 percent indicated they had not voted. As usual, voting is overestimated in the survey, the average turnout in these countries being 72 percent.[10]

Table 2.2 presents the results of the logistic regression (see appendix E for a description of the variables). The regression includes all the major socioeconomic characteristics as well as dummy variables for eight of the nine countries.[11] The country dummy variables control for the impact of macro factors such as those examined in chapter 1. I wish here to determine the specific effect of individuals' socioeconomic characteristics, after taking into account the fact that turnout is particularly low or high in a given country.

Wolfinger and Rosenstone have shown that education is the most powerful predictor of voting in the United States. The CSES data indicate that the two most crucial socioeconomic determinants of voting are education and age. The gap between the least and the most educated and between the youngest and the eldest is a huge 20 points. The propensity to vote increases substantially with age and education.

The third most important characteristic of voters is that they tend to be religious. People who regularly attend religious services and who say they are very religious are more likely to vote. Finally, turnout is slightly higher among those who are married and with a higher income.

These are the patterns that prevail when all countries are combined. I have also run separate regressions for each country. Each country has its own peculiarities. Furthermore, voters (and abstainers) tend to have starker characteristics in the two countries (Poland and the United States) where turnout is particularly low, and relationships tend to be especially weak in Australia, the country with the highest turnout (and compulsory voting). This being said, the coefficient for age is positive in each of the nine countries, the coefficient for education in eight (the exception being Spain), and the coefficient for religiosity in eight (the exception being Australia).[12] The most important socioeconomic characteristics that are associated with voting are strikingly similar among these nine countries.

Why is it that the better educated, the eldest, the most religious, the richest, and those who are married are more likely to vote? There is certainly a host of factors involved but one characteristic that these groups share is that they tend to be integrated in society. The socioeconomic profile of voters and abstainers provides support for a sociological interpretation of the act of voting as expressing one's sense of belonging to the larger community.

Table 2.2. The Determinants of Voting in Nine Democratic Countries (1996–97): Australia, Czech Republic, Great Britain, Israel, Poland, Romania, Spain, Taiwan, and United States (Logistic Regression)

Variables	Logistic Coefficient (SE)		Impact[a]
Education	1.90***	(.16)	.22
Age	0.03***	(.002)	.20
Religiosity	0.96***	(.11)	.10
Income	0.43***	(.09)	.05
Married	0.46***	(.06)	.05
Union	0.31***	(.08)	.03
Student	0.40**	(.16)	.04
Woman	-0.10*	(.06)	-.01
Unemployed	0.08	(.12)	.01
Housewife	-0.02	(.11)	.003
Retired	0.01	(.10)	.001
Poland	-1.55***	(.09)	-.23
Australia	3.09***	(.28)	.17
USA	-0.98***	(.10)	-.13
Taiwan	1.33***	(.15)	.11
Spain	1.17***	(.14)	.10
Czech Republic	0.88***	(.12)	.09
Israel	0.83***	(.16)	.08
Romania	0.55***	(.12)	.05
Constant	-1.51	(.16)	
Adjusted pseudo R^2	.30		
Percent correct prediction	84.7%		
N	11,521		

Source: CSES Data, 1996–2000. For description of variables, see appendix E.

* Significant at the .10 level (two-tailed test)

** Significant at the .05 level (two-tailed test)

*** Significant at the .01 level (two-tailed test)

[a]For each variable, I calculated the probability that each individual will participate under two scenarios: first assuming that the variable takes its lowest value, then assuming that the variable takes its highest value, all other variables remaining at their observed values. The reported impact is the difference between the two average probabilities, across the entire sample. For more details, see Rosenstone and Hansen (1993, 73).

These results cannot tell us whether the rational choice model provides a compelling explanation of why people vote. This will be the object of chapters 3, 4, and 5. The findings suggest, however, that considerations that lie outside the model may play an important role.

Conclusion

Most people vote in national elections and a good majority are regular voters. Many people vote in just about every election and most of them have already decided that they will vote by the time the election campaign starts. These findings do not fit well with the image that is often portrayed by the rational choice model of a citizen who makes her choice whether to vote or not at the margin, on the basis of small changes in perceived benefits or costs. These findings do not invalidate the rational choice model but they suggest that the decision to vote or not to vote may depend to a good extent on deep values that induce people to go to the ballot box whatever the specific context of a given election.

The better educated, the eldest, the most religious, the richest, and those who are married are more likely to vote. There are certainly many reasons for these patterns but the most common characteristic shared by all these groups is that they tend to be better integrated in their social milieu. These results do not tell us anything as such about the validity of the rational choice model but they give some support to an alternative sociological interpretation.

With these contextual pieces of information in mind, we may now proceed to a more direct test of rational choice.

CHAPTER 3

Do People Believe that Their Vote Could Be Decisive?

We have seen in which countries turnout is particularly high and in which it is particularly low. I have identified which socioeconomic and institutional characteristics are most closely linked with turnout. I have also examined variations in the propensity to vote at the individual level. I have portrayed the socioeconomic profile of voters and abstainers.

It is now time to return to the initial question posed in the introduction, that is, the capacity of the rational choice model to account for individuals' decision to vote or not to vote. The core model has three basic parameters: B, the benefits of voting; P, the probability of casting a decisive vote; and C, the costs of voting.

This chapter focuses on P and the following on C. I do not devote a chapter to B because it is, in my view, an unproblematic factor. The rational choice model predicts that people are more likely to vote when the election is perceived to matter a lot, that is, when they believe that who wins will make a big difference to them. I will show that this hypothesis is largely borne out.

This should be construed as positive support for the theory. At the same time, however, I do not think too much should be made of this, as it boils down to saying that the more important the election the higher the turnout. This is fine, but it was well known before rational choice theorists told us about it.

From this perspective, the P term is crucial. This is the factor that traditional studies of electoral participation did not include, even indirectly, and the reason why only rational choice views voting as a paradox. According to rational choice, individuals should estimate the probability that their vote decides who wins and take that probability into account when they decide to vote or not to vote. As we have seen, because that probability is bound to be minuscule in an election with a very large number of electors, the theory predicts that most people will abstain in national elections. The fact that most people vote is the paradox that leads many to conclude that the theory should be discarded.

That conclusion does not necessarily follow. People might vote even if P matters under either of the following circumstances. First, people may consider the probability of casting a decisive vote and this may make them lean toward abstention but other factors, sense of duty, for instance, may induce them to vote anyway.

The second possibility is that people vote on the basis of P but systematically overestimate the probability of casting a decisive vote. That possibility was suggested by Riker and Ordeshook (1968, 38), who wrote, "[I]t is likely that, for many people, the subjective estimate of P is higher than is reasonable, given the objective circumstances." Why would it be so? Many people find it very difficult to understand probabilities (Kahneman, Slovic, and Tversky 1982), so perceptions may be at variance with reality.

Why would most people tend to overestimate rather than underestimate probabilities? According to Riker and Ordeshook, they do mainly because official propaganda repeatedly tells people that an election could be decided by a few votes. But the fault could also be with the individuals. Much research has shown that people tend to overestimate the frequency of rare events, so that tiny probabilities tend to be inflated (Quattrone and Tversky 1988). Perceptions of probabilities are also tainted by wishful thinking. Those who identify with a party, for instance, tend to be optimistic about the probability of that party winning the election (Johnston, Blais, Brady, and Crête 1992, 207; Uhlaner and Grofman 1986). Likewise, expectations about exchange rates are biased: those in exporting sectors expect a decline while those in imports expect an increase, both groups forming expectations of changes that are favorable to them (Ito 1990).

This leads me to address two questions related to P. First, do people overestimate the probability of casting a decisive vote? Second, do perceptions of P affect the propensity to vote? The combination of the two questions yields four scenarios: (1) P is overestimated and affects voting; (2) P is overestimated but does not affect voting; (3) P is not overestimated but affects voting; (4) P is not overestimated and does not affect voting.

Scenarios 1 and 3 would both offer some support for the rational choice model. Under scenario 1, it would have to be explained why people overestimate P. As there is a cost involved in trying to estimate P accurately, people may rationally decide not to invest in such activity and to rely on simple intuitions, which may be off the mark. Overestimation could also reflect wishful thinking. Whatever the case, finding that people vote (in part) because they wrongly believe they might cast a decisive vote could buttress the model.[1]

Under scenario 3, people would vote even though they correctly perceive they are extremely unlikely to cast a decisive vote. If they still vote, this would imply that P has less weight than other factors, such as sense of duty. This would still provide support to the theory. Under scenarios 2 and 4, finally, P does not matter at all, and we would have to conclude that one critical element of the rational choice model is invalid.

I proceed in the following way. Most of the empirical literature has used proxies for P. The two most popular proxies have been the size of the electorate and the closeness of the election. The reasoning is that the smaller the electorate and the closer the election, the greater the probability of casting a decisive vote. I review previous research on the impact of size and closeness on turnout, and I discuss the implications of those results. If size and closeness matter, does it entail that P affects turnout?

I then turn to more direct measures of P. A few studies have attempted to tap people's perceptions of the probability of their casting a decisive vote. These studies allow us to determine whether P tends to be overestimated and to find out whether, all things being equal, perceptions of P are correlated with voting.

The last section deals with minimax regret. The minimax regret hypothesis has been proposed by Ferejohn and Fiorina (1974) as an attempt to rescue the rational choice model. The assumption is that when probabilities are unknown, people resort to different decision procedures. One such procedure is to attempt to minimize potential regret. The individual would thus consider how much regret she would have if she voted and her vote was not decisive versus if she did not vote and her vote would have been decisive. She will decide to vote if she is more concerned with the latter than with the former. In other words, the person votes because she would feel awful if she did not vote and her preferred candidate lost by one vote.

I have outlined the many problems associated with minimax regret. It is not a theoretically satisfactory solution. Yet it could be that this is the way people feel about voting and that, in spite of its theoretical inadequacies, minimax regret offers one compelling explanation for why most people vote. Again, I review the evidence and render my verdict.

Do Size and Closeness Matter?

Rational choice reminds us that, all things being equal, the probability of casting a decisive vote decreases as the size of the electorate increases. This leads to the prediction that the size of the electorate is negatively correlated with turnout. I review below the evidence on this hypothesis.

It is also the conventional wisdom that turnout tends to be higher when an election is close than when it is not close. Is conventional wisdom right? If so, how much does closeness matter? And if closeness matters, how much support does it give to the rational choice model?

Closeness can be measured in two different ways, objectively and subjectively. Objective measures are based on the actual results of the election (or of the previous one) and assume that citizens are able to anticipate those results correctly. Subjective measures are based on survey questions tapping perceptions of the closeness of the race.

I begin with studies based on objective measures. Some of these studies have looked at both size and closeness, others have looked at one or the other.[2] Some have been cross-sectional, others longitudinal, and still others have been based on pooled data. Some have examined national elections, others subnational ones.

Table 3.1 summarizes the evidence. Before assessing that evidence, I need to discuss the methodological problems that arise in the case of cross-sectional studies of turnout within the United States. Many of these studies compare turnout in presidential elections across the various states. The standard rational choice prediction is that turnout will be higher in smaller states. The fact is, however, that, because of the electoral college, citizens of small states have a smaller chance of casting the vote that would decide who will be elected president (see Wolfinger 1994, 78). The implication is that American presidential elections do not offer an appropriate test for the impact of size on turnout and are not reviewed here. I have made one exception to that rule, the study by Kau and Rubin (1976), because they have included as a control variable a relative power index that takes into account the electoral college. We do expect turnout to be higher in smaller states, controlling for the number of members of the electoral college.

The same problem arises with respect to congressional or gubernatorial elections that are held at the same time as presidential elections, since the decision to vote in a congressional or gubernatorial election hinges very much on the decision to vote in the presidential election. When it comes to ascertaining the relationship between size and turnout, therefore, the only relevant studies are those that pertain to congressional or gubernatorial elections that do *not* take place at the same time as presidential elections.

Table 3.1. The Impact of Size and Closeness: Review of Studies

Study	Object	Size	Closeness
A. Cross-National			
Powell (1982)	23 countries, average turnout, 1958–76	No	No
Capron and Kruseman (1988)	26 countries	Yes	N.I.
Blais and Carty (1990)	20 countries, 509 elections	Yes	Yes
Black (1991)	18 countries, average turnout, 1980s	N.I.	No
Blais and Dobrzynska (1998)	91 countries, 321 elections	Yes	Yes
B. Cross-Sectional: United States			
Barzel and Silberberg (1973)	Gubernatorial, 1962–1968	Yes	Yes
Silberman and Durden (1975)	House, 1962 and 1970	Yes	Yes
Tollison et al. (1975)	Gubernatorial, 1970	No	Yes
Kau and Rubin (1976)	Presidential, 1972 (state results)	Yes	No
Crain and Deaton (1977)	Presidential, 1972 (state results)	N.A.	Yes
Caldeira and Patterson (1982)	Congress, Iowa and California, 1978	N.I.	Yes
Patterson and Caldeira (1983)	Gubernatorial, 1978–80	N.I.	Yes
Foster (1984)	Presidential, 1968–80 (state results)	N.A.	No
Kenney and Rice (1986)	Presidential primary, 1976–80 (state results)	N.I.	No
Tucker (1986)	Congress, Washington, 1976–82	N.I.	Yes
Crain et al. (1987)	Congress, 1982	N.I.	Yes
Hansen et al. (1987)	School districts, Oregon, 1970–73	Yes	N.I.
Crain et al. (1987)	Congress, 1982	N.I.	Yes
Cox and Munger (1989)	House, 1982	N.I.	Yes
Filer et al. (1993)	Presidential, 1948, 1960, 1968, 1980	N.I.	Yes
C. Cross-Sectional: Other			
Rosenthal and Sen (1973)	French constituencies, 1958–68	N.I.	Yes
Seidle and Miller (1976)	British constituencies	N.I.	Yes
Chapman and Palda (1983)	Canadian provincial constituencies, 1972–78	N.I.	Yes
Denver and Hands (1985)	British constituencies, 1959–79	N.I.	Yes
Darvish and Rosenberg (1988)	Israel municipal, 1978, 1983	N.I.	Yes
Rallings and Thrasher (1990)	British local, 1981–89	N.I.	Yes
Eagles (1991)	Canadian constituencies, 1980–88	N.I.	Yes
Kirchgässner and Schimmelpfennig (1992)	British and German constituencies, 1987	No	Yes
Birsch (1993)	Canadian constituencies, 1980	No	Yes
Matsusaka and Palda (1993)	Canadian constituencies, 1979–80	Yes	Yes
Cox et al. (1995)	Japanese constituencies, 1967–90	N.I.	Yes
D. Longitudinal			
Settle and Abrams (1976)	U.S. presidential, 1968–72	N.I.	Yes
Gray (1976)	U.S. gubernatorial, 1968	N.I.	Yes
Capron and Kruseman (1988)	U.S. presidential, 1900–1980	No	Yes
Blais (see chap. 1)	19 countries, 1960–95	N.I.	Yes

Note: N.I.: Not included in the analysis. N.A.: Not applicable because it is a presidential election or a congressional or gubernatorial election that was held at the same time as a presidential election. See the text for an explanation.

The situation is different in the case of closeness. Here there is no problem with respect to presidential elections, or congressional and gubernatorial elections that are *not* held at the same time as presidential elections. We should expect a higher turnout where the election is closer. The situation is more ambiguous with respect to congressional and gubernatorial elections that do take place at the same time as presidential elections. In those cases, voters should be sensitive first and foremost to the closeness of the presidential race in their state and secondarily to the closeness of the congressional or gubernatorial race. Unfortunately, existing studies have looked only at the latter. I nevertheless include these studies in my review, since the closeness of the congressional or gubernatorial race should at least marginally (positively) affect turnout.

As table 3.1 shows, the verdict is crystal clear with respect to closeness: closeness has been found to increase turnout in 27 of the 32 different studies that have tested the relationship, in many different settings and with diverse methodologies. There are strong reasons to believe that, as predicted by rational choice theory, more people vote when the election is close.

The evidence is more ambiguous in the case of size. The hypothesis that turnout decreases with the size of the electoral unit has been confirmed in eight studies but is disconfirmed in five others. This provides some limited support for the hypothesis, but the conclusion must be that the jury is still out on this question.

All the studies reviewed in table 3.1 are based on objective measures of closeness.[3] It can be argued, however, that what really matters is the *perception* that an election is going to be close and that the most meaningful indicator is electors' subjective expectations about the outcome of the election. The real question is whether people are more likely to vote when they perceive the race to be close.

A number of studies have examined the relationship between perceptions of closeness and the propensity to vote. All these studies have been conducted in the United States. The first one was by Riker and Ordeshook (1968). They tested a model whereby citizens decide to vote on the basis of B, P, and D, using the American National Election Studies (NES) of 1952, 1956, and 1960. They show that, controlling for B and D, those who perceive the election to be close are somewhat more likely to vote.[4]

Ferejohn and Fiorina (1975) came to different conclusions. Using the NES of 1952, 1956, 1960, and 1964, they tested two alternative versions of the rational choice model: the standard utility version where the decision to vote depends on $B^{\star}P$, and the minimax version where only B matters. Their findings show the minimax model to perform better, thus suggesting that P, measured here again as the perception that the election is close, does not matter.

As Aldrich (1976) has demonstrated, however, their results depend to a great extent on their exclusion of unregistered voters, on response error in vote report, and on which aspect of closeness is measured. The findings are broadly supportive of the closeness hypothesis when these corrections are made.[5]

Frohlich, Oppenheimer, Smith, and Young (1978) tested a complex model built on proxies of B, P, C, and D to predict turnout in the 1964 presidential election. The proxy for P is the perception that the election is close and the authors indicate that the omission of that variable "reduces the model's ability to predict turnout significantly" (191).

Two other studies (Silver 1973; Ashenfelter and Kelley 1975) seem to indicate that closeness does not matter, but include interest in the campaign as a control variable. In my view, this is a case of overcontrol. It is quite possible that a close election arouses interest in a campaign, which then produces a higher turnout. Controlling for interest does not allow us to capture the full impact of closeness.[6] Finally, in both studies, closeness has the expected sign, and in one instance (Ashenfelter and Kelley 1975) it reaches a weak level of statistical significance (10 percent, one tail). These two studies should not be construed as disconfirming the hypothesis that closeness matters.

The bulk of the evidence supports the hypotheses that turnout decreases with size and increases with closeness. These two patterns are precisely those that would be predicted by rational choice theory. But how strong a support is this for the theory? The question is whether such results make sense only under rational choice or whether other theories can provide competing and perhaps even more compelling explanations.

Let us start with size. It would seem that turnout is slightly larger when the electorate is relatively small. According to rational choice, this is because the probability of casting a decisive vote is greater. Could it be for other reasons? The answer has to be yes. It may well be, for instance, that citizens of smaller communities tend to be more integrated into community life and that they are more likely to vote because they are more socially integrated (see Milbrath and Goel 1977, 110; Eagles and Erfle 1989). The fact that size matters is also consistent with the sociological model of voting.

What about closeness? Does the fact that turnout increases when there is a close race entail that some electors are induced to vote out of the belief that they might cast a decisive vote? Not necessarily. But I would argue that closeness as a concept belongs to the rational model. When an election is close, individual votes matter more. The finding that closeness enhances turnout constitutes prima facie evidence in support of rational choice. We need to uncover, however, why closeness matters. Could it be for reasons other than citizens' perceptions of the probability of casting a decisive vote?

One potential interpretation is that the stakes are higher for the parties and candidates in a close election, and parties and candidates drive turnout up by spending more energy in mobilization efforts. A number of studies have examined the separate impact of mobilization—usually measured in terms of spending—and closeness on turnout. With one exception (Jackson 1996), their findings are consistent (Seidle and Miller 1976; Tucker 1986; Cox and Munger 1989; Rallings and Thrasher 1990; Berch 1993; Matsusaka and Palda 1993): both variables have an independent impact.

The implication is that closeness fosters turnout in part because parties and candidates spend more, but that closeness remains significant even after controlling for party spending. In short, the impact of closeness *cannot* be imputed entirely to mobilization. Contrary to what Aldrich (1993) seems to indicate, strategic politicians cannot explain away the impact of closeness.

The culprit could also be the media. The media may find close elections more worthy of coverage and accord them more attention, thus arousing citizens' interest and turnout. But this begs the question of why the media would be more inclined to cover a close election. Would it not be because their audience finds close elections more interesting to follow? And is not a close election more interesting because it could be decided by a few votes, or, who knows, by a single one?

I conclude that closeness matters and that this is consistent with rational choice theory. The fact remains, however, that closeness is only a proxy for P. What really matters is how people perceive P.

Do People Overestimate the Probability of Casting a Decisive Vote?

In the rational choice model, P indicates the subjective probability of casting a decisive vote. Should we not ask people what probability they assign to their vote deciding who wins the election? Surprisingly enough, until recently no study had followed that route. Robert Young and I have tried to fill the gap.

The first study was done in 1993, during the Canadian federal election. Questionnaires were administered to students in ten classes at two universities, the Université de Montréal (hereafter Montreal) and the University of Western Ontario (Western). The classes were in three different disciplines: political science, economics, and sociology. Five panel groups were administered three questionnaires, two during the campaign and one after the election, while the other five were administered only the post-election questionnaire. The total number of respondents was 1,459 (see appendixes C and D).

The questionnaires included the following two questions: "What do you think the chances are, roughly, that *your vote* will determine which candidate wins the election in your riding?" and "Again, what do you think the chances are that *your vote* will determine which party wins the election in Canada as a whole?"[7] We offered eight possibilities, from one chance in 10 to one chance in 100,000,000.

Table 3.2 shows the distribution of responses to these two questions. With respect to P at the riding level, the modal and median response is one chance in 100,000. With respect to P at the national level, the modal response is one chance in 100,000,000, and the median response one chance in 10,000,000.

Do people overestimate P? In order to answer the question we need to establish the true value of P. The problem is, of course, that it is impossible to establish that value with any degree of accuracy. It is possible, however, to provide an approximation.

Canada has about 50,000 voters, on average, in a constituency. The simplest estimation is that the probability of casting a decisive vote is one chance in 50,000. This estimation is probably too pessimistic, however. As a matter of fact, most electoral contests are relatively close: in two-candidate contests, the winner's share of the vote is typically much closer to 50 percent than to 100 percent. Taking that into account, the probability of casting the decisive vote is likely to lie somewhere between one chance in 10,000 and one chance in 50,000.

Different sets of empirical evidence tend to support such a view.[8] First, the historical evidence. From 1945 to 1997 (inclusive), there have been seventeen federal elections in Canada. The total number of seats has varied between 245 and 301. This yields a total of 4,626 constituency elections during that period. One of those 4,629 elections did produce a tie. In the Quebec riding of Pontiac-Temiscamingue in 1963, the returning officer elected Paul Martineau, who had obtained 6,448 votes, exactly as many as Paul Oliva Goulet. In that election each of the 6,448 individuals who had voted for the winner could reason that they had cast the decisive vote, since if they had not voted Mr. Martineau would have lost. This means that out of the 158 million votes cast in federal elections between 1945 and 1997, 6,448 were decisive. Ex post, the probability of casting a decisive vote in all elections held between 1945 and 1997 has been one chance in 25,000.

It is possible to provide another estimate by looking only at the results of the 1988 election, which directly preceded the one in 1993. There were 295

Table 3.2. Perception of Determining Outcome

Riding

Response	N (%)		
	T1	T2	T3
1 chance in 10	17 (2)	15 (2)	21 (2)
1 chance in 100	23 (3)	14 (2)	13 (1)
1 chance in 1,000	72 (9)	48 (7)	93 (9)
1 chance in 10,000	141 (17)	106 (15)	176 (18)
1 chance in 100,000	160 (19)	156 (22)	201 (22)
1 chance in 1,000,000	87 (10)	84 (12)	92 (9)
1 chance in 10,000,000	60 (7)	53 (7)	62 (6)
1 chance in 100,000,000	83 (10)	106 (15)	124 (13)
Don't know	192 (23)	136 (19)	182 (18)
Refuse	9 (1)	7 (1)	25 (3)
Total	843	725	989

Canada

Response	N (%)		
	T1	T2	T3
1 chance in 10	19 (2)	12 (2)	15 (2)
1 chance in 100	8 (1)	6 (1)	8 (1)
1 chance in 1,000	17 (2)	7 (1)	13 (1)
1 chance in 10,000	16 (2)	19 (3)	25 (3)
1 chance in 100,000	34 (4)	32 (4)	59 (6)
1 chance in 1,000,000	87 (10)	63 (9)	94 (10)
1 chance in 10,000,000	190 (23)	172 (24)	219 (22)
1 chance in 100,000,000	261 (31)	249 (34)	325 (33)
Don't know	201 (14)	157 (22)	203 (14)
Refuse	10 (1)	8 (1)	28 (2)
Total	843	725	989

elections in as many ridings. In five ridings, the margin of victory was less than 100. In those five ridings, a total of 114,285 votes were cast for the winning candidates, 0.86 percent of all votes cast in that election. These votes, of course, proved not to be decisive, but as the margin of victory was less than 100 one could estimate that their ex ante probability of being decisive was one chance out of 100.[9] Taking that into account, the probability of casting a decisive vote in 1988 was one chance in 12,000.

But perhaps it was not reasonable to extrapolate in 1993 on the basis of the 1988 election. The 1993 election was much less close than the one in 1988. In 1993 the percentage point difference between total votes for the leading and second parties was 22; it was 11 points in 1988. As a matter of fact, there were only two ridings in 1993 where the margin of victory was less than 100. In those two ridings, a total of 30,837 votes were cast for the winning candidates. Applying the same calculus as the one just used for 1988, the probability of casting a decisive vote in 1993 would appear to have been one chance in 45,000.

It is clear from these different calculi that it is impossible to arrive at a precise estimate of P. Looking at different kinds of evidence leads to different results. These differences, however, should not be exaggerated. All our results buttress our initial point that P lies somewhere between one chance in 10,000 and one chance in 50,000, which is probably all the information people need to know when they decide whether they should vote.

From that perspective, our findings indicate that most students did not overestimate P. The "true" P at the riding level is somewhere between one chance in 10,000 and one chance in 100,000 but is closer to the former. The median response is one chance in 100,000. In fact, there seems to be a propensity to underestimate P, as the median response is more pessimistic than what the empirical evidence suggests: the chances might have been slightly better than what most students believed.[10]

There are a number of caveats, however. First, it could be that university students have a better grasp of probabilities than the general population. I present below other pieces of evidence based on surveys of representative samples of the electorate. Second, the fact remains that some respondents clearly overestimate P. Between 10 and 15 percent perceive P to be one chance in 1,000 or more at the constituency level and to be greater than one chance in 1,000,000 at the national level. It could be that some people vote because they overestimate P.

Third, around 20 percent of the students could not answer the question. This could mean that they had never thought about this, which of course would imply that P does not matter. But it could also reflect their reluctance to provide a number when it is really impossible to know what that probability is.[11] This calls for another approach to measure P, one that we have used in subsequent studies whose findings I report below.

Fourth, there is the possibility that on the first question measuring P at the constituency level, the middle categories were more often chosen because a number of respondents who did not really have an opinion guessed that the truth was more likely to lie in the middle than at the extremes. Fifth, perceptions of P are not correlated at all with perceptions of the closeness of the election.[12] Theoretically, there should be at least a moderate correlation between the two, as the probability of casting a decisive vote increases with the closeness of the outcome. This raises the possibility that probabilities are just too difficult to grasp for some and that the information we obtain when we ask people to express their perceptions in terms of numbers is not very reliable. Again, this would seem to call for other types of questions to check the robustness of the findings.

In this study, we also conducted an experiment. In five of the ten classes, we presented a ten-minute lecture on the paradox of voting.[13] The paradox, we said, arises when economic notions of rationality are applied to politics. We then briefly outlined the benefits and costs of voting, stressing that any individual's vote can make the benefits accrue only if that vote is decisive, and that the probability of that occurring is extremely small. No precise probability was provided but the point that P was very small was emphasized. The lecture concluded that it appears irrational to vote, within that perspective, and the fact that most people do vote is a paradox that has led to a debate in political science about whether the theory ought to be rejected or amended.

Did the presentation have an impact on students' perceptions of P? To find out, we regressed panel respondents' estimates of P[14] in the second (campaign) and third (post-election) questionnaires on the same estimates provided in the first questionnaire, plus a dummy variable that equals 1 for those exposed to the presentation. The dummy variable comes out with a significant coefficient of −.08. Everything else being equal, those who were exposed to the presentation gave a score that was .08 lower, on a scale from 0 to 1. As the average score was .41, this corresponds to a relative difference of 20 percent.[15] This is a substantial impact.

A number of students, then, were led to revise downwards their estimate of P after hearing the presentation. The latter seems to have induced some to think they might have been overestimating P. This result is intriguing. While the overall distribution of responses reveals little overestimation, some students reacted to the presentation as if they believed they had been overestimating P. It is difficult to draw clear conclusions.

In reaction to this first study, Thalheimer (1995) conducted a small exploratory study in which she tested another approach (see appendix F). She interviewed 125 students lurking the cafeterias, lunch counters, and a pub at the Université de Montréal between February 23 and March 10, 1995. At the time, a referendum on Quebec sovereignty was expected to be held sometime in the year (it took place in October).

Instead of asking her respondents to indicate their estimate of P by choosing among a number of probabilities, Thalheimer first resorted to an open-ended question: "How, approximately, do you evaluate the chances that your vote will decide whether it is the Yes or No side that wins the referendum? One chance in . . ." This had the advantage of not structuring the responses. Out of 125 students, 15 percent could not provide any number. Among those who did give a number, the median response was one chance in 1,000,000.[16]

Such a response appears reasonable. One could expect between four and five million citizens to vote in the referendum; to say that the chances are one in 1,000,000 was perhaps the most sensible answer to give at the time.[17] Here again, there is no evidence of systematic overestimation of P at that point in time. On the other hand, one student out of three thought that the chances of casting the decisive vote were better than 1 in 100,000, which appears to have been an overly optimistic estimate. The open-ended question, then, suggests that overestimation may be more frequent than the first study indicated.

This finding was reinforced by the results obtained with respect to two other questions. Because she knew that many people find fractions and probabilities confusing, Thalheimer asked her respondents to ascertain the chances of casting a decisive vote in qualitative terms: whether that chance was very strong, fairly strong, fairly weak, or very weak. And for those who indicated that the chances were weak, she followed with a question asking whether the chances were practically nil. If P was, as I have just argued, in the vicinity of one chance in 1,000,000, the right answer to those questions was that the chances are very weak and indeed practically nil.

Thalheimer found that nine of her respondents thought that the chances of casting a decisive vote were strong. And among those who answered that the chances were weak, nineteen said that they were *not* practically nil. This gives twenty-eight students, 22 percent of the total sample, who overestimated P. This estimate is slightly lower than the one based on the open-ended question about the probability of a decisive vote. Clearly, most students do not overestimate P, but a substantial minority, one out of three or four, does.

The study contained still another question concerning P. Early in the questionnaire, after having asked respondents whether they had voted in the previous two elections, Thalheimer asked them whether they had ever thought about the possibility that if they did not vote their candidate would lose by one vote. Forty respondents, 32 percent of the sample, said yes.

This result can be construed in two ways. On the one hand, it could be argued that in order to be affected by P, electors must have tried somehow to estimate it, and that this result shows that for the great majority of people P just does not matter. On the other hand, it could be that those who had thought about the possibility in fact believed that P is not practically nil and thus overestimated it. And indeed there is a moderate correlation ($+.17$) between having thought about the possibility and saying that the chances of casting a decisive vote are not practically nil.

Thalheimer's study, then, partly confirms but also qualifies the findings of the Blais-Young study. Both indicate that the majority of students do not overestimate P. But whereas the Blais-Young study suggests that overestimation is confined to a small minority (in the order of 10–15 percent), Thalheimer's more qualitative approach yields a higher estimate, somewhere between 20 and 35 percent.

These two studies dealt with student samples. What about "ordinary people"? Blais and Young did a study using a representative sample of the population of Quebec during the 1995 referendum on sovereignty. A sample of 1,004 electors were interviewed during the last week of the campaign, and 926 of them were briefly reinterviewed right after the referendum (see appendix G).

We pursued a strategy similar to the one followed by Thalheimer. We first asked whether the chances that the Yes or the No side would win by a single vote were very high, somewhat high, somewhat low, or very low. The referendum was very close. The polls were showing the two camps neck and neck, and the No side finally won with 50.6 percent of the vote, a majority of 52,000 votes. Yet, even with such a close race, the probability of a tie or a margin of one remained extremely low. Still, 22 percent of the sample said the chances of the referendum being decided by one vote were very or somewhat high, and another 30 percent thought they were only somewhat low, not very low. For all those who said the chances were low, we followed up with a more specific question about whether the chances were absolutely zero, almost zero, or just low. The responses were fairly evenly distributed among the three categories: 29 percent said absolutely zero, 34 percent almost zero, and 37 percent just low.

We might debate whether the appropriate response was absolutely zero or almost zero. The probability is not really zero but it is so close to it that both answers appear reasonable. Answering that the chances are just low, not almost zero, does appear, however, overly optimistic. If we combine those who answered the initial question by saying that the chances were high and those who said in response to the follow-up that they were just small (not almost zero), then we have 486 individuals, 48 percent of the total sample, who were overestimating P.

This is a much higher estimate than those coming out of the two previous studies. This is partly due to the fact that overestimation is negatively correlated with education: the percentage overestimating P among those with a university degree is just 37 percent. But this could also reflect the fact that as the polls were indicating a very close outcome it became less unreasonable to believe that the chances of casting a decisive vote were not that tiny.

These results have to do with a referendum. Are perceptions of P different in an election? To address this question, we decided to perform a similar analysis of the provincial election that was held in British Columbia on May 28, 1996. Turnout in that election was 72 percent. A random sample of 804 respondents were interviewed in the last week of the campaign (see appendix H).

We again asked our respondents what they thought were the chances that the election in their riding would be decided by a single vote. The election was a close one. The incumbent New Democratic Party (NDP) won the election, being elected in thirty-nine ridings out of seventy-five, but they obtained fewer votes than the Liberals. The race was close in a number of constituencies. Still, no race was decided by a single vote; only in one riding was the gap between the first two candidates less than 100, and the probability of casting a decisive vote remained quite low.

Nevertheless, 15 percent of respondents felt that the chances of the election in their riding being decided by a single vote were very or somewhat high, and another 26 percent said somewhat low, not very low. To all those who answered that the chances were low, we put a follow-up question about whether the chances were absolutely zero, almost zero, or just low; the percentages choosing these three options were 26 percent, 32 percent, and 42 percent respectively.

If we combine, as we have done in the case of the Quebec referendum, those who said the chances were high and those who answered to the follow-up question that the chances were just low, not almost zero, we get 379 individuals, 47 percent of the total sample, who were overestimating P. The equivalent percentage in the Quebec referendum was 48 percent. In these two instances, about half the electorate seems to believe it is possible that their vote could make the difference.[18] Of course, these two cases are instances of very close contests. The evidence tells us, however, that in close contests a good number of people overestimate P.

Are those who expect a close outcome more likely to overestimate the probability of casting a decisive vote? We find the correlation in both instances to be weak. In the case of the Quebec referendum, 43 percent of the few who did not think the outcome would be close were unwilling to acknowledge that P was practically nil, against 50 percent among those expecting a close outcome. The equivalent percentages for the British Columbia election were 39 percent and 53 percent. The weakness of the relationship is puzzling, since the probability of a tie depends on the closeness of the outcome. This raises questions about the validity and reliability of our measure of P.

In both studies, we also included a question as to whether the respondent had thought about the possibility of casting a decisive vote. Thirty-three percent said they had entertained such a thought in the case of the Quebec referendum and 38 percent in the British Columbia election.[19]

I explored perceptions of P in still another fashion. I conducted with Kim Thalheimer a more extensive study of the reasons for voting among regular voters. We interviewed, in the spring of 1996, 108 regular voters in the metropolitan Montreal area.[20] We asked them whether it could happen *one day* that an election is won by one single vote and that their vote could decide who wins the election. As many as forty-five respondents, 42 percent of the sample, would not dismiss that possibility.

Clearly, many people do not have well-formed opinions about the probability of casting a decisive vote. In fact, only one-third report having thought about such a possibility. And when they are asked to estimate the probability in quantitative or qualitative terms, a clear majority is willing to admit that the probability is very small. At the same time, however, a substantial minority of electors is prone to overestimate P and to believe that their vote might be decisive.

Does P Matter?

The bottom-line question, of course, is whether, whatever the amount of overestimation that takes place, people decide to vote or to abstain on the basis of their perception of P. To respond to that question, I use two approaches. The first is simply to ask people whether they would vote if they were absolutely sure there was no chance their vote could be decisive. If P matters, they should answer they would abstain.

Responses to such questions must be interpreted with caution. It is not altogether clear that voters really understand what motivates them to vote or abstain, or are able to tell how they would behave in hypothetical situations. Such responses remain, however, suggestive of people's spontaneous reactions.

Thalheimer (1995) put the following question to her 125 students: "If you were completely certain that there is absolutely no chance that your ballot decides the outcome of the referendum, would you vote?" Nine students, all of whom intended to vote, said they would not vote if they were completely certain their vote could not make a difference. It would thus seem that P was decisive for 7 percent of the students.

Such results suggest that P may matter for only a small minority of electors. One caveat is in order, however. It may be that some people say they would still vote because in their mind there will always be a small chance that their vote could be decisive. We have signs of this in Thalheimer's study. All those who told her they would vote even if they were sure there was no chance that their vote could be decisive were asked to explain their decision. The majority referred to a sense of duty, something I will examine in chapter 5. Seven individuals, however, said they would turn out because if everybody thinks their vote doesn't matter few people will vote and consequently the chances of one ballot being decisive increase. Seven other individuals used the "in case" argument, clinging to the you-never-know notion and saying that they would vote just in case their ballot happened to be decisive. These fourteen individuals simply did not accept the premise of the question. We cannot assume that they are insensitive to P. All in all, 23 students out of 125, almost one out of five, thus seemed to be affected by P.

Blais and Young repeated the same approach in their study of a representative sample during the last week of the Quebec referendum. Respondents were asked if they would vote if they were absolutely sure there was no chance their vote could decide which side wins. Forty individuals, 4 percent of the total sample, said they would not vote. Among those who actually voted, only 3 percent indicated they would not vote. The implication is that turnout would have been three percentage points lower if P were assumed to be zero.

Perhaps P did not matter much in the referendum because the stakes were perceived to be so high. It is interesting to see whether the same pattern emerges in a more typical election. We repeated the same question in our study of the 1996 election in British Columbia. Sixty-eight respondents, 9 percent of the sample, said they would not vote if they were absolutely sure their vote could not make a difference. Among those who said they were certain or likely to vote, only 3 percent, exactly the same percentage as in the Quebec referendum, answered that they would not vote.

We pursued a similar strategy in our interviews with regular voters in the Montreal area. We asked our 108 respondents if they would vote if they were sure there was absolutely no chance their vote could be decisive. Only two of them indicated they would not vote. In their explanation for why they would vote, however, five individuals expressed themselves in a way that suggests they are not insensitive to P. Three respondents indicated that their vote could close the gap, one rejected the premise of our question, saying that "you never know [whether your vote will be decisive]," and a fifth seemed not to understand the question, as she said she would vote so that her candidate wins. The bottom line, here again, is that P does not appear to have much impact.

We asked our regular voters still another question, that is, whether they are more inclined to vote when an election is close. In this case, twenty-five respondents, 23 percent of the sample, indicated that indeed they are more inclined to vote when an election is close. And their explanations are revealing: "my vote has more opportunity to count," "you know your vote will be more meaningful," "one has the impression that the vote has more weight," "your vote would seem to have more impact," "I feel my vote may have an influence."

All these individuals said they would vote even if they were certain that their vote would not be decisive. Yet a good minority of regular voters, and many more irregular voters I would assume, admit a close election is more enticing. And it is more enticing because one's vote seems to count more. This comes close to saying that P matters.

In short, few people say they would not vote if they were absolutely sure there was no chance their vote could be decisive. More people acknowledge, however, that they are more inclined to vote when an election is close, because their vote seems to count more. This suggests that P may matter at least marginally.

A second approach, more standard in social research, is to determine if perceptions of P have an independent effect on the decision to vote. In the core rational choice model, as explained in the introduction, the decision to vote is predicted to depend on $B^{\star}P$ and on C. The analyses that are presented below include two other factors that may affect the propensity to vote but that lie outside the rational choice model: D, the sense that voting is a duty, and I, the overall level of interest for politics.

The first study is that of students' turnout in the 1993 Canadian election. Table 3.3 summarizes the findings concerning B and P. The dependent variable is whether the respondent voted or not, which is assumed to depend on B, P, C, D, and I. I have also included two control variables that had an additional independent impact on the vote: those students who were on our panel groups were more likely to vote, while turnout was lower at Western than at Montreal.[21]

Table 3.3 shows the results. I distinguish B_c, P_c, B_n, and P_n as electors may have perceptions of the benefits of having their candidate or party win and of the probability of casting the decisive vote for the specific contest in their own constituency and for the whole national election.

In the upper section of table 3.3, P is a dummy variable that equals 1 for those who overestimate it, that is, those who said that the chances of casting a decisive vote at the constituency level were one chance in 1,000 or more and those who said that the chances of casting a decisive vote at the national level were one chance in 100,000 or more. In the first equation, I have re-

Table 3.3 The Impact of P and B on Voting among University Students in 1993: Logistic Regressions

	B_c*P_c	B_n*P_n	B_c	P_c	B_n	P_n
Direct measure of P: Chances						
B_c*P_c and B_n*P_n	.10	.35				
B_c and P_c			.97***	.01		
B_n and P_n					1.11**	.12
B_n and P_c				.17	1.12**	
Indirect measure of P: Closeness						
B_c*P_c and B_n*P_n	1.62***	.19				
B_c and P_c			.80*	.84**		
B_n and P_n					1.05**	-.12
B_n and P_c				.85**	1.00*	

* Significant at the .10 level (two-tailed test)
** Significant at the .05 level (two-tailed test)
*** Significant at the .01 level (two-tailed test)

Note: B_c indicates how important it is to respondents, on a scale from 0 to 10, which candidate wins in their constituency. B_n indicates how important it is on the same scale which party wins in the country as a whole. Both scales were transformed to 0 to 1.

Chances is a dummy variable that equals 1 for those who said that the chances that their vote would determine which candidate wins in their constituency was one chance in 1,000 or better (P_c) and for those who said that the chances that their vote would determine which party wins in the country as a whole was one chance in 100,000 or more (P_n).

Closeness indicates how close the election was perceived to be on a scale from 0 to 1, in the respondents, constituency (P_c) and in the country as a whole (P_n).

The regressions also include C, D, I, and two dummy variables that equal 1 for those who had also answered a campaign questionnaire (Panel) and who attended the University of Western Ontario (Western). For more details, see Blais and Young (1996).

gressed voting on $B*P$, as entailed by the rational choice model, at both the constituency and national levels. The results indicate that at neither level is $B*P$ significant. In equations 2-4, I have regressed voting on B and P independently. It can be seen that the decision to vote is affected by B but not by P. I have tried different operationalizations of P, such as scores on a 0 to 1 scale, but in all cases P (or $P*B$) remained nonsignificant. That study suggests that P does not matter.

Another set of findings needs to be considered, however. In the lower section of table 3.3, the direct measure of P is replaced by the perceived closeness of the election, the usual proxy for P. It should be recalled that perceived closeness is only weakly correlated with the perceived probability of casting a decisive vote.

The results are more positive for rational choice. When I rely on closeness as an indicator of P, then $B*P$ at the constituency level becomes clearly significant. The following equations indicate, however, that an additive model, in which electors are assumed to consider independently the importance they attach to the election at the national level on the one hand and the closeness of the race in their constituency on the other hand, performs even better.[22]

Turnout does seem to be positively affected by the perceived closeness of the election in the constituency. Why should closeness matter but not our direct measure of P? My interpretation is that closeness is a good proxy for something akin to P. Perhaps, then, P, or something akin to it, matters in spite of the negative evidence we have come up with when it is operationalized in a more direct fashion. There is no support, however, for the hypothesis that the effect of B and P is multiplicative rather than simply additive.

Two additional questions in our study allow us to explore in greater depth how students assessed the value of their vote. We asked them to indicate their agreement or disagreement with a number of statements. One was "So many people vote that my vote means hardly anything." This could be construed as yet another measure of P. Seventy-three percent of the students agreed with the statement, and those who heard the presentation were more prone to agree. Yet, when we added that measure to our model, it did not have an independent impact on the vote.

The second statement was the following: "My own vote may not count for much, but if all people who think like me vote, it could make a big difference." Ninety-four percent of the students agreed with the statement. Responses were strongly correlated with sense of duty. For those who believe it is the duty of every citizen to vote, the statement provides another reason to vote. But agreeing with the statement could also reflect self-delusion. Interestingly, that variable comes up significant when it is incorporated into our model, which opens the possibility that some people vote because they believe that somehow their own vote counts.

Let me turn, finally, to our surveys of the 1995 Quebec referendum and of the 1996 election in British Columbia. Turnout in the referendum was extraordinarily high: 93.5 percent. Turnout in Quebec elections is usually around 80 percent. Turnout in the previous referendum on sovereignty-association, held in 1980, had been 85 percent. By any criterion, turnout in the 1995 referendum was astonishing.

Why? One reason has to be that the stakes were perceived to be extremely high. When we asked our respondents, in the last week of the campaign, what difference it made, for them personally, which side wins, 39 percent said it made an enormous difference, and 40 percent said a great difference; only 11 percent and 9 percent said a small difference and no difference, respectively. Still, that can hardly be the whole explanation. It cannot explain, in particular, why turnout was much higher than in the previous referendum in 1980.[23]

A second plausible reason was that the outcome was a very close one. The No side won with a very thin edge: it got 50.6 percent of the vote. And the polls were all pointing to an extremely close outcome. This was epitomized by the headline of the very last public poll: "50-50!" As a consequence, 49 percent told us they expected a very close outcome and another 44 percent predicted it to be somewhat close; only 2 percent thought it would not be close at all. At first sight at least, it would seem reasonable to suppose that closeness did foster turnout.

We can test our model about the determinants of voting. The decision to vote is assumed to depend on B^*P, C, D, and I. Before considering the results, it is important to keep in mind that turnout in the election was 93.5 percent and that in our sample 96 percent said they had voted. We have only thirty-six individuals who indicated they had not voted. There is very little variance, and in such circumstances it is difficult for any relationship to achieve statistical significance.

Table 3.4 shows the findings concerning B and P. Neither variable is statistically significant. Note, however, that B has the expected sign, is close to achieving statistical significance,[24] and that its logistic coefficient is not substantially different from the one observed in table 3.3. The situation is different in the case of P. The logistic coefficients are systematically weak and never come close to being significant. But note that the most direct measure (chances) yields the worst result (a coefficient with the wrong sign). Interestingly, we get at least the right sign when we use as an indicator of P not respondents' perceptions of the likelihood of casting a decisive vote but rather whether they had actually thought about that possibility.

We may thus conclude that the decision to vote or not to vote in the Quebec referendum was affected by B but that it is not clear that P, even as represented by closeness, mattered. This last finding is perplexing. We have seen that in a great majority of studies perceived closeness does seem to foster turnout. Furthermore, it is hard to believe that the extraordinarily high turnout in the referendum was not partly due to the extremely close contest.

The most plausible explanation is, in my view, that when we have so little variance it is extremely difficult for variables that have only a marginal impact on the vote to emerge as statistically significant. When B comes out as only marginally significant, we should not expect much from P.

What about the 1996 British Columbia election? Table 3.5 shows the re-

Table 3.4. The Impact of P and B on Voting in the 1995 Quebec Referendum: Logistic Regressions

	$B^{\star}P$	B	P
Direct measure of P: Chances			
$\quad B^{\star}P$	-.13		
$\quad B$ and P		.90	-.22
Direct measure of P: Possibility			
$\quad B^{\star}P$	.26		
$\quad B$ and P		.88	.38
Indirect measure of P: Closeness			
$\quad B^{\star}P$	.65		
$\quad B$ and P		.85	.39

* Significant at the .10 level (two-tailed test)
** Significant at the .05 level (two-tailed test)
*** Significant at the .01 level (two-tailed test)

Note: B (Benefits) is the respondent's score on a scale from 0 to 1: the scale is made up of two questions about how much change sovereignty would bring about in general and about how much difference it would make personally for the respondent.

Chances is a dummy variable that equals 1 for those who said that the chance of casting a decisive vote was high or only small (not absolutely or close to zero).

Possibility is a dummy variable that equals 1 for those who said they had thought about the possibility that their vote could be decisive.

Closeness is a dummy variable that equals 1 for those who expected the outcome to be close.

The regressions also include C, D, and I.

sults. The dependent variable is the probability of voting as expressed in the last week of the campaign.[25]

Consider first the findings with the direct measures of P. There is no support for the multiplicative model in which voting is assumed to depend on $B^{\star}P$. It can also be seen that the propensity to vote does not increase with P; in fact, P has the wrong sign in three equations out of four.

Once again, the results are more interesting when we rely on closeness as a proxy for P. Once again also, the additive model outperforms the multiplicative one. What is most interesting in this case is that the perceived closeness of the race at the provincial level seems to matter more than the perceived closeness at the constituency level. This does not fit the "pure" rational choice model: whether the provincial race is close or not should not matter if the local race in the constituency is not close. Electors in British Columbia appear to have reacted differently. Perceiving the provincial election to be a close contest made people feel that individual votes could count. Note also that the impact of P cannot be explained away by the role of stra-

Table 3.5. The Impact of P and B on Voting in the 1996 British Columbia Election: OLS Regressions

	B_c*P_c	B_n*P_n	B_c	P_c	B_n	P_n
Direct measure of P: Chances						
B_c*P_c	.01					
B_c and P_c			.07***	-.02		
B_n and P_c				-.02	.07**	
Direct measure of P: Possibility						
B_c*P_c	.01					
B_c and P_c			.07***	-.03*		
B_n and P_c				-.03*	.07***	
Indirect measure of P: Closeness						
B_c*P_c and B_n*P_n	.003	.06**				
B_c and P_c			.04	.004		
B_n and P_n					.07***	.06*
B_c and P_n			.07***			.07**
B_n and P_c				.004	.06**	

* Significant at the .10 level (two-tailed test)
** Significant at the .05 level (two-tailed test)
*** Significant at the .01 level (two-tailed test)

Note: B_n is the respondent's score on a scale from 0 to 1: the scale is made up of the question about how much difference it would make personally for the respondent which party wins in the province as a whole. B_c is the respondent's score on the same scale. It indicates how much difference it would make personally for the respondent which candidate wins in her constituency.

Chances is a dummy variable that equals 1 for those who said that the chance of casting a decisive vote was high or only small (not absolutely or close to zero).

Possibility is a dummy variable that equals 1 for those who said they had thought about the possibility that their vote could be decisive.

Closeness indicates how close the election was perceived to be on a scale from 0 to 1, in the respondent's constituency (P_c) and in the province as a whole (P_n).

The regressions also include C, D, and I.

tegic politicians concentrating their efforts in certain constituencies, since it is perceptions of the province-wide race that mattered.

Does P matter then? If we were to look only at the hard evidence as to whether there is a significant relationship between direct measures of P and voting, the answer would be an unequivocal no. The fact that these direct measures of P are weakly related to perceived closeness is, however, perplexing. It is telling that closeness seems to foster turnout in almost every study and that this relationship cannot be explained away by political mobilization. There remains a significant relationship between closeness and turnout even after party spending is controlled for. And, whatever the parties and the media do, people themselves say they feel more inclined to vote when the election is close, as many regular voters have told us in open-ended interviews.

If people are more inclined to vote when the election is close, it is because they have the impression that their vote "counts" more. This does not mean that they think specifically about the possibility that the election may be decided by a single vote. In fact, it not clear what precisely goes on in people's minds; it seems to be a vague feeling that each vote counts more. That may not be exactly the kind of reasoning that rational choice imputes to voters, but it is akin to it.[26]

There is another reason not to dismiss the impact of P on turnout. There is strong evidence that electors take into account the various candidates' and parties' probability of winning when they make up their mind which party or candidate they will support. This is called strategic voting, whereby one votes for a second-preferred party (candidate) rather than the first-preferred choice because the former has a better chance of winning the election. The existence of strategic voting has been documented in a great number of studies (Alvarez and Nagler 2000; Blais and Nadeau 1996; Abramson, Aldrich, Paolino, and Rohde 1992; Black 1978; Cain 1978; Fisher 1973; Niemi, Whitten, and Franklin 1992).

Let us take the example of a plurality election with only three candidates. Let us assume that an individual perceives her preferred candidate as being the least likely to win the election. Data from the 1988 Canadian election indicate that 30 percent of people who find themselves in such a situation decide to vote for their second-preferred candidate (Blais and Nadeau 1996). And the propensity to vote strategically increases when the second choice is perceived to have a much better chance of winning than the first choice, and when the race between the second and third choices gets closer.

A good number of voters are concerned not to waste their vote on a candidate who has no chance of winning. The implication is that many people (implicitly) think their vote could make a difference, and decide to vote for a candidate who is not their most preferred because of P. If P enters into the calculus of choosing which candidate to support, why would it not be part of the calculus of deciding whether to vote or not?

My verdict, therefore, is that P matters. It matters, however, only at the margin. A close election is likely to increase turnout by a few percentage points, but the fact remains that most people vote in a national election even if the outcome of that election is a foregone conclusion. And P does not matter exactly as the rational choice model assumes. People do not multiply B by P and they rely on the vague notion that their vote might count more in a close election rather than on an estimate of the probability that their vote could be decisive.

Do (Some) People Vote on the Basis of Minimax Regret?

It is possible to salvage the rational choice model even if P did not matter.[27] The most important attempt along these lines has been offered by Ferejohn and Fiorina (1974), who suggest that some electors may be unable or unwilling to estimate P, given the great uncertainty that surrounds it. While they know that there is a possibility of casting a decisive vote, they cannot tell how likely or unlikely that possibility is. As a consequence, some electors resort to a minimax regret calculus rather than utility maximization. Such individuals compare the regret they would feel if they voted and their vote proved not to be decisive with the regret they would feel if they did not vote and subsequently found out that their vote would have been decisive. If the former is greater than the latter, they abstain; if it is smaller, they vote.

I reviewed in the introduction the major criticisms that have been addressed to this model. Ferejohn and Fiorina (1975, 925) have acknowledged these difficulties but argue that the model may offer an apt description of at least some people's reasoning. To support their claim, they test two versions of the rational choice model, the standard utility one where the decision to vote depends on B^*P (P corresponding to perceived closeness) and a second one where only B matters. The second version is shown to perform better, thus indicating that P does not matter. The fact that P does not matter, suggests, according to Ferejohn and Fiorina, that the minimax regret model, in which electors do not estimate P, is superior.

Such a conclusion is dubious for at least two reasons. First, as I have indicated earlier and as Aldrich (1976) has shown, the findings are more supportive of P when a number of corrections are made. Second, their test could be construed as questioning the validity of the expected utility model but it does not provide any positive support, as such, for minimax regret. A more direct test is called for.

Such a direct test is offered by Kenney and Rice (1989). They asked a sample of respondents in two cities the following question: "Please tell me whether you ever worry that if you don't vote your favorite candidate might lose by one vote—your vote?" Over one-third of the respondents said, "Yes," qualifying as potential minimax regret decision-makers. And these minimax regret respondents were significantly more likely to have voted in the previous election (1984) and to intend to vote in the forthcoming one (1986). This is an interesting finding. The study, however, has one major limitation: it does not examine other factors that may affect turnout, and it is thus impossible to determine whether minimax regret has an independent effect, controlling for these other factors.

A second study, by Dennis (1991), does test the minimax hypothesis at the multivariate level. Using data collected in Wisconsin during the 1984 presidential campaign, Dennis finds that the minimax measure is not significant when other psychological variables are added. Some of the questions used by Dennis are, however, problematic,[28] thus casting some doubt on the findings.

Our 1993 study of university students did include a question on minimax. Students were asked to indicate their degree of agreement or disagreement with the following statement: "I would feel really terrible if I did not vote and my candidate lost by one vote." The question is similar to the one used by Kenney and Rice but it is more concrete: it focuses on the upcoming election rather than asking whether they *ever* thought in terms of minimax.

Considerable numbers of respondents agreed with the minimax statement: 33 percent strongly agreed and another 38 percent agreed. There was also a moderately strong correlation between the minimax measure and the propensity to vote. Yet, in the multivariate analysis, minimax regret was found not to have any independent impact on the vote (see Blais, Young, Fleury, and Lapp 1995). The main reason is that there is a relatively strong correlation between minimax and sense of duty. Those who feel it is the duty of every citizen to vote would, of course, feel terrible if they did not vote. For many, agreeing with the minimax statement is a mere reflection of a generalized sense of civic duty. When we control for that sense of duty, minimax does not have independent explanatory power.

The verdict must thus be that there is little empirical support for the minimax regret hypothesis.

Conclusion

What have we found? First, there is little doubt that closeness fosters turnout. We may not know precisely how and why this happens but the relationship cannot be explained away by the role of strategic politicians. This pattern is clearly consistent with the rational choice model.

The evidence with respect to *P* as such is more ambiguous. Many people find probabilities confusing, so that beliefs about *P* may be fuzzy or inconsistent. We have, nevertheless, tried to tap electors' perceptions of *P*. We have asked students to choose among eight options, from one chance in 10 to one chance in 100,000,000. With representative samples of the population in two different settings (a referendum in Quebec and an election in British Columbia), we have asked respondents to describe what they perceived to be their chance of casting the decisive vote on a continuum from very high to absolutely nil.

The survey among university students suggested little overestimation of *P*. This may be due in part to the fact that the sample was highly educated. It may also be an artifact of the question. Perhaps the most telling result is that hearing the presentation made students revise *P* downwards by 20 percent. Many students reacted as if they had been slightly overestimating *P*.

The studies of the 1995 Quebec referendum and of the 1996 British Columbia election produced startling results. Close to half the respondents in both cases would not acknowledge the fact that their chance of casting a decisive vote was close to zero. This leads me to conclude that there is substantial overestimation of *P* in the population. Perhaps these two contests were so close that people were exceptionally overly optimistic about *P*,[29] but the point remains that many people are prone to overestimate *P*.

When it comes to ascertaining the impact of *P* on voting, things are more complicated. In three different studies, direct measures of *P* did not have any independent impact on voting. I am reluctant, however, to conclude that *P* does not matter. I have doubts about the validity of the measure of *P* utilized in the first study. I have greater confidence in the more qualitative approach followed in the other studies, but the results are still negative. The nil findings obtained in the Quebec referendum can easily be accounted for: the extremely high turnout makes it almost impossible for a factor that is likely to play only at the margin to come out statistically significant. But the negative results observed in British Columbia cannot be easily dismissed.

This is not sufficient, however, to conclude that *P* does not matter. It is not sufficient because we know that closeness affects turnout and that if there is such a relationship it is not only because of political mobilization by the parties. I have shown that regular voters themselves acknowledge being more inclined to vote when the election is close and that the reasons they give boil down to the perception that their vote counts more. This may not be exactly the kind of reasoning that rational choice assumes people go through and the reasoning may be somewhat confused, but it is sufficiently akin to it. Furthermore, this kind of reasoning is consistent with the well-documented presence of strategic voting. When they vote, some people seem to be concerned not to waste their vote on a candidate who has no chance of winning. In the same manner, when it comes to deciding whether to vote or not to vote, some people are more likely to vote when they perceive the race to be close. In my view, this amounts to assuming, implicitly, that one's vote could possibly be decisive.

It is thus reasonable to believe that *P* matters. At the same time, the evidence points to a small impact. *P* cannot account for the fact that most people vote in national elections, but it does seem to play at the margin.

Finally, the results support the view that the impact of *B* and *P* is additive rather than multiplicative. This suggests that the calculus of voting is less sophisticated than the rational choice model would lead us to believe. People do not make up their mind on the basis of expected benefits in the strict sense of the term. They are just somewhat more inclined to vote when they feel the election is important and/or there is a close race.

CHAPTER 4

What Is the Cost of Voting?

The rational citizen decides to vote or not to vote on the basis of whether, in her estimation, the expected benefit outweighs the expected cost. But what is the cost of voting? In the model, this cost corresponds, on the one hand, to the amount of time one feels she needs to spend assembling and digesting the information about candidates and parties in order to decide which party or candidate to vote for and, on the other hand, to the time spent going to the poll, voting, and returning.

Rational choice theorists have concluded that it is irrational to vote because they have assumed that the cost of voting, while not large, is not extremely small. But how do citizens themselves assess this cost? How much time does it take to vote? How much time does it take to get the information to decide how to vote? And how do people value the opportunity cost of these activities?

There are very few concrete data available on how people perceive the cost of voting. In fact, data on the cost of voting are as scant as those on perceptions of P. I fill some of the gaps and provide new survey evidence on this.

There are two possibilities. First, the subjective cost could be nil. In that case, because P is not zero, it would become rational to vote. Under such a scenario, it would have to be explained, however, why people do not perceive any opportunity cost in the act of voting.

Second, the cost could be very small, but not nil. In that case, it would seem irrational to vote since expected benefits are bound to be minuscule in a large electorate. The rational choice model could, however, be salvaged by two kinds of arguments. It could be that people vote, in spite of the fact that costs exceed expected benefits, because of other nonrational considerations, such as the feeling that they have a moral obligation to vote. Or it could be that it is precisely because costs are so small that people don't bother to calculate and compare benefits and costs, as proposed by Barry (1978).

The chapter has three sections. The first presents some descriptive information on how people perceive the cost of voting. The second ascertains to what extent perceived costs affect the propensity to vote. The third examines Barry's proposition that rational choice fails to explain the decision to vote because the stakes are too low.

How Small Is the Cost of Voting?

Few would argue that voting is a very demanding activity. In most democracies, the authorities do all they can to facilitate the act of voting. In most countries, citizens have only to answer a short questionnaire to become registered on the electoral list; to go to a polling station that is usually located close to where they live; and to indicate on a ballot which party(ies) and/or candidate(s) they wish to support. These activities are supposed to require very little time and effort. But how much time does it actually take to vote? And how easy or difficult do citizens find it to go and vote? The empirical literature has failed to address these questions. I present below the evidence I have assembled, which sheds some light on people's perceptions.

Voting also entails information costs. Citizens must garner information to determine which candidate or party would best represent their views and interests. As Downs (1957, chap. 11) has pointed out, acquiring such information is costly. Citizens must decide how much to invest in information-gathering.

According to Downs, the energy and time invested in information-gathering depends on three factors. First, the importance one attaches to making a correct as opposed to an incorrect decision. Second, the expected marginal return: how likely is it that new bits of information will alter her judgments? Third, the marginal cost of acquiring new bits of information.

The upshot is that most people are unlikely to invest much in acquiring new information. They merely aim at becoming minimally informed. Still, there is a cost involved. If an individual decides, at the outset of a campaign, that she will not vote, she will be able to spare some time and effort that she would have had to invest if she had decided that she would vote. This is referred to as the information cost of voting, and it is a difficult cost to ascertain. The person must figure out what she would have done if she had decided at the outset that she was not going to vote. I have tried to measure this information cost as well, and I present the results below.

Let us start with the cost of voting as such. Robert Young and I put the following question to our sample of students two weeks before the 1993 Canadian election: "How difficult do you think it would be for you to go and cast your vote?" Only 10 percent responded that it would be difficult or very difficult. Clearly, for the great majority the cost was very small: 45 percent indicated it would be very easy, another 45 percent opting for easy. A "very easy" answer might suggest that the cost is about nil. It could thus be that for half the students there is no perceived cost in the act of voting as such.

Our questionnaire included another question on the cost of voting. We asked our respondents whether they agreed with the statement that "it is so easy to vote that I don't see any reason not to." Seventy-two percent agreed (34 percent strongly agreed). Responses to this question do not merely tap perceptions of cost. In fact, the question is strongly correlated with questions measuring sense of citizen duty (Blais and Young 1996). But it is also separately and independently correlated with the question on the difficulty of voting. The fact that three-quarters of the students could not see *any* reason not to vote is certainly telling.

Our studies of representative samples of electors during the 1995 Quebec referendum and the 1996 British Columbia election allow us to probe further into perceptions of cost. In these two surveys 64 percent (in Quebec) and 66 percent (in British Columbia) told us it is *very* easy to vote (another 31 percent and 24 percent, respectively, said it is somewhat easy). Again, this could indicate that, for the majority of people, the perceived cost is simply nil.

In both studies, we asked an additional question about how much time they thought it would take them to go to the poll, vote, and return. In Quebec, 52 percent estimated it would take them a quarter of an hour, and another 35 percent said half an hour; the equivalent percentages in British Columbia were 44 percent and 43 percent. The average estimated time is 25 minutes in Quebec and 27 minutes in British Columbia.[1] This might be an underestimation of the real time it takes.[2] But it is the subjective cost that matters, and that subjective cost is quite small. As expected, the less time one expects it will take to go and vote, the more likely she is to find it very easy to vote.[3]

We asked these two questions again in Quebec, after the referendum. We might still expect people to underestimate the actual time, but the bias could be reduced, after people have had the opportunity to go through the actual experience of going to the poll and voting. Instead, we find that relatively few people revised their estimate upwards, and as many (in fact, a few more) revised it downwards, so that the average reported time, after the fact, was 23 minutes, compared with the average expected time of 25 minutes.

It is also interesting to see whether having voted in previous elections affected perceptions of cost. Previous to the 1995 referendum, there had been two elections in Quebec, the 1994 provincial election and the 1993 federal election, as well as the 1992 referendum on the Charlottetown Accord. Among our respondents, 71 percent said they had voted in each of these three contests, 16 percent claimed to have voted in two, 5 percent in one, and 8 percent in none. Those who had never voted tended to perceive a higher cost.[4] Only 39 percent of them expected it would take only 15 minutes to vote, and only 45 percent thought it was very easy to vote, compared to 52 percent and 66 percent respectively among those who had previously voted. Moreover, the real difference is between those who had voted at least once and those who had never voted: the percentages finding it very easy to vote are almost as high (60 percent) among those who had voted once or twice as among those who had voted in each of the three ballots (68 percent). The same pattern emerges in the British Columbia data set. These data suggest that those who had never voted were inclined to overestimate the cost of voting.

These findings show that for the majority of electors the cost of the act of voting, as such, is very small. For 84 percent of our Quebec sample and 87 percent of the BC respondents, the expected time involved is half an hour or less, and for 64 percent and 66 percent respectively, voting is deemed to be very easy.

But there are also information costs. In the two surveys, we asked the following question: "Do you find it very easy, somewhat easy, somewhat difficult, or very difficult to get information to decide how to vote?" In Quebec 41 percent said it was very easy and 40 percent somewhat easy; in British Columbia the percentages were 50 percent and 32 percent. This tells us two things. On the one hand, information costs are perceived to be relatively small. On the other hand, they are perceived to be somewhat higher than the cost of voting as such.[5]

Are perceptions of information costs correlated with perceptions of the cost of the act of voting? In part. Among those who find it very easy to vote, 52 percent in Quebec and 64 percent in British Columbia also find it very easy to become informed. This gives a group of 34 percent of the sample in Quebec and of 43 percent in British Columbia who find it very easy both to get the information and to vote. It could be that for these people, the cost of voting is practically nil.

I have probed this question further in the open-ended interviews with regular voters. We asked them, as we had done in the referendum study, how much time it takes them to vote. But we also asked them how much time it takes them to get information to decide how to vote, something we had not asked in the referendum study. It is a difficult question, forcing respondents to sort out the time they devote to obtaining the specific information that is directly relevant to the vote decision. The overwhelming majority of respondents could not provide even an approximate answer. Quite a few pointed out that they usually have made up their mind by the beginning of the campaign, so that from their point of view, there was no information cost. Others said that they always keep up with politics, whatever the case; they do not feel they bear any cost either. For the great majority of voters, then, the perceived information cost is simply nil.

This question was followed by an even more difficult one which was designed to tap whether electors perceive any opportunity cost in voting. The question was the following: "If you did not vote, you would save some time. Do you think you could do something enjoyable or useful instead?" If someone cannot think of anything she could do instead of becoming informed and voting, her opportunity cost of voting is, practically speaking, nil. Interestingly enough, about two-thirds of our respondents said No. Many of them responded, "Not really," indicating that of course in principle they could do something else but that, practically speaking, there was no opportunity cost. As one colorful interviewee told us, "Something pleasant in 15 minutes? Not really." Some other answers are as revealing: "Well, I don't think I'm so busy that the time I spend voting would become a problem"; "It is obvious that one could do something pleasant or useful but that does not bother me. This is not about saving time"; "They give me an hour off of work, so it does not matter." But the quote I prefer the most is the following: "Bad question. I don't think that way." The implication is obvious: for most voters the perceived cost of voting is, indeed, practically nil.[6]

The evidence reviewed here shows that the perceived cost of voting is very small. The issue is whether that cost is very or extremely small, or even almost zero, but it is unfortunately impossible to measure costs with the degree of precision that would be required to distinguish among these possibilities. The various results presented above strongly suggest, however, that for a number of voters the perceived cost is just nil, and that for many others it is extremely small.

How Much Does Cost Matter?

There is little doubt that one reason why so many people vote is that the perceived cost of voting is very small. Indeed, as table 4.1 shows, in each of the three surveys we have conducted the perceived cost of voting affects turnout, even after taking into account benefits, the probability of casting a decisive vote, political interest, and sense of duty.

Table 4.1. The Impact of Cost on Voting

	Cost
a. University students in 1993: Logistic regression	-2.09***
b. 1995 Quebec referendum: Logistic regression	-2.66**
c. 1996 British Columbia election: OLS regression	-.10**

** Significant at the .05 level (two-tailed test)
*** Significant at the .01 level (two-tailed test)
Note: In *a* Cost indicates, on a scale from 0 to 1, the extent to which respondents disagreed with the following statement: "It is so easy to vote that I don't see any reason not to." In *b* and *c* Cost is the respondent's score on a scale from 0 to 1; the scale is made up of three questions about how much time it takes to go to the poll, vote, and return, how easy it is to vote and how easy it is to get information to decide how to vote.
    The regressions also include *P, B, D,* and *I*.

But how powerful a factor is cost? How much would turnout decrease if costs were to increase? And what kind of cost matters the most? Perhaps the best way to address these questions is to run some simulations.

Here again, I start with our experimental study among university students in the 1993 Canadian election. In that study, the measure of cost used is the degree of agreement or disagreement with the statement, "It is so easy to vote that I do not see any reason not to." Suppose that strongly agreeing with that proposition reflects the perception that there is no cost at all involved in voting, while just agreeing with it corresponds to a perceived small cost. We may ask ourselves what would have happened if everybody had perceived at least some small cost, that is, if all those who strongly agreed with the statement had "merely" agreed with it. My simulation reveals that turnout would have been reduced by about two points.[7]

But perhaps a simulation with our other measure of cost, which directly asked how easy or difficult it would be to vote, is more telling. Again we may suppose that those who indicated it is very easy to vote perceive no cost at all in voting. What would have happened if all of them had perceived some small cost, that is, if they had responded that it is easy, rather than very easy? According to that simulation, turnout would have declined by four points. This may not be a huge impact but it is not negligible either, as it merely reflects the effect associated with moving from a cost of close to zero to a cost that is very small.

Our studies of the 1995 Quebec referendum and of the 1996 British Columbia election allow us to examine the impact of cost in greater depth, and with representative samples. I rely here on a scale, from 0 to 1, made up of three questions about the time it takes to vote, the ease of voting, and the ease of getting information to decide how to vote. The median score on this scale is 0.2 in both Quebec and British Columbia, indicating that the median elector perceives the cost to be quite low; this corresponds to a situation where voting is expected to take between 15 and 30 minutes, to be very easy, and becoming informed is construed as somewhat easy.

What would happen if the median score were 0.4, that is the median situation were one in which it takes 45 minutes to vote, and it is somewhat easy to vote and to become informed? Our data indicate that if everyone's score on cost increased by 0.2, turnout would be reduced by two points in both cases.

In the open-ended interviews of regular voters, I explored the matter in another fashion. We asked our respondents if they would vote if it took them one or even two hours. All in all, nine respondents indicated they would not vote if it took one hour and 36 balked at the idea of devoting two hours to voting. The last result is particularly interesting. At the lower end of the scale, the impact of cost is relatively marginal, but the willingness to vote does decline when voting is construed to be painful. Moreover, it must be kept in mind that our study dealt only with regular voters; we may assume that irregular voters are even more sensitive to considerations of cost.

We may therefore conclude that one reason why so many people vote is that the perceived cost of voting is very low. As the case of the United States shows, quite a few people would not be willing to make much effort to become registered on the voting list to begin with. And many more would stay home if they had to wait for hours in the polling station.

Outside unusual circumstances, however, marginal increases in cost seem to matter only marginally. My various simulations suggest that turnout would decrease by only a few percentage points if voting became a little less easy or if it took one hour instead of 30 minutes to vote.

Perhaps the best illustration of this is the negligible impact of weather conditions on the vote. It is usually taken for granted that turnout is depressed when the weather is bad (see Grofman 1993, 102). The evidence, however, is much more ambiguous. The most thorough study, by Knack (1994), shows that rain has no effect whatsoever among those with a high sense of civic duty (almost half the electors) and reduces turnout by only a few percentage points among those with a weaker sense of duty: the overall impact is minimal. People may not be willing to vote at any cost, but minor inconveniences such as rain or a queue deter only a few.

Is There a Threshold in the Cost of Voting?

The final question that needs to be examined flows from Barry's suggestion that rational choice fails to explain why people vote, but for a very good reason: it is not rational to calculate expected benefits and costs when both are bound to be very low. This amounts to arguing that rational choice is a useful model in general but not in the specific case of voting. I defer a thorough discussion of that position until the last two chapters, and especially the conclusion.

There is a more specific hypothesis that can be deduced from Barry's suggestion, which I wish to test here. Simply put, it should follow that the predictions of the rational choice model hold only for those who are faced with nontrivial costs. This entails that B and P should be more closely related to voting among those whose cost of voting is not practically nil.

Table 4.2 tests this proposition with three different data sets, the 1993, 1995 and 1996 studies. The regressions reported in table 4.2 include the standard variables (B, P, C, D, and I), plus two interaction-effect terms: B^*C and P^*C. The expectation is that the interactive variables will be positive, which would indicate that B and P play a more important role for those whose cost of voting is more substantial.

Table 4.2. Testing Interaction between Cost, Benefits and Probability

a. University students in 1993: Logistic regression

B_n	1.30
P_c	1.06
Cost	-1.27
Cost * B_n	-.76
Cost * P_c	-.46

b. 1995 Quebec referendum: Logistic regression

B	2.21*
P	.65
Cost	1.91
Cost * B	-5.39
Cost * P	-1.11

c. 1996 British Columbia election: OLS regression

B_c	.03
P_n	.08*
Cost	-.13
Cost * B_c	.20
Cost * P_n	-.07

* Significant at the .10 level (two-tailed test)
** Significant at the .05 level (two-tailed test)
*** Significant at the .01 level (two-tailed test)
Note: For description of variables see tables 3.3, 3.4, 3.5, and 4.1.

The regressions also include D, I, and, in the case of *a*, two more variables, Panel and Western.

It can be seen that the interactive variables are not significant in any of the equations. I also tested interactive models in which C was dichotomized so that all those whose score on C was 0.3 or above (or 0.4 or above) were distinguished from all others: the interactive variables proved to be systematically nonsignificant. The hypothesis that B and P matter only for those with higher costs has to be rejected.

It does not seem possible, then, to salvage the theory with a more complex interactive model in which electors are assumed to calculate expected benefits only when the cost of voting becomes nontrivially small.

Conclusion

For most people most of the time the subjective cost of voting is extremely small. And some do not perceive any cost at all. This is certainly one of the reasons so many people vote.

This could be construed as providing a solution to the paradox of voting. For many electors, C equals zero. Even if B^*P is extremely small, it is still greater than C. This solution, however, is not really satisfactory, because the evidence suggests that when there is a (small) cost, most people continue to vote. In our interviews of regular voters, the overwhelming majority were undeterred by the perspective of having to devote one full hour to voting. And the impact of bad weather on turnout is strikingly small. My conclusion is that marginal increases in C reduce the propensity to vote only marginally.

CHAPTER 5

Is It a Duty to Vote?

Is voting only a *right,* and is it up to each individual to decide whether it is in her best interest to vote or to abstain, or is it also a *duty,* such that every citizen, in the absence of other compelling reasons such as illness, should feel obliged to fulfill her responsibility, as a member of a democratic society, to vote? In most countries, as we saw in chapter 1, the law does not make voting compulsory. The implication seems to be that voting is construed to be a right that citizens should feel free to exercise or not to exercise.

The situation is more ambiguous, however. In about one democratic country out of five, the law officially declares that voting is not only a right, but also an obligation.[1] Even in those countries where voting is not compulsory, while it is acknowledged that every individual has the right not to vote, it is also alleged that citizens should feel some moral obligation to vote. To use a religious analogy, not voting can be construed as a venial sin: it is a wrong, one that weak human beings should be urged not to commit but may be forgiven for if they indulge in it.[2]

As far as I can tell, there has been no systematic study of that official discourse. Personally, I remember quite vividly Catholic priests in their Sunday sermons telling parishioners that it was up to them to decide which party or candidate to vote for but insisting that it was their duty to cast a vote.[3] I also remember (less vividly) reading election eve editorials that supported a given candidate or party but added that the most important thing is that each citizen votes, regardless of her views.

What interests me is not the public discourse as such but how people themselves feel about the issue. I review the evidence and present new data on people's views about whether voting is a duty or not. I also assess how much turnout can be accounted for by such a sense of duty. Finally, I examine the hypothesis that the rational choice model performs better for those without a strong sense of duty.

There is the risk that duty encompasses a host of different motivations. Riker and Ordeshook (1968), in particular, refer to D as reflecting many kinds of psychic gratification, including the enjoyment of going to the poll. To be useful, the concept must have a precise meaning. I define duty as "the belief that not voting in a democracy is wrong." Sense of duty thus corresponds to an ethical judgment that voting is right and not voting is wrong. If someone votes out of a sense of duty, she votes because her conscience tells her she ought to vote; she would feel ashamed and guilty if she were not to vote.

A sense of duty entails adherence to a norm that establishes that voting is right and not voting is wrong. The crucial question is whether the norm that not voting is wrong is fully internalized by people. People may agree superficially with the norm without really internalizing it. The empirical test of whether people adhere to the norm is whether they would feel they were doing something wrong if they were not to vote. If someone votes out of a sense of duty, she would consider herself as having committed a sin, albeit a venial one, if she had not voted.[4]

As I will show, most people agree with the statement that voting is a duty. It is important, however, to assess the depth of that sentiment. It could be mere lip service to the dominant public discourse. It could also be mere rationalization: those who vote are led, after the fact, to admit they are doing the right thing. We have to determine whether a sense of duty is really a powerful motivating force.

But why do people feel it is wrong not to vote? The crucial underlying consideration is, I think, a belief in democracy. People value democracy, and the right to vote in a free and fair election is the most basic democratic right. People believe that a society in which people have the right to vote is a better society than one in which people do not have such a right.[5] Society has bestowed on them a right, which they regard highly. As they cherish the right to vote, they would feel they were not living up to their principles if they acted as if this right was not important, that is, if they did not vote.

There are loose ends in this chain of reasoning. It is perfectly rational for someone to value democracy strongly but not to vote because whether or not she votes will not make democracy more or less sustainable. But this is not how *moral* people reason. Moral people think in terms of what the good citizen should do. Since she believes that it is a good thing that those who govern be chosen through a fair and honest election, and since the cost of voting is small, the good citizen will conclude that voting is the right thing to do and not voting is wrong.

The Sense of Duty

How widespread and strong is the feeling that it is a moral duty to vote? Until the late seventies, the U.S. National Election Studies used a battery of four questions intended to tap the sense of citizen duty. Americans were asked whether they agree or disagree with the following four statements:

1. "It isn't so important to vote when your party doesn't have a chance to win."

2. "A good many local elections aren't important enough to bother with."

3. "So many people vote in the national elections that it does not matter much to me whether I vote or not."

4. "If a person doesn't care how an election comes out he shouldn't vote it."

These questions do not directly establish the existence of a sense of duty. Instead, they measure whether something other than self-interest is at work. Statements 1 and 3 ask whether it is worth voting when P equals zero. Over the years, between 85 and 90 percent of respondents have expressed disagreement with these statements. This confirms that the great majority of people believe it is meaningful to vote even if P is zero. Perhaps question 1 comes closest to directly measuring sense of duty, with the implication being that it is important to vote in *all* elections.

Statement 2 measures the importance attached to local elections and is not of great interest here. Statement 4 tests whether it is worth voting when B is zero. On average over the years, around 50 percent have said they disagreed with the statement. The fact that disagreement is less widespread here confirms that B is perceived to be a more legitimate factor in the voting decision than P.

Half of Americans say that one should vote even if in her view it does not matter at all who wins. For half of the electorate, indifference is not a sufficient reason for abstaining. This provides a conservative estimate of how widespread sense of duty is. It is a conservative estimate because it is quite possible to believe that one should normally vote but that the obligation does not hold when there is no real choice, in other words, when all the candidates or parties are perceived as being equally unacceptable.

Perhaps even more interesting are the results of a survey done by the National Opinion Research Center in 1944. Americans were asked the following question: "Do you regard voting more as a duty you owe your country, or more as a right to use if you want to?" As many as 59 percent chose "duty," and only 36 percent "right" (see Dennis 1970, 827). This does not tell us how powerful such a feeling is, but it does convey the message that for the majority of people voting is construed as a duty.

The same pattern holds outside the United States.[6] Stoetzel (1955) reports that a clear majority of electors in France feel that when they vote they are carrying out a duty.[7] When people in a British constituency were asked "whether you don't have to vote unless you feel like it, or whether voting is a duty, 82 per cent replied that they thought voting a duty" (Rose and Mossawir 1967, 189).

Robert Young and I explored the same kinds of feelings in three different surveys. In our survey of university students in the Canadian election of 1993, we asked them whether they agreed with a number of statements that tap such sense of duty.[8] Table 5.1 reports the percentage agreeing and strongly agreeing with these statements. The most straightforward statement is that "it is the duty of every citizen to vote." The overwhelming majority (84 percent) expressed their approval; even more revealing is the fact that 43 percent indicated they strongly agreed. Support for the assertions that "it is important to vote even if my party or candidate has no chance of winning" and that "in order to preserve democracy, it is essential that the

Table 5.1. Sense of Duty among University Students (1993), in Quebec Referendum (1995) and British Columbia Election (1996)

	Percentage Agreeing		
	University Students	Quebec	BC
"It is the duty of every citizen to vote."	84 (43)[a]	99 (83)[a]	92 (72)[a]
"It is important to vote even if my party or candidate has no chance of winning."	92 (46)[a]		
"In order to preserve democracy, it is essential to vote."	93 (50)[a]		
"In order to preserve democracy, it is essential that the great majority of citizens vote."		99 (85)[a]	96 (79)[a]
"If you did not vote, would you feel that you had neglected your duty as a citizen?"		84 (60)[b]	70 (39)[b]
"If I did not vote, I would feel guilty."	49 (16)[a]		
"If you did not vote, would you feel guilty?"		74 (38)[c]	71 (31)[c]

[a]The numbers in parentheses indicate the percentages agreeing strongly with the statements.
[b]The first numbers indicate the percentages saying "enormously" or "a lot." The numbers in parentheses indicate the percentages saying "enormously."
[c]The first numbers indicate the percentages saying "very" or "somewhat" guilty. The numbers in parentheses indicate the percentages saying "very."

great majority of citizens vote" is even stronger, being close to unanimous. One statement elicited weaker support: "If I did not vote, I would feel guilty." Even there, however, half the students admitted they would feel some guilt.

There are different ways to read these results. One cautious interpretation is that about half the students adhered to the norm that voting is a duty. The most telling result, in my view, is the fact that as many as 43 percent *strongly* agreed with the direct statement that it is the duty of every citizen to vote.

These findings hold for a student sample, and it is difficult to know whether they can be generalized to the population at large. We therefore asked the same kinds of questions to representative samples of the electorate in the 1995 Quebec referendum and in the 1996 British Columbia election. Two of the questions were identical to those asked in 1993; we tapped again the degree of agreement with the statements that "it is the duty of every citizen to vote" and that "in order to preserve democracy, it is essential that the great majority of citizens vote."

Support for these two propositions is simply overwhelming. We also observe greater support during the Quebec referendum than at the time of the British Columbia election. This probably reflects the extraordinary circumstances of the Quebec referendum, in which turnout was so exceptionally high. The fact remains, however, that even in British Columbia as many as 72 percent of the sample strongly agreed with the statement that it is the duty of every citizen to vote.

The Quebec and British Columbia surveys included two additional questions designed to tap sense of duty. These two questions were couched in more personal and direct terms. It might be somewhat easy to agree with the abstract statement that it is the duty of every citizen to vote. These two additional questions invited respondents to think about how they would feel if they were not to vote: would they feel that they had neglected their duty? Would they feel guilty?

As can be seen in table 5.1, 84 percent of respondents in Quebec and 70 percent in British Columbia indicated that they would feel they had neglected their duty "enormously" or "a lot." These numbers are very close to those who strongly agree with the statement that it is the duty of every citizen to vote. We probed further and asked our respondents if they would feel guilty if they did not vote. This is a tougher question because we are asking people to acknowledge that by not voting they would be doing something wrong. We also know from our pretests and open-ended interviews that some people hate the word "guilty," in good part because it has religious connotations. Still, we find that around 70 percent would feel at least somewhat guilty; 30 percent would even feel very guilty.

These data support the view that, for most people, not voting is defined as something that is wrong. It may not be a very serious wrongdoing, and most would not feel very guilty if they did not vote, but it would, nevertheless, be on a par with a venial sin.

It is interesting, in this respect, to determine what kind of people are more likely to adhere to the norm that voting is right and not voting is wrong. Table 5.2 shows that, unsurprisingly, sense of duty is strongly correlated with level of political interest. What is even more interesting, however, is that, controlling for political interest, sense of duty is greater among women and increases with age and religiosity.[9]

The feeling that voting is a moral obligation is more widespread among people who are prone to think in terms of morality and principles. Religious people are concerned about what is right and wrong, and so it is not surprising that they believe there are certain duties one should carry out, voting being one of them. Similarly, there is evidence that women attach greater importance to ethical issues than men; women, for instance, seem to pay greater attention to ethical considerations when choosing an employer (Frank 1996).

Finally, people are more likely to construe voting as a citizen duty as they grow older. On the one hand, their sense of attachment to their community increases, which makes them more inclined to think about duties toward the community. On the other hand, they have more exposure to the dominant norm that the good citizen ought to vote.

The skeptics might argue that these are just words and that they do not mean much. I disagree. The personal open-ended interviews we have conducted with regular voters have convinced me that the sense that it is a civic duty to vote is deeply ingrained. Fortunately, we also have some evidence that this feeling translates into actual behavior.

One piece of evidence comes from an experiment conducted by two economists during the first lecture of a basic course in microeconomics, held five days before the 1994 German election (Guth and Weck-Hanneman 1997). Students in the course were asked to indicate on a form what amount, between DM 0 and DM 200, they would be willing to accept in return for selling their voting rights. They were told that after they had filled in the form a price would be randomly selected between DM 0 and DM 200, and that four of those who had indicated a price equal to or below the selected price would be randomly chosen to be paid in exchange for not voting, that is, for destroying their voting card and leaving their identity card over the weekend.

How would someone who believes that voting is a moral obligation react to such an experiment? Obviously such a person should refuse to sell her

Table 5.2. The Determinants of Sense of Duty

	OLS Coefficient (SE)		
Variables	a. *Students 1993*	b. *Quebec 1995*	c. *BC 1996*
Political Interest	.16*** (.02)	.21*** (.02)	.24*** (.03)
Women	.00 (.01)	.03** (.01)	.07*** (.02)
Education	—	.02 (.03)	.04 (.03)
Age	—	.0001** (.00)	.003***(.00)
Western	-.12*** (.01)	— —	
Income	—	.05** (.02)	—
Religiosity	.04** (.02)	—	.05** (.02)
Constant	.77*** (.02)	.63*** (.02)	.40*** (.03)
R^2	.12	.14	.20
N	808	857	742

* Significant at the .10 level (two-tailed test)
** Significant at the .05 level (two-tailed test)
*** Significant at the .01 level (two-tailed test)
Note: Duty corresponds to respondents' score on a scale from 0 to 1. In *a* the scale is made of three questions measuring sense of duty: whether respondents think it is the duty of every citizen to vote, whether it is essential to vote to preserve democracy and whether they would feel guilty if they had not voted. In *b* and *c* the scale is made up of four questions tapping whether respondents think it is the duty of every citizen to vote, whether it is essential to vote to preserve democracy, whether they would feel guilty and having neglected their duty if they had not voted.

Political interest indicates, on a scale from 0 to 1, how interested the respondent is in politics.

Women is a dummy variable that equals 1 for women and 0 for men.

Education is a scale from 0 to 1 where 0 corresponds to those who have no secondary education and 1 to those who have a university doctorate.

Age is the age of the respondent.

Western is a dummy variable that equals 1 for students at the University of Western Ontario and 0 for students at the Université de Montréal.

Income is a scale from 0 to 1 where 0 corresponds to those whose annual income is $20,000 or less and 1 for those whose annual income is more than $80,000.

Religiosity is a scale from 0 to 1 where 0 corresponds to those for whom religion is not at all important in their life and 1 to those for whom it is very important.

voting rights. In this case, students could do so by returning the form empty or by indicating a price over DM 200, which ensured that they could not be chosen to be paid.[10] Ninety did the latter, five the former. Only 52 out of 147 students actually wrote in a number between DM 0 and DM 200.

In a postexperimental questionnaire, the great majority of those who refused to sell their vote indicated that they considered it immoral to sell one's right to vote. We do not know exactly why they hold such a view, but a plausible explanation is that they believe that in the absence of other compelling circumstances it is one's duty to vote. And it is revealing to note that among seven reasons to vote suggested in the post-experimental questionnaire, the one that was chosen most frequently is "it is a civil duty to preserve democracy."

The feeling that voting is a moral obligation and that not voting implies a failure to fulfill one's civic duty is widespread and strongly ingrained in the population. The only issue is how widespread and strong that feeling is.

I would surmise that about half the citizens in democracies have a strong sense of duty. Half of Americans believe that people should vote even if they don't care how an election comes out. About 70 percent of electors in British Columbia and 80 percent in Quebec would feel they had neglected their civic duty enormously or a lot if they did not vote. These figures could reflect lip service to what is clearly a dominant norm, but I would argue that for about half the electors in most democracies there is a deep feeling that it is wrong not to vote.

Perhaps it is fitting to add a word of caution. Many people feel a strong sense of duty to vote. At the same time, however, most have not thought through why they have such a feeling, and the fact remains that not voting is considered only a venial sin. Sense of duty is, to some extent, malleable.

We have evidence of such malleability in our experimental study among university students. As explained in chapter 3, in five of the ten classes we gave a short presentation on the paradox of voting, in which we summarized how rational choice looks at the decision of whether to vote or not to vote. In the presentation, we talked about P, B, and C, but made no reference at all to D.

It turned out that the presentation had the effect of reducing students' sense of duty. This effect was entirely indirect, as the presentation was silent on that factor. It would appear that framing the voting act as something reasonable people could contemplate not doing led some to reconsider whether voting ought to be viewed as a duty. The feeling that one has a moral obligation to vote is not immutable.

One should not overstate the softness of this sense of duty, however. The impact of our presentation was only .06 on a 0 to 1 scale; as the average initial score was .77, this corresponds to a relative impact of less than 10 percent. And this is among a young group in which political attitudes are likely to be less ingrained. The conclusion must remain that for the population at large sense of duty is strong and firm.

Table 5.3. The Determinants of Voting among University Students (1993), in the Quebec Referendum (1995) and in the British Columbia Election (1996)

	Logistic Coefficient (SE)		OLS Coefficient (SE)
Variables	a. *Students 1993*	b. *Quebec 1995*	c. *BC 1996*
Benefits	1.00* (.52)	.85 (.72)	.07*** (.03)
Probability	.85** (.41)	.39 (.60)	.07** (.03)
Cost	-2.09*** (.39)	-2.66** (1.11)	-.01** (.04)
Duty	3.27*** (.66)	4.49*** (.94)	.41*** (.04)
Interest	.89* (.46)	.003 (.73)	.14*** (.03)
Panel	.43* (.23)	—	—
Western	-1.48*** (.29)	—	—
Constant	-1.53** (.68)	-.50 (.82)	.41*** (.04)
Adjusted pseudo R^2	.40	.19	—
Percent correct prediction	81.38	95.87	—
Adjusted R^2	—	—	.31
N	607	799	682

* Significant at the .10 level (two-tailed test)
** Significant at the .05 level (two-tailed test)
*** Significant at the .01 level (two-tailed test)

Note: Benefits is the respondent's score on a scale from 0 to 1. In *a* it indicates how important it is to respondent, which candidate wins in the country as a whole. In *b* the scale is made up of two questions about how much change sovereignty would bring about in general and about how much difference it would make personally for the respondent. In *c* it indicates how much difference it would make personally for the respondent which candidate wins in her constituency.

In *a* Probability indicates how close the election was perceived to be on a scale from 0 to 1, in the respondent's constituency. In *b* it is a dummy variable that equals 1 for those who expected the outcome to be close. In *c* it indicates how close the election was perceived to be on a scale from 0 to 1 in the province as a whole.

Cost is the respondent's score on a scale from 0 to 1. In *a* it indicates the extent to which respondent disagreed with the following statement: "It is so easy to vote that I don't see any reason not to." In *b* and *c* the scale is made up of three questions about how much time it takes to go to the poll, vote, and return, how easy it is to vote and how easy it is to get information to decide how to vote.

Duty corresponds to respondent's score on a scale from 0 to 1. In *a* the scale is made of three questions measuring sense of duty: whether respondent thinks it is the duty of every citizen to vote, whether it is essential to vote to preserve democracy, and whether she would feel guilty if she had not voted. In *b* and *c* the scale is made up of four questions tapping whether respondent thinks it is the duty of every citizen to vote, whether it is essential to vote to preserve democracy, and whether she would feel guilty and having neglected their duty if she had not voted.

In *a, b,* and *c* Interest is a scale from 0 to 1, measuring how interested the respondent is in politics in general.

Panel is a dummy variable that equals 1 for those who had also answered a campaign questionnaire and Western is a dummy variable that equals 1 for those who attended the University of Western Ontario. For more details, see Blais and Young (1996).

Duty as a Motivation to Vote

Many people believe they have a moral obligation to vote. It remains to be shown that the belief is powerful enough to induce them to vote even if sometimes they might be tempted to stay home.

The first piece of evidence that sense of duty does induce people to vote is presented in table 5.3. The table shows that in each of our three studies, controlling for the perceived benefits and costs of voting as well as level of political interest, duty is strongly correlated with turnout.

Again, it is possible to illustrate the impact of this factor with simulations. Our respondents scored very high on our duty scale, the averages being respectively .81, .83, and .76. What would have happened if there had been no sense of duty at all, that is, if everyone had scored 0? Our simulations suggest that turnout would have been depressed by 46 points in 1993,

Table 5.4. The Determinants of Voting among University Students in 1993

	Logistic Coefficient (SE)			
Variables	Low Level of Duty		High Level of Duty	
Benefits	1.93***	(.65)	-.26	(1.01)
Probability	1.57***	(.54)	-.54	(.73)
Cost	-3.66***	(.59)	-.48	(.64)
Interest	.75	(.59)	2.23**	(.91)
Panel	.11	(.29)	1.56***	(.48)
Western	-1.98***	(.40)	-1.16**	(.47)
Constant	.89	(.62)	1.33	(.97)
Adjusted pseudo R^2	.38		.18	
Percent correct prediction	73.76		91.08	
N	282		325	

* Significant at the .10 level (two-tailed test)
** Significant at the .05 level (two-tailed test)
*** Significant at the .01 level (two-tailed test)
Note: Benefits indicates how important it is to respondent, on a scale of 0 to 10, which candidate wins in the country as a whole. The scale was transformed to 0 to 1.

Probability indicates how close the election was perceived to be on a scale from 0 to 1, in the respondent's constituency.

Cost indicates, on a scale from 0 to 1, the extent to which respondent disagreed with the following statement: "It is so easy to vote that I don't see any reason not to."

Interest is a scale from 0 to 1, measuring how interested the respondent is in politics in general.

Panel and Western are dummy variables that take the value of 1 for those who had answered a campaign questionnaire and who attended the University of Western Ontario respectively. For more details, see Blais and Young (1996).

Table 5.5. The Determinants of Voting in the 1995 Quebec Referendum

Variables	Logistic Coefficient (SE)			
	Low Level of Duty		High Level of Duty	
Benefits	1.56**	(.75)	.34	(1.86)
Probability	.33	(.68)	1.23	(1.15)
Cost	2.81**	(1.25)	-2.95	(2.43)
Interest	1.01	(.79)	-1.14	(1.79)
Constant	1.45*	(.80)	4.55**	(2.22)
Adjusted pseudo R^2	.11		.02	
Percent correct prediction	92.29		98.85	
N	364		436	

* Significant at the .10 level (two-tailed test)
** Significant at the .05 level (two-tailed test)
*** Significant at the .01 level (two-tailed test)
Note: Benefits is the respondent's score on a scale from 0 to 1: the scale is made up of two questions about how much change sovereignty would bring about, in general and about how much difference it would make personally for the respondent.
   Probability is a dummy variable that equals 1 for those who expected the outcome to be close.
   Cost is the respondent's score on a scale from 0 to 1: the scale is made up of three questions about how much time it takes to go to the poll, vote, and return, how easy it is to vote, and how easy it is to get information to decide how to vote.
   Interest is a scale from 0 to 1, measuring how interested the respondent is in politics in general.

by 47 points in the Quebec referendum, and by 30 points in the British Columbia election. According to these estimates, about one elector out of two or three voted because of a sense of duty.

The overriding importance of duty is demonstrated even more strikingly in tables 5.4, 5.5, and 5.6. In these tables I reran the equations presented in table 5.3 separately for those with a low and a high sense of duty. What emerges from these tables is that B, P, and C do a much better job of explaining the vote among those with a weak sense of duty than among those who feel a strong moral obligation to vote. The latter tend overwhelmingly to vote and the few who abstain do so for reasons that have little to do with rational choice.

Among those with a weak sense of duty, the rational choice model performs much better. In British Columbia, for instance, benefits matter three times as much among those with a low sense of duty. Perhaps even more interesting is the fact that the closeness of the election becomes almost as important as costs in this group.

These tables convey a simple but crucial message. In order to make

Table 5.6 The Determinants of Voting in the 1996 British Columbia Election

	OLS Coefficient (SE)	
Variables	Low Level of Duty	High Level of Duty
Benefits	.17*** (.04)	.05** (.02)
Probability	.16*** (.05)	-.01 (.03)
Cost	-.14** (.07)	-.07* (.04)
Interest	.24*** (.05)	.03 (.02)
Constant	.52*** (.05)	.94*** (.03)
Adjusted R²	.16	.04
N	403	276

* Significant at the .10 level (two-tailed test)
** Significant at the .05 level (two-tailed test)
*** Significant at the .01 level (two-tailed test)
Note: Benefits is the respondent's score on a scale from 0 to 1 ; it indicates how much difference it would make personally for the respondent which candidate wins in her constituency.

Probability indicates how close the election was perceived to be on a scale from 0 to 1 in the province as a whole.

Cost is the respondent's score on a scale from 0 to 1: the scale is made up of three questions about how much time it takes to go to the poll, vote, and return, how easy it is to vote, and how easy it is to get information to decide how to vote.

Interest is a scale from 0 to 1, measuring how interested the respondent is in politics in general.

sense of why people vote, it is necessary at the outset to distinguish people according to their sense of duty. Among those with a strong sense of duty, the great majority vote and the few who abstain do so for reasons that appear idiosyncratic. Among those with a weak sense of duty, the rational choice model is quite helpful.

Some might object that if people feel compelled to vote, it is not so much because they honestly believe that it is a *moral* obligation to vote but rather because they perceive that there is a widespread norm that people should vote, and that it is in their best interest to conform to that norm in order to establish or maintain their reputation of good citizen. The norm is not really internalized by citizens, they just obey it because if they did not vote they would be frowned upon by their family and friends. From that perspective people vote not out of a deep sense of duty but rather because of social pressures.

Robert Young and I explored this possibility in our three studies. In our 1993 survey we asked our students whether they agreed with the statements that if they did not vote their family and their friends would think badly of them. Only 18 percent thought so in the case of their family and 8 percent in the case of their friends. Among these students, then, social pressures to vote appear to be weak. The fact, however, that most of the pressure seems to come from parents rather than from the peer group suggests that things could be somewhat different for the population at large.

Our other two surveys, conducted among representative samples of the population, indicate that some people feel that not voting would not be well perceived. In Quebec in 1995 and in British Columbia in 1996, we included the following question: "If you did not vote, do you think that your friends and family would disapprove very much, disapprove somewhat, approve somewhat, approve very much, or do you think they would not care at all?" Close to half the respondents in the two surveys—47 percent in Quebec and 43 percent in British Columbia—said they would anticipate some disapproval. The majority of them would expect mild—not strong—disapproval, which makes sense if not voting is only a venial sin. There exists some social pressure to vote. And such pressure should exist if there is a widespread norm that not voting is wrong. If people genuinely believe that in principle every citizen should vote, they should disapprove if their friends and relatives decide not to vote. These data tell us not only that the norm exists but that people are aware that it is shared by their social milieu.

The question, therefore, is what matters the most, the personal belief that voting is a moral obligation or the perception that abstaining would be disapproved by one's milieu? The answer is clear, it is the former. If we add our measure of social pressures to the regressions in table 5.3, it proves to be nonsignificant in each case, and the impact of duty is left unaffected.[11] I conclude that it is an internalized sense of duty and not the presence of social pressures that induces people to vote.

Duty as the Main Reason to Vote

I probed the power of duty as a motivation to vote in yet another fashion in a study of regular voters in Montreal conducted with Kim Thalheimer (Blais and Thalheimer 1997). In that study we tried to establish, for each of the 108 respondents, the main reasons he/she voted. To establish whether duty was an important consideration, we relied on questions 15a, 15b, 15c, and 16a (see appendix I). In order to be construed as voting out of a sense of duty, an individual had to say that for her personally it is a duty to vote, *and* that it is an important duty, *and* that it is a duty to vote in all elections,[12] and that she would feel like having failed her duty as a citizen if she were not to vote.

An amazing number of respondents fulfilled each of these four conditions: 92 persons out of 108, or 85 percent of the sample. This is prima facie evidence that duty is an important consideration for most voters.

This study allows us to go further and to establish which reason is the most important motivation to vote for each of our 108 individuals. Duty may be a reason to vote for 92 respondents, but for how many is it the *main* reason?

This question requires that other reasons for voting be explored. In our questionnaire, we had sets of questions that were designed to determine whether each of the components of the rational choice model, B, P, and C, seemed to matter in the decision to vote. We also wanted to check whether the individual might be inclined to vote because of social pressure or out of habit. The questionnaire also included a number of open-ended questions that invited the respondent to explain, in her own words, the reasons why she votes (see appendix I).

On the basis of the rich and textured information assembled in the questionnaire, Kim Thalheimer and I determined the most important motivations for voting for each of the 108 individuals interviewed. We came to the conclusion that sense of duty was the main reason for 79 of them, or 73 percent of the sample.

How can we reach such a conclusion? We carefully read the full material of each interview and, in each and every case, came to an agreement (after some discussion) on what seemed to be the most important reasons why that individual usually votes and on the ranking of these reasons (for a more elaborate presentation of the methodology and of the results, see Blais and Thalheimer 1997).

I present below three of the respondents for whom duty appears to be the main factor, so that readers can appreciate how we have formed our judgments. I indicate, as much as possible, the precise words that people used, because they provide important cues about how they view the act of voting.

Respondent A: Duty

Respondent A typifies those individuals who vote solely out of a strong sense of duty. She is a forty-two-year-old divorced woman with a high school education. She describes herself as an informed citizen who is very interested in politics, who always votes, and who keeps up to date on the subject through newspapers and television news.

Throughout the interview, Respondent A spontaneously refers to "civic duty," "obligations," and "democratic rights" as the main reasons why she heads to the polls. In fact, in our first open-ended question, she immediately lists "the duty of every citizen" as her first and foremost reason for voting (Q4).

Respondent A also boasts a perfect score when it comes to our battery of questions measuring the duty factor. She labels voting as being a "very important duty" and believes it a moral obligation to vote in each election (Q15a–c). Indeed, she maintains that if one believes in democracy one absolutely has to vote (Q16b). She also reveals that, if she didn't vote, she would feel guilty and would feel as though she had neglected a civic responsibility (Q16c and Q16a).

Her responses to our questions measuring other factors explaining turnout equally point to duty as her single important motive for casting a ballot. Without hesitation, Respondent A quips "definitely" when asked if she would vote if it took up to two hours (Q13c). Correspondingly, she denies voting out of social pressure or habit, countering that voting is "a duty that I make for myself. . . . A pleasure, even" (Q18 and Q20). While she admits to having thought, in an election, that it would change absolutely nothing if one party won instead of another, Respondent A says she turned out regardless because "it is still my duty to do so" (Q7). And when asked if she would vote even if there would be absolutely no chance that her vote would decide who won, she replies yes because "I make it an issue of conscience. For me it's an obligation, it's my choice, my expression and I don't want anybody to take away that right" (Q12).

Respondent A admits to neglecting school board elections and to subsequently feeling that she has neglected her civic duty. On this subject, she remarks, "I realize that it is still an election and that our participation is expected, and that in a certain way I hinder democracy."

Respondent B: Duty and Benefits

Respondent B is an avid consumer of news who acknowledges a strong interest in politics. He is a middle-aged, married man who holds some postsecondary education.

Two factors explain why this regular voter and a number of individuals like him turn out. A strong sense of duty is the primary reason why Respondent B goes to the polls, followed closely by the benefits he perceives in one party being elected instead of another.

This individual's answers to our questions measuring duty clearly show a heightened sense of obligation when it comes to voting. He asserts that the act is "absolutely" a personal duty (Q15a) and one that he further values as being "very important" (Q15b). He confirms it to be a duty to vote in all elections (Q15c), believes that those—including himself—who neglect to vote fail to meet a civic obligation (Q15d and Q16a), and thinks that if one believes in democracy, one must vote (Q16b). Likewise, Respondent B contends he would experience feelings of guilt if he were to abstain (Q16c).

In our open-ended questions examining motives for voting, this interviewee continually alludes to the duty factor, speaking freely of a sense of responsibility toward society and invariably stressing the importance of exercising his democratic right (Q4, Q12, Q18, and Q28). In these questions, references to a sense of duty pop up first and most often.

Further answers supplied by the respondent to these open-ended questions also reveal the benefit factor ranking a close second as grounds for voting. In fact, Respondent B does state that he votes "for what [he] believes in" and to "give support to [his] candidate" (Q4 and Q12). This motive invariably follows the initial admission of turnout due to a strong sense of duty and comes up somewhat less frequently.

In our other questions exploring the weight of the benefit factor, Respondent B firmly declares that "sure it makes a difference" which party is elected (Q6). He also offers an unqualified "no" when asked if he has ever thought in an election that it would change absolutely nothing if one party won instead of another (Q7).

Other possible factors appear to have little impact on Respondent B's decision to vote. When questioned about the probability of casting the decisive ballot, Respondent B maintains he votes notwithstanding, for two reasons: because it is still "very important that you . . . exercise your democratic right" and in order to back his candidate (Q12).

Nor is cost an issue. On this subject, Respondent B discloses that he spent short of three hours in the last plebiscite to exercise his franchise (Q13). He further adds, "If it took me five hours and I thought my party was right, I would wait five hours."

Social pressure and habit, the last factors tapped for, equally come up naught with Respondent B, repudiating the suggestion that voting is a routine tendency or that he may have bowed to any external influence.

Respondent C: Duty and Cost

The third case, that of Respondent C, is representative of those individuals in our survey who vote from two main considerations, first, duty and second, cost. Respondent C is a married woman in her fifties who professes to be somewhat interested in politics while admittedly lacking exposure to any political news, whether that be on television, on the radio, or in the newspapers. She lays claim to some postsecondary education and designates her religion, Catholicism, as being very important.

Respondent C customarily votes and declares early on in our interview that she considers the act a responsibility each citizen must fulfill. Performing this civic duty, she explains, is part of a personal set of basic principles she deeply values and adheres to (Q4).

Respondent C further rates highly in terms of a strong sense of duty, as measured by Q15 and Q16. Viewing voting as a "very important" civic obligation for her personally (Q15a–b), this interviewee answers that the deed must be accomplished for each election (Q15c). In her opinion, citizens who believe in democracy ought to vote (Q16b) and those who default fail to fulfill their civic responsibility (Q15d). She applies this same rule to herself (Q16a), adding that, were she to slight the electoral process, she would feel guilty: "Yes, and then some!" (Q16c).

Cost is the second consideration governing Respondent C's decision to vote. She figures that, since the polling station is quite close by, it takes her approximately 10 minutes to go to the polls, vote, and return. When asked if she would exercise her right if it took one hour to do so, Respondent C doesn't immediately balk at the idea. Rather, she responds, "Yes, probably, because at work, they always give us the time to go." However, when we push this interviewee further, she flatly rejects the prospect of spending two hours to vote, indicating that cost is indeed a consideration. The fact, however, that she would probably vote if it took one hour suggests that it is not as potent a factor as duty.

In terms of the other elements tapped by our study, the benefits component clearly lacks any influence in Respondent C's decision to vote. In effect, she scoffs at the notion that it changes things if one party is elected instead of another (Q6) and dismisses any difference between political parties, calling them "all the same." Correspondingly, Respondent C allows for casting a ballot even when B is nil since the act of voting is nonetheless an "obligation to society, as a citizen" (Q7).

As for the probability of an election being decided by a single ticket, Respondent C hasn't even considered that possibility and doubts it could ever happen (Q9–Q11). She also concedes that she would vote even if the probability of her casting the decisive ballot were zero, owing to "civic obligation" (Q12).

While Respondent C admits to relying heavily upon her husband to determine which candidate will obtain her support, she stops short of admitting to having buckled under any pressure from her spouse to vote (Q17). This respondent does reveal that she has headed to the ballot box despite preferring not to, but she refutes having done so to please someone else. Rather she says she went "to perform my personal duty." *Habit* is the last factor this respondent categorically rejects as even a partial explanation for her behavior, insisting that the action, in her case, is in no way routine (Q20).

These are only three individuals. But in our judgment a strong majority of our respondents vote mainly because they feel they have a moral obligation to vote. Every one of these individuals we classify as voting on the basis of duty told us that it is an important duty to vote, that it is a duty to vote in each election, and that they would feel they had failed to fulfill their duty if they were not to vote.

This is not all. Among the 78 respondents who vote mainly because of duty, 71 agreed with the statement that if one believes in democracy, one absolutely has to vote. Only two respondents plainly rejected the statement. One woman said that each person is free to have her opinions, thus indicating an unwillingness to pass judgment on others' behavior. One responded "not necessarily" and two others "don't know," one adding: "It depends on the person. A person might feel that their vote doesn't mean anything even in a democracy. I can only speak for myself." A few persons thus nuance, but the bulk of those who vote out of a sense of duty think that if you believe elections are a good thing, you should express your faith by casting a vote.

It is also interesting to see how these people reacted when we asked them whether they would feel guilty if they did not vote. The great majority would feel guilty: only 18 respondents said they would not feel guilty. But many wanted to qualify their Yes or No. Among those who indicated they would feel guilty, many added qualifiers such as "probably," "a little," or "somewhat." And quite a few of those who denied feelings of guilt did so because the word seemed too strong. Their responses were "not to the point of feeling guilty," "not necessarily," "well, guilty, it is not that serious." Perhaps most revealing is the following answer given by a respondent who thinks it is a very important duty to vote in all elections and who would feel she had failed to fulfill her duty if she did not vote: "Well, guilty? No. I would feel in disagreement with myself. I would act against my principles." This respondent obviously would feel she was doing something wrong if she did not vote. She refrains from using the word "guilt," probably because it has religious connotations, but the reasoning is the same: given her beliefs, she feels she ought to vote, and not voting would be equivalent to doing something wrong.

Could it be that a sense of duty is not the real driving force that leads these people to vote, that this is simple rationalization? I cannot rule out the presence of some rationalization, but other pieces of evidence strongly suggest that people genuinely feel a moral obligation to vote. Among these 78 individuals, all said they would vote if it took one hour, and only 16 changed their minds if it took two hours. The sense of duty is not unlimited but it is quite strong. Likewise, it is revealing that among the 32 respondents who could think of one election in which they had come to the conclusion that it would change *absolutely* nothing which party wins the election, only two decided to abstain. In those cases where B equals 0, it is hard to make sense of why people vote other than because they feel a moral obligation to do so.

In principle at least, those who believe it is their duty to vote should feel obliged to vote in all elections. As a matter of fact, however, turnout is considerably lower in municipal and school-board elections, as we have seen in chapter 1. Does it follow that the moral obligation does not hold for all kinds of elections? If so, could it be that sense of duty is not as powerful as I have depicted it to be?

We probed these questions by asking our respondents whether they usually vote in municipal and school-board elections and by exploring their reasons for not voting. In that case, we inquired about feelings of guilt.

Overall, 85 percent of those respondents we have characterized as voting mainly out of duty regularly vote in municipal elections. The sense of moral obligation does extend to local elections. And turnout is higher among those respondents than among the other regular voters we interviewed for whom duty is not the main consideration: turnout for municipal elections in the latter group is 73 percent. The propensity to vote in municipal elections is greater when one believes it is a duty to vote.

We have, however, 12 individuals who do not vote regularly in municipal elections even though they indicated they felt an obligation to vote in all elections. Is this a contradiction? I do not believe so. Aside from one individual who was under the false impression that only property owners had the right to vote in municipal elections, the most often professed reasons for not voting are simply the lack of information and concern.

What this suggests is that the moral obligation to vote is believed to apply to all elections in which the stakes are deemed to be relatively important. And the stakes are defined in terms of broad issues, not narrow personal interest. From that perspective, federal and provincial elections are always important, and people feel they should vote in them, even if it may not change anything with respect to who wins a particular election. If it is important, one should vote, even if B is nil. For most voters with a strong sense of duty, municipal elections are also considered to be important, so they vote. The minority who thinks they are not really relevant feel free not to vote.

What about school-board elections? Only 32 percent of our respondents with a strong sense of duty regularly vote in these elections. Turnout is the same (33 percent) among those for whom duty is not a prime motivation, which suggests that in these elections duty has no leverage. Once again, many individuals explained their not voting as resulting from a lack of information and concern: 17 of them explicitly referred to the fact that they did not have children of school age. For example, take the man, aged 59, who indicates his children are no longer in the school system and points out that he has lost touch with the milieu; when asked whether he feels that he is not fulfilling his duty when he does not vote in a school-board election, he says no, because "I have done my share in the past." Or the single woman who says that she did not know she had the right to vote and adds that she does not feel guilty since she does not have children. Some of these individuals would probably go so far as to argue that it is improper for someone who does not have children to vote in these elections. One's sense of duty is toward the community, and many people do not feel part of the school community.

But why exactly do people feel it is a moral obligation to vote? Many have not thought this question through. The kinds of responses given to the open-ended questions are, however, quite revealing. Take the woman, aged 51, whom we have characterized as voting essentially out of duty, like Respondent A. In response to the first open-ended question asking her to explain in her own words why she votes, she replies, "It is a citizen duty. It is important to vote because we are always dissatisfied with our politicians. We must express our opinion." Later on, when she is asked whether she would vote even if she was sure her vote would not be decisive, she unequivocally answers yes and adds, "It is something we owe to society. We live in a democracy and people must vote. What would be the use of a democracy if nobody votes?"

For many people like this woman, voting is an expression of faith in democracy. This is why almost everyone agreed with the statement that if one believes in democracy, one absolutely has to vote. The (mostly implicit) reasoning seems to be the following: "Not exercising my right to vote would mean that I do not value that right very much. As I strongly believe in democracy, it is my duty to vote."

For some people, voting also expresses an attachment to the community. The woman just quoted said that voting is something we owe to society. Another man explained his voting by a sense of civic duty and immediately added, "I am interested in what happens to my country." In the same vein, some sovereignist Quebeckers told us that they did not feel the same obligation to vote in federal elections. Someone who does not feel Canada to be her country is unlikely to believe that she owes anything to that community.

There are thus two kinds of motivation underlying the sense of duty to vote. The first is more personal: voting is something one should do because one believes in democracy. The second is more social: voting is something one should do because one cares about the community.

In this study, then, around 70 percent of regular voters seem to vote mainly because of a sense of duty. These results need, of course, to be corroborated by other studies. For the time being, I take it to be a first approximation of the importance of that motivation.

This does not mean that sense of duty explains everything. We must keep in mind, in particular, that the study dealt only with regular voters. As we have seen in chapter 2, regular voters typically constitute 60 percent of electors. Almost by definition, an irregular voter does not vote out of a sense of duty; a person who believes it is a moral obligation to vote feels impelled to vote in all (important) elections. The proportion of electors who vote out of a sense of duty would thus be around 40 percent. This estimate is not too different from the one I arrived at above on the basis of survey evidence.

Conclusion

One citizen out of two feels that voting is a moral obligation and would feel guilty if she were not to vote. The underlying reason is that it is great to live in a society where people have the right to vote and not voting would amount to an implicit admission that one does not truly believe in electoral democracy. Consistent with that interpretation is the fact that sense of civic duty is deeper among women, and older and more religious people, that is, among those who are more prone to think in terms of morality and principle.

Duty is the overriding motivation for about half of those who vote and a clear majority of regular voters. Those with a strong sense of duty almost always vote and those who abstain, at a particular election, do so for idiosyncratic reasons. It is only among those with a weaker sense of duty that rational choice provides a compelling explanation of the decision to vote. Among the latter, it does make sense to assume that the propensity to vote increases with B and P and decreases with C.

Many people have not thought through why they feel it is wrong not to vote. Their sense of duty may be somewhat malleable. But most strongly believe in democracy, and their conscience tells them they ought to vote. There is some social pressure to vote, since the norm that not voting is wrong is so widespread. The evidence indicates, however, that people vote because they genuinely believe it would be wrong not to vote, not because they are concerned about maintaining their reputation of good citizens.

Some readers may wonder whether survey respondents who say that it is the duty of every citizen to vote are not just delivering the socially appropriate response. It is a social norm that one behaves for selfless reasons, and sense of duty certainly appears selfless. Or, alternatively, could it be that once people have voted, they rationalize their behavior by referring to the widespread norm that voting is a duty?

It would be foolish to suppose that survey responses are not affected by social norms or that no rationalization takes place. And these biases may affect some of the findings reported here. This being said, it is difficult to argue that sense of duty is not a powerful motivation for voting.

The bottom line is that it seems impossible to make sense of many findings if we reject the notion of duty. If duty were mere rationalization, how to account for the fact that half of university students, many of whom had never voted before, agreed with the strong statement, "If I did not vote, I would feel guilty"? If responses were merely picking up lip service to social norms, how does one explain that women and more religious persons, and not the better educated, feel a stronger sense of duty? And how should we explain that in an experiment among students taking a course in economics a clear majority of participants refused as much as DM 200 in order to retain their right to vote? Is not the plausible reason that they considered it immoral to sell their right to vote?

Perhaps the most telling evidence is provided in tables 5.4, 5.5, and 5.6. It can be seen that, in three separate studies, sorting out people according to the strength of sense of duty allows much clearer relationships to emerge. It is only when we focus on those whose sense of duty is weaker that B, P, and C can be shown to truly affect the decision to vote or to abstain. These results make sense. We should not expect those who conceive of voting as a moral obligation to calculate benefits and costs. And it is for exactly the same reasons that, according to Knack's (1994) findings, rain depresses turnout only among those with a weaker sense of civic duty.

It is not only with respect to voting that sense of duty appears to be a crucial motivating factor. Recent work has shown that tax compliance hinges to a great extent on an internalized sense of duty to obey laws (Scholz and Pinney 1995; Scholz and Lubell 1998).[13] Not only are those who have a strong sense of duty more likely to comply with the law but they "systematically overestimate the likelihood of being caught by the IRS if they cheat" (Scholz and Pinney 1995, 491).

I conclude that for many people voting is not only a right, it is also a duty. And the belief that in a democracy every citizen should feel obliged to vote induces many people to vote in almost all elections. That sense of duty is not shared by everyone. It may vary from one country to another. It can also vary over time.

If I am right, the recent decline in turnout documented in chapter 1 could flow from a decline in the sense of duty. Unfortunately, we have very little evidence to confirm or disconfirm that hypothesis. Some U.S. data are suggestive, however.

Earlier on, I referred to four questions about sense of duty that had been included in the American National Election studies until the late seventies. The last of these four questions, in which people are asked whether they agree or disagree with the statement that "if a person doesn't care how an election comes out that person should not vote in it," was also included in the 1980, 1984, 1988, and 1992 election studies.

About half of respondents typically disagree with the statement, an indication that they consider voting a civic duty. There is some evidence, however, that sense has weakened recently. In the six surveys (1952, 1956, 1960, 1972, 1976, and 1978) conducted before 1980, the average percentage disagreeing with the statement was 52 percent.[14] In the three surveys done after 1980, the average is 44 percent. There is an indication that slightly more Americans are willing to concede that people who do not care should not feel obliged to vote.

Sense of duty may be weakening somewhat, and this should not surprise us. The process of secularization, in particular, has nourished a sense of moral relativism that makes it more difficult for people to be certain that voting is good and not voting is wrong. The point should not be overstated. The evidence presented in this chapter indicates that many people still construe the act of voting as a moral obligation. It could be, however, that this sense of duty is slowly eroding and that turnout is going downward in the long term.

CHAPTER 6

Do People Free Ride?

The decision to vote or not to vote is only one of many decisions that citizens are faced with in a democracy. And it is not the most demanding or significant from the citizen's point of view. Other decisions raise problems that are similar to those I have discussed in the previous chapters.

Suppose someone is greatly concerned with the quality of the environment. This person has to ponder what she should do about it. More specifically, she may wonder whether she should join an environmental group that is in the process of being formed in her city.

According to rational choice theory, the decision to participate or not to participate in a group is basically the same as the decision to vote or not to vote. The individual will join the group only if the expected benefits outweigh the costs. The costs in this case would be the membership fee and the time and energy devoted to the group's activities. The benefits correspond to the improvement in the quality of the environment that the group is likely to bring about.

The rational individual has to weigh the potential benefits that her own personal contribution will bring about, B^*P, that is, she has to assess the probability that whether she joins or not will be *decisive* in whether the group is formed and in whether it is successful in reducing pollution. According to the theory, even if a person is convinced that the group will bring about a great improvement in the quality of the environment and even if she is strongly concerned with environmental issues, she will not join the group because whether she becomes a member or not will not make a significant difference in the end, and because, being a soccer mom, she has very little free time available. She *free rides*. She hopes to reap the benefits of the group getting formed and contributing to the reduction of pollution without paying the cost.

Abstaining is a form of free riding.[1] When someone votes, she decides not to free ride.[2] As we have seen, most people decide not to free ride in elections because they feel they have a moral obligation to vote. These people do not calculate benefits and costs; they think about what is right and what is wrong. They have other motivations than those assumed by rational choice, and in the case of voting these other motivations override "rational" considerations.

Voting is cheap. It can be done in less than half an hour. Most other forms of participation are more demanding. Could it be that when the stakes, and more specifically the costs, are higher, people are more prone to free ride? Could it be that, as Barry (1978) has suggested, rational choice does not perform well with respect to voting because the stakes are too low?

These are the questions I address in this chapter. As we will see, much can be learned by examining other kinds of behavior that raise questions similar to the ones tackled in the previous chapters. We need to know whether people behave differently in other contexts, and whether rational choice faces the same problems in other domains.

I start by presenting the theoretical debate on this issue. Olson's *The Logic of Collective Action* (1965) is the seminal contribution on the question of free riding. I briefly summarize Olson's position and the debate it has spurred. My concern is to assess how much or little people free ride in other realms of life. Much of the work in this area is experimental. I first review the evidence provided by experimental studies and then consider the nonexperimental literature.

The Logic of Collective Action

Olson's main argument is that "unless the number of individuals in a group is quite small, or unless there is coercion or some other special device to make individuals act in their common interest, rational, self-interested individuals will not act to achieve their common or group interest" (Olson 1965, 2).

Olson invites us to consider the case of a large industry in which all producers are convinced that they would greatly benefit from a government program to help the industry. To obtain such assistance from government, the industry would have to set up a lobbying organization. According to Olson, it would be irrational for any producer to sacrifice time and money to support an organization that will benefit the entire industry. Every producer will reason that her own contribution will not be decisive in whether the lobby is successful or not. As a consequence, each individual decides not to participate, to free ride. If there is a successful lobby, she will enjoy the benefits without having to suffer the cost. If the effort to organize a lobby fails, at least she will have avoided the cost of trying to organize it.

According to Olson, the propensity to free ride occurs primarily in large groups. Free riding is not a major problem in small groups, especially if "there are members who would be better off if the collective good were provided, even if they had to pay the entire cost of providing it themselves" (Olson 1965, 34). I deal here only with the implications of Olson's model in large groups.[3]

Does this entail that no large group will be formed? It would seem so. But large groups do exist. Is rational choice able to account for their existence? Olson proposes a solution, the byproduct theory. His argument is that large groups can be formed if there are "selective incentives," that is, benefits that accrue only to those who join the group. Labor unions, for instance, exist in part because of "compulsory membership, picket lines, and violence" (Olson 1965, 72), and in part thanks to selective incentives, such as various forms of insurance, welfare benefits, and seniority rights that are made available only to those who join the union.

Two main criticisms have been addressed to the byproduct theory. First, the theory runs the risk of becoming tautological, as Barry (1978, 33) points out. At one point, Olson (1965, 61) acknowledges that anything can be construed as a selective incentive: social status, social acceptance, and psychological and moral incentives. It is true that he refrains from using the latter types of incentives so that the theory does have some bite, but he remains unclear as to what precisely can and cannot count as selective incentive.

The second criticism, even more important, comes from Fireman and Gamson (1979). The argument is very simple: organizations can either provide collective goods *and* selective benefits that accrue exclusively to their members, or only the latter. Clearly, providing only the latter will be cheaper, and organizations that specialize in those private goods will drive out of business those that attempt to provide collective goods as well. As one reviewer candidly put it, the criticism is "so devastating for Olson's account of collective action, that my immediate reaction was to believe it must be wrong. I have not, as yet, been able to figure out what is wrong" (Udehn 1993, 248).

The verdict must be, then, that Olson fails to explain why large groups get formed. This does not mean that the theory is basically flawed. The approach may well explain why so few large groups get formed.[4] The bottom line, however, is that from a strict economic rationality perspective, such groups should not exist. There must be other kinds of motivations.

Among these other kinds of motivations, moral considerations deserve

a special treatment. Olson himself acknowledges the existence of such motivations. He admits that his model may not be very useful for the study of
"non-economic" organizations (Olson 1965, 159–65). And he explicitly refers
to such feelings as "the sense of guilt, or the destruction of self-esteem, that
occurs when a person has forsaken his moral code" (Olson 1965, 61).

Moral considerations, I have argued, are the most compelling motivation to vote. Most people vote because their conscience tells them that
someone who believes in democracy ought to vote. Is it because people believe they would be committing some kind of sin by not doing anything
about pollution that they join environmental groups? Are such motivations
sufficient to override the propensity to "rationally" free ride? Do most
people abstain from free riding?

The Experimental Evidence

There have been countless experiments on the question of collective action.
I will focus on those that most directly deal with the propensity to free ride.
Here is a standard experiment:

> We created seven-person public goods problems under such laboratory
> circumstances. After they signed the necessary release form, subjects were
> seated around a large table and read instructions. Each was given a $5
> promissory note and was told that he or she could contribute that $5
> toward a bonus of $70 to the group as a whole. This bonus would be
> distributed equally so that each group member would receive $10. A
> specified minimal number of contributions was required for the bonus to
> be distributed; if the number of contributions was not forthcoming, there
> would be no bonus. Subjects made the decision between contributing and
> not contributing simultaneously, anonymously, and only once. . . . If the
> subject had not contributed the $5 and the bonus was produced, the net
> payoff was $15; if the subject had contributed and the bonus was pro-
> duced, the net payoff was $10; if the subject had not contributed and not
> enough other subjects had contributed to produce the bonus, the payoff
> was $5; and if the subject had contributed and not enough others had, the
> net payoff was zero. (Dawes, Orbell, Simmons, and Van de Kragt 1986,
> 1174–75)[5]

Three experiments were conducted, the first two in Eugene, Oregon, and
the third in Logan, Utah. In the first experiment, the required number of
contributions for the bonus to be distributed was set to 3, in the last two it
was set to 5. I first report the overall findings for the three experiments. The

third experiment produced some peculiar results, the meaning of which I discuss below.

What should the rational individual choose to do in such an experiment? She should free ride and not contribute to the bonus. She would reason that if enough others contribute she will get the bonus anyway and will have saved the $5 contribution, and that if not enough contribute and no bonus is produced she will at least have saved $5.

Such reasoning assumes that each individual's contribution will not be critical. If the required number of contributions is 5 and the player is certain that exactly four of the six other participants will contribute, the rational choice is to contribute. But if the probability of being decisive is less than .5—and it is difficult to see why it should not be—the rational player should choose not to contribute.

What do the authors find? About half the participants contributed, and thus decided not to free ride.[6] Why? One possible reason is that those who contributed overestimated the probability that their choice would be decisive. The researchers tapped these perceptions in their third experiment. They asked the players to assess the likelihood that among the six others in the group exactly four will choose to contribute and that they would thus be decisive, the likelihood that fewer than four will contribute (their own contribution then being futile), and the likelihood that more than four will (their own contribution being redundant).

On average, the participants thought there was one chance out of five that their contribution would be critical. If the probability of each player contributing is around .5, the overall likelihood that exactly four out of six contribute is precisely one out of five. From that perspective, perceptions of P appear to be reasonable. But only 23 percent contributed in the third experiment in which these perceptions were tapped, and none of the five groups had at least four contributions. This suggests that, in the same way as electors overestimate the probability of their casting a decisive vote, at least some players were too optimistic in their estimation that their decision would be critical.

Moreover, those who chose to contribute perceived the probability of being critical to be higher than those who did not contribute (the average perceived probability was .29 among the former and .18 among the latter). It would thus seem that one (small) reason why people do not free ride is that they overestimate the probability of being critical to the success of the collective movement.

One intriguing result reported in that study is the remarkably higher level of free riding that took place in the third experiment. Less than half the participants chose to free ride in each of the first two experiments, but the great majority (77 percent) did in the last. The authors offer no explanation for this odd finding. Could the reason be that the last experiment was conducted in another city? I find it hard to believe that the political culture of Utah would be so distinct from that of Oregon. And if it were so, it would mean that the decision to free ride or not hinges on cultural factors, an interpretation that does not fit well with the rational choice model.

The third experiment differed from the first two in one important respect: it was the only one in which perceptions of the probability that exactly four, fewer than four, or more than four of the other six players will contribute were tapped. Could it be that the mere fact of asking such questions induced the players to free ride?

Think back to the experiment Robert Young and I conducted with students (see chapter 3). A short presentation on the paradox of voting, in which we forced students to think about the minuscule probability of casting a decisive vote, induced a number of them not to vote, that is, to free ride. The same kind of effect would seem to have occurred in the Dawes et al. experiment: forcing the players to think about the probability of their contribution being futile or redundant induced them not to contribute.

Why would there be such an effect? It could be that many people do not think through the strategic implications of such situations. Suppose you are a subject in one of the first two experiments in which you are not asked about your perception of probabilities. You may be struck by the fact that the best collective outcome is one in which the required number of contributions is met and you may be inclined to assume, without thinking much about it, that everyone will make sure that the condition is met. And you decide to contribute. I am not suggesting that everyone is reacting like that. It is surely not the case, since even in the first two experiments close to half the players chose to free ride. But it could be that a good proportion of those who did not free ride in the first two experiments had not actually figured out that they would be better off free riding.

If this interpretation is correct, what are the implications? There are two possible reactions. One is to infer that many people do not spontaneously reason like the model assumes: many do not normally think about the probability that their decision will be decisive. The other is to argue that when people "really" understand the collective action problem, the great majority rationally decide to free ride. Both arguments have some validity.

The findings I have presented and discussed pertain to what the researchers called the standard game. The experiment included two variants of that game: the "money-back guarantee" and the "enforced contribution." Under the money-back guarantee situation, "subjects were told that if they contributed their $5, but there were not enough other contributions to ensure provision of the bonus, their $5 would be returned. Thus there was no way in which subjects could lose their contribution. However, they could still free ride on the contribution of others." Under the enforced contribution variant, "no subject could leave the experiment with more than $10," which is "logically equivalent to forcing all to contribute $5 if the bonus is provided." This meant that "there was no opportunity to free ride" but "subjects could still lose their contributions and be 'suckered'" (Dawes et al. 1175).

Both variants make contributing somewhat more appealing. With the money-back guarantee, one was sure not to be "suckered"; with the enforced contribution, one was sure others could not make more money by free riding. Of the two, the latter, the enforced contribution, proved to yield the lowest level of free riding: only 23 percent did not contribute, compared to 77 percent in the standard experiment.

What the enforced contribution situation provided, and not the money-back guarantee, is an insurance that the public good, if it were to be delivered, would be fairly shared by all the players. This suggests, and this is supported by many other experiments, that perceptions of fairness are very important when people ponder whether they should free ride or not. When someone believes many people will be able to benefit from a public good without having anything to pay, the willingness to contribute weakens.

The following lessons can be drawn from this experiment:

1. People do free ride: a good half of the participants chose not to contribute to the bonus.

2. People do not free ride as much as predicted by rational choice theory. Obviously some other motivations drive people to contribute even though personal interest calculations would dictate free riding.

3. Among these other motivations, conceptions of fairness are especially important. The enforced contribution game yielded little free riding precisely because there was the guarantee that the benefits and costs of the public good would be shared equally by all the players.

4. People do not always correctly perceive the benefits of free riding, and this is one reason why they contribute to the public good to a greater extent than rational choice would predict. When the researchers forced the participants to think about the probability that their contribution would be futile or redundant the propensity to free ride increased.

Another interesting study was conducted by Andreoni (1995). In the *Regular* experiment, subjects are given 60 tokens and are asked to divide their tokens between the individual and the group "exchanges." Each group is composed of five members. Every token invested in the individual exchange earns one cent. Every token invested in the group exchange earns one-half cent; in this case, however, every member gets one half-cent for each token invested by the whole group.

What should a rational player decide to do? She should reckon that she gets a higher return on her investment in the individual exchange and thus put all her tokens in that exchange, hoping that the other four members will contribute to the group exchange, from which she will benefit. In other words, she should free ride. Andreoni reports that, in the first round, only 20 percent of the subjects do precisely that, and that 56 percent of the total tokens are invested in the group exchange. Free riding occurs, but to a much lower extent than the rational choice model would predict.

In Andreoni's experiment, as in many others, there were 10 rounds: each subject was asked to make a new investment decision in each round. Subjects were told that after each round they would be reassigned to a new group of five participants, who will not have been members of the same group in the past. The amount of free riding does increase over time; by the tenth round, 45 percent do not contribute to the group exchange and 74 percent of the total tokens are invested in the individual exchange. As subjects learn about the game, free riding becomes more frequent.

The experiment had two other variants. In the *Rank* condition, "subjects get paid based on how their experimental earnings rank in comparison to the other subjects in the group. The subject with the highest experimental earnings gets the highest monetary payments, with payments decreasing with rank" (Andreoni 1995, 894). In this situation, the rational choice, like in the Regular condition, is to free ride. But there is something more. In the Regular condition, someone who contributes to the public good (the group exchange) makes the group better off; in the Rank condition, she does not, as the total earnings of the group are predetermined. There are thus no incentives for reciprocal altruism.

As expected, the amount of free riding increases substantially in the Rank condition: 35 percent of the subjects do not contribute to the group exchange in the first round; this rises to 93 percent in the last round. There are still some subjects who invest in the group exchange, for no clear reason. These people are assumed to contribute to the public good out of confusion. The data suggest that there is an important amount of confusion in the first round, but that confusion recedes as subjects repeat the game.

There were two differences between the Regular and the Rank conditions: in the latter, subjects are informed about their rank and they are paid on the basis of their rank. The difference between the behavior observed under the two conditions could stem from information as such, apart from payment.

To explore this possibility, Andreoni created a third condition in the experiment, called *RegRank*. In this condition, "subjects get all the same information on their rank . . . that the Rank subjects get, but they get paid according to their experimental earnings, just like the Regular subjects do" (Andreoni 1995, 894). In this situation, the players who contribute to the group exchange can see that they earn less than those in the group who free ride but they can also observe that their contribution does make the group better off overall. "As a result, the difference in cooperation between RegRank and Rank will provide a measure of the minimum amount of cooperation that would be attributable to kindness" (Andreoni 1995, 895). Unsurprisingly, the amount of free riding in the RegRank situation falls somewhere in between that in the Regular and the Rank situations.

Andreoni's conclusions are clear and simple: "[O]n average about 75 percent of the subjects are cooperative, and about half of these are confused about incentives, while about half understand free-riding but choose to cooperate out of some form of kindness" (Andreoni 1995, 900).

This study confirms that one important reason why free riding is not more prevalent is simple confusion. People do not quite get it; they do not always make the elementary calculus assumed by the experiment. The study also shows that confusion is not the whole story. Some other motivation, which Andreoni calls "kindness," is at work. This seems to be the only way to account for the fact that free riding is much less frequent in the RegRank condition than in the Rank. Andreoni confesses not being certain about the exact motivation, but assumes it is some form of benevolence.

The experiment also indicates that free riding increases from early to late rounds. This is often interpreted as a learning process: as the subjects better understand the game, they become more rational. Andreoni's study shows that there is indeed some learning. But the data reveal that over rounds 1–6 the amount of confusion declines rapidly, but free riding only slightly increases. This suggests the following explanation: "When individuals who start off confused learn the dominant strategy, it appears that they may first try to cooperate but then eventually turn to free-riding. This could suggest that, for some subjects, kindness may depend on reciprocity" (Andreoni 1995, 897-98). A substantial number of subjects in these experiences refrain from free riding because of other motivations, which have been called altruism, benevolence, kindness, or fairness by various authors. But could it be that the reasons why many subjects contribute to the public good are less angelic than they might appear?

This question has been addressed most pointedly in other games which, although they are not of a collective action nature, appear to elicit the same kind of benevolent behavior. I refer here to ultimatum and dictator games. In the ultimatum game, every individual is randomly paired with another player. They are told that a given amount of money, typically $10, is to be divided between the two subjects. The first player proposes how this amount should be split between the two players; the second player either accepts or rejects the proposal. If she accepts, the proposal is carried out. If she rejects, both players get nothing.

How should rational players behave in this game? The proposer should reason that if she proposes to keep $9 and to give her counterpart $1, it will be the counterpart's interest to accept, since she will be better off accepting than declining the offer (she will get $1 instead of nothing). Game theory thus predicts that most proposers will offer a $9/$1 split and that most of these offers will be accepted.

As a matter of fact, the most frequent outcome is an equal split between the two players, which suggests that some other motivation is at work. The most plausible consideration seems to be some sense of fairness. Fairness can play in two different ways. A proposer in this game can offer to split the amount equally because she thinks it would be wrong to get more than her counterpart. But she could also reason that if she proposes an unequal split, her counterpart is likely to reject an offer that she will construe to be unfair, that she is willing to lose money in order to make the proposer pay for her "unacceptable" behavior. Proposers thus offer equal splits because they believe in fairness or because they believe others believe in fairness, or both.[7]

In the dictator game, the proposer decides how the money is to be split between the two players; the second player does not have any say in the outcome. The "rational" solution is obviously for the proposer to keep all the money for herself, especially as all the players are anonymous and the counterpart is in another room. In a typical experiment (Forsythe, Horowitz, Savin, and Sefton 1994), only 20 percent of the "dictators" keep all the money for themselves. Proposers, however, come out somewhat less generous than in the ultimatum game: the modal offer is to give the second player $3. It would seem that "dictators" attempt to be "fair" but at the same time can hardly resist the temptation to take some (but not undue) advantage of their dominant position.

It would thus appear that concern with fairness (and others' perceived concern with fairness) prevents many people from trying to keep the whole pie for themselves in ultimatum and dictator games. This interpretation has been challenged most forcefully by Hoffman, McCabe, Schachat, and Smith (1994, 349). They propose the following alternative explanation:

> In such simple experiments, particularly the dictator game, subjects may ask themselves (unconsciously): What is the experimenter's objective? (1) They may think that their actions in this game will affect the experimenter's decision to have them participate in future experiments. (2) They may think they will be chosen to participate in future experiments, but they may be concerned that their current decision will affect which later experiments they are selected for. (3) They may be concerned about appearing greedy and being judged so by the experimenter.

The argument boils down to the view that if subjects do not try to maximize their monetary gains in the experiment it is because they wish to maintain a reputation of being a moral person in the experimenter's eye. This is very similar to the attempt by some rational choice authors to solve the paradox of voting by referring to social pressures and the desire to maintain a reputation of a good citizen. I have shown, in the last chapter, that there is little support for the impact of social pressures and that the feeling that it is wrong not to vote is strongly internalized by a substantial fraction of the electorate. The question in the case of these experiments is whether willingness to share with others reflects a genuine sense of fairness or simply social pressure.

To explore these issues, Hoffman et al. varied the experiments in three ways. First, in half of the groups the experiment is presented as an "exchange between a seller and a buyer" rather than as "division." The expectation is that self-regarding concerns are deemed to be more legitimate in the context of an exchange. Second, instead of being chosen randomly, proposers (who, in these games, are likely to make more money) were selected on the basis of rankings on a current events quiz. Third, in one dictator game the experimenters resorted to a "double blind," which assured subjects that the experimenters could not find out about their decision.

The authors show that each modification, as expected, decreased the propensity of proposers (or sellers) to be generous toward their counterpart. The impact of these modifications is, however, modest, at least in the case of ultimatum games. When the game is presented as an exchange between a seller and a buyer, and when the seller is selected on the basis of rankings on a current events quiz, the modal offer is a $6/$4 split, rather than a perfectly equal split. This indicates that when one has performed better in some "fair" contest, she is inclined to believe she deserves to get slightly more money. This in no way shows that fairness does not matter. It is rather that fairness does not necessarily mean absolute equality. But note that the modal response is still closer to an absolutely equal split than to the dominant option ($9/$1) predicted by game theory.

The double blind variant seemed to have greater impact in the dictator game. When subjects are guaranteed full anonymity, a majority of them keep the full amount for themselves, whereas in the standard experiment the modal offer is to give the second player $3. This leads the authors to conclude that "the presence of the experimenter . . . can be one of the most significant of all treatments for reducing the incidence of self-regarding behavior" (Hoffman et al. 1994, 371).

This conclusion is challenged by Eckel and Grossman (1996). They argue that by imposing double anonymity, Hoffman et al. "have removed virtually all motivation for donating money to one's partner. The decision makers cannot identify each other, nor do they have enough information to know if their partner is poor or otherwise deserving of generosity" (183).

Eckel and Grossman replicated the Hoffman et al. experiment, but with the following modification: "the anonymous partner in the next room is replaced by a charity, the local branch of the American Red Cross." They report that, on average, subjects keep $7 for themselves and give $3 to the Red Cross, compared to a $9/$1 split when the counterpart is anonymous. Even when they are assured that their decision is completely anonymous, the subjects seem to feel it would be unfair for them not to give some nontrivial amount to a deserving organization.

The attempt to explain away the amount of cooperation that takes place in experiments as a mere reflection of social pressure to please experimenters simply does not work. People refrain from purely selfish behavior because they feel it is wrong to be selfish. This does not mean that people are completely unselfish. In Andreoni's experiment, most subjects invested some tokens in both the individual and the group exchange.

The conclusion has to be that people have mixed motives. They calculate (imperfectly) according to their own self-interest but they also attempt to follow their conscience, to do what (they believe) is right and not to do what (they believe) is wrong. Sometimes, these two sets of considerations conflict; people then try to accommodate them as much as possible.

It must be pointed out that the stakes in these experiments are relatively low: in a typical experiment, the rational players who free ride may win $10 more than those who choose to collaborate. Furthermore, "it is indeed a systematic if not often replicated fact in experimental data that increasing the stakes . . . reduces the contribution rate in dilemmas" (Ledyard 1995, 169).

What do we learn, then, from the propensity to free ride in experimental settings? In his extensive review of the literature, Ledyard (1995, 121) sums up the major findings:

1. In one-shot trials and in the initial stages of finitely repeated trials, subjects generally provide contributions halfway between the collectively optimal level and the free riding level.

2. Contributions decline with repetition.

3. Face-to-face communication improves the rate of contribution.

He concludes by offering "some personal conjectures and beliefs" (172):

(1) *Hard-nosed game theory cannot explain the data.* . . . Even the most fervent economic experimentalist cannot force rates of contribution much below 10 percent. . . . If these experiments are viewed solely as tests of game theory, that theory has failed. (2) *Contributions are however certainly responsive to marginal selfish payoffs.* . . . (3) *Altruism or group-regarding preferences cannot explain the data.* . . . (4) *It is possible to provide an environment in which at least 90% of subjects will become selfish.* . . . (5) *It is possible to provide an environment in which almost all of the subjects contribute toward the group interest.* . . . (6) *There appear to be three types of players:* . . . players who act pretty much as predicted by game theory with possibly a small number of mistakes, a group of subjects who will respond to self-interest . . . if the incentives are high enough but who also make mistakes and respond to decision costs, fairness, altruism, etc., and a group of subjects who behave in inexplicable (irrational?) manner. Casual observation suggests that the proportions are 50 percent, 40 percent, 10 percent in many subject pools. (172–73)

This is, in my view, a fair verdict. I would take issue with statement 3, that altruism does not explain the findings. Ledyard is not himself consistent on this point, as he acknowledges, in statement 6, that altruism may play some role. And Andreoni's fine experiment, published after Ledyard's review, has shown that "kindness" matters.

If Ledyard is right, and I tend to agree with him, around half the subjects in collective choice experiments behave more or less as rational choice would predict, almost as many are tempted to free ride but try to follow what their conscience tells them is the right thing to do and often underestimate the probability of their participation being futile or redundant, and a small group reacts apparently completely irrationally.

If this is the pattern, it must be concluded that the rational choice model, though it has clear limits, performs better in the case of collective choice experiments than in the case of voting. I have argued in the previous chapter that the model is irrelevant for about half the voters, who have a strong sense of civic duty. In the experiments I have reviewed here, the model, while incomplete, is nevertheless an essential component of a full understanding of what people do.

The Nonexperimental Evidence

Collective action experiments are contrived: in real life, people are seldom faced with the choice of investing in an individual or group exchange. And these experiments are almost always conducted among students, whose behavior may be peculiar in some respects. Does rational choice perform better or worse in real-life situations?

As indicated at the outset, the typical dilemma for an individual is whether she should join a group or movement or, if she is already a member, how much she should get involved in the activities of the group. A number of studies have looked at this dilemma from a rational choice perspective.

The most prolific author on this topic is Karl-Dieter Opp. Opp (1986) first studied participation in the antinuclear movement in and around Hamburg, Germany.[8] His analysis is based on a survey of 398 opponents of nuclear power. The dependent variable is protest activity, which indicates the frequency of specific kinds of protest action performed by the respondents.

Opp relies on a "broad" rational choice model, which includes "expressive elements like enjoying demonstrating and getting support from reference persons" (90). In this model B is personal discontent with atomic energy, the extent to which a person feels threatened by it, P is the perception that one can have a personal influence on the use of atomic energy, and C is the perception that one could be arrested, registered, or injured by the police. Note that the opportunity cost of protesting, the time and energy invested, is not measured.

The model includes quite a few other variables. Opp reasons that people may not feel personally threatened by nuclear power stations but be strongly opposed to them; such sentiments are called political discontent. Or the real incentive for protest could be the altruist perception that *others* would be harmed by atomic power stations. There is the feeling that one ought to do something about the problem. This is measured by a battery of items, one of them being, "If I were not active against atomic power stations, I would have a bad conscience." This obviously corresponds to the famous D factor.

Two variables refer to the impact of social pressure. There is "the subjective probability of reference persons expecting an individual to participate" (91) and the value of positive sanctions from the private social environment. The last two factors are psychological gratifications, a general disposition to protest and the degree to which participating in protest activities is pleasant.

Opp finds that the B^*P factor is significant: it provides, in fact, the strongest predictor of protest activity. The real issue, however, concerns the relative role of B and P. The fact that people who feel more threatened by nuclear power stations are more likely to protest is not very surprising. The rational citizen should reckon, however, that the probability that her personal involvement will be decisive is practically nil and should thus stay home.

Obviously, most of the survey respondents did not think in these terms. Indeed, only 46 percent agreed with the statement that "the activity of a single person against the erection of atomic power stations cannot prevent the development of the use of nuclear energy." As in the case of turnout, we have evidence here that quite a few people overestimate P.[9]

But does P have an independent impact on the propensity to protest? It is hard to tell. Opp indicates that the bivariate correlation of protest with B^*P ($r = .57$) is greater than with B alone ($r = .51$). The difference, however, is small, and Opp does not show whether, in the multivariate regression, B^*P performs better than B alone, nor whether the multiplicative model performs better than an additive one. My own reading of the evidence is that P hardly matters.

C is measured by the probability of negative sanctions by the police. The variable emerges as significant, but with the wrong sign. It would seem that the perception that one might be arrested induced people to become more active. As Opp notes, in the antinuclear movement police action confirms belief in state repression and strengthens willingness to get involved. This is, of course, the opposite of what rational choice theory would predict.

Three other variables come out as significant: the feeling that one ought to do something, the perceived expectations of others, and the perceived pleasure of participation. It is particularly interesting that the D factor, the feeling that if one is opposed to nuclear power, one should do something about it, affects the propensity to get involved. Moral considerations come into play here, as in the case of voting. There is, however, an interesting difference: while D appears to be the overriding consideration that induces people to vote, it would seem that B, the perception that nuclear power is a major threat, is the most crucial incentive for participation in the antinuclear movement.

Overall, Opp's data do not support the hard-core rational choice model. It is true that the B factor proves to be extremely important, but P is grossly overestimated and does not seem to matter much anyway, and people seem to be induced to participate when C increases.

A second study, by Finkel, Muller, and Opp (1989), examines the general propensity to become involved in legal and illegal protest. The authors propose and test two models to explain why individuals participate in collective action, both models being capable, according to the authors, of overcoming the free-rider problem.

The first model, which they call the personal influence model, simply relaxes the assumption that P is close to zero; according to the authors, "those with a strong sense of political efficacy may believe they make a difference because of their resources and political expertise" (Finkel, Muller, and Opp 1989, 888). They add that individuals will be inclined to participate only if "feelings of personal efficacy are coupled with the perception that the group as a whole is likely to succeed" (888). There are thus two Ps, the traditional one indicating personal decisiveness and one indicating the likelihood of group success.

The second model, collective rationality, has two variants. In one variant, individuals reason that it is a moral duty to participate because free riding is collectively irrational. We have here the famous D term. Again, however, the authors add a new twist. They argue that individuals will decide to fulfill their duty only if the probability of group success is relatively high.

According to the second variant, individuals come to believe in the "unity principle," that is, they reason that the participation of everyone is necessary to obtain the public good. Here, the individuals' utility and that of the group "become indistinguishable, and each individual will participate if the overall potential for group success appears high" (888).

These models are tested with survey data, collected from November 1987 to January 1988, from a national sample and two samples of protest-prone communities in the Federal Republic of Germany. The personal influence model is supported for both legal and illegal protest, while the collective rationality model is supported only for legal protest.

Are these results consistent with a rational choice model? The authors think so. While they acknowledge that the implications are complex and that the findings do not fit with the standard assumptions of rational choice, they argue that, according to their findings, "individuals are maximizing utility based on their preferences for public goods and the constraints on realizing their preferences represented by their own perceptions of personal influence, acceptance or rejection of the beliefs promoting collective rationality, and the opportunities for successful collective action afforded by the environment" (901).

I would qualify this optimistic assessment. First, the fact that some people participate out of a sense of moral duty cannot be construed as support for a rational choice model. Second, the study did not tap the perceived cost of participation, thus leaving out a crucial element of the calculus.

But the authors' claim that "procedurally rational individuals may calculate a positive expected utility for participation that outweighs the free ride" (901) rests very much on the finding that P matters:

> [I]ndividuals appear to participate in whatever form of behavior promises the greatest chance of success. Moreover, the interaction effects demonstrated in the multivariate models are clearly compatible with procedural rationality. In the personal influence model, individuals who feel personally efficacious are unlikely to participate unless the group as a whole can also succeed, and individuals who believe that the group can succeed but feel personally inefficacious are likely to stay at home and free-ride. (901)

Let us look closely at these results. Perception of personal influence is measured by a question asking respondents the amount of influence (from no influence to great influence) they could personally have if they were to get involved in a number of protest activities. The mean score on the personal influence scale is .46, indicating that on average people think they can exert "some" influence.

The finding that perceptions that one can personally have some influence do affect the propensity to participate is broadly consistent with the rational choice model. According to the model, however, people should rely not on vague conceptions of political influence; they should think hard about whether their personally getting involved or not is likely to change anything. The question asked by the authors did not get directly at the *decisiveness* of one individual's participation.

It is interesting, in this respect, that personal influence seems to matter more in this study than in Opp's earlier one on the antinuclear movement, in which P was measured more directly by questions such as whether respondents agreed with the statement that "the activity of a single person . . . cannot prevent the development of the use of nuclear energy." We have here perhaps the same pattern as in voting: the more direct measures of P yield less satisfactory results than the more indirect ones. This suggests that while people do think about whether their vote or protest may "count" in some sense, they do not necessarily ask themselves whether their own individual vote or action may prove to be decisive.

Finally, Finkel, Muller, and Opp make much of the fact that the interaction effects they find correspond exactly to the predictions of the rational choice model. It must be pointed out, however, that they do not explicitly test, as they should have done in my view, whether their interactive model performs better than the simple additive one. They indicate that "additive specifications yielded no better fit to the data" (899) but they do not say that they performed less well. And I would argue that if the two sets of specifications provide equal fit, the simpler additive model should be retained. It is up to rational choice researchers to demonstrate that a multiplicative model is superior to the additive one. I have seen no evidence to support the claim.

In short, the Finkel, Muller, and Opp study provides only limited support for the rational choice model. They show that B and P matter, though in the case of P people seem to reason somewhat differently from what the model assumes. It is not clear at all that people think in terms of decisiveness nor that they pay equal attention to B and P. Furthermore, other nonrational considerations, especially moral ones, come into play.[10]

Rational choice has also been used to explain the decision to participate or not in the quintessential political group, the party. The most important study from this perspective is that of Whiteley (see Whiteley, Seyd, Richardson, and Bissell 1994; Whiteley 1995).[11] The study is based on a survey of Conservative party members in Britain. The dependent variable is the respondent's level of activism in the party (A).

Whiteley starts with the simplest model in which $A = (P^{\star}B) - C$. Whiteley notes that P may not be as infinitesimally low in this case as it may be in the case of voting or protest activity. First, party activists have direct access to policymakers. Second, while there is a large number of party members, some of the collective goods the party may provide are in the form of local policy outputs for which "the active contribution of a few individuals can play a decisive role" (220). The data show that both terms ($P^{\star}B$ and C) are significant, with the expected signs.

Whiteley then moves to an extended version that encompasses "selective incentives." He distinguishes three such incentives, related to "outcome," "process," and "ideology." The outcome incentive corresponds to "the private returns from participation associated with the aim of building a political career" (221). The process incentive "measures the extent to which party members enjoy participation, since it provides an opportunity to meet like-minded people, and to learn about the political process at first hand" (221). The ideological incentive is the reward one gets from "express[ing] deeply held beliefs in company with other like-minded beliefs" (222). The results indicate that each of these incentives affects the propensity to be active.

In a third stage, Whiteley considers three other incentives that "are not consistent with a rational actor model" (222): "group efficacy," "social norms," and "expressive motives." First, party members may calculate the benefits and costs of political action at the level of the group, as Finkel, Muller, and Opp (1989) suggest. Whiteley, however, argues, rightly in my view, that "this 'collective rationality' does not accord with the method-ological individualism essential to rational choice models" (223). Likewise, party activists may be reacting to social norms, more specifically to the per-ceived opinions of others; such a reaction, according to Whiteley, is unlikely to reflect a thoughtful calculation of benefits and costs. Finally, expressive motives indicate members' emotional attachment to the party. Whiteley finds that group efficacy and expressive motives affect party activism, but that social norms do not.

Whiteley argues that the results "support the conclusion that the vari-ables in a rational choice model of participation clearly play an important role in explaining why some individuals are active while others are not" but that they "also show that a purely rational actor model provides an incom-plete explanation of political action; important motives for participation ex-ist in high-cost types of activities, which are inconsistent with the rational actor model" (227).

This is a fair conclusion. The verdict, however, is somewhat vague. The important and difficult question is: how good a model is it? At first sight, the rational choice model performs very well. The extended rational choice model includes six variables, and each of them comes out significant. This is an impressive result. It is true that the model is incomplete, that other fac-tors come into play, but is that not the fate of any model?

A closer look at the results leads to a more nuanced verdict. Let us start with the hard-core model. It is true that both $B*P$ and C are significant, and that the former comes out as the most important factor of all. But it must be said that C is just barely significant.[12] It is certainly intriguing that in the two nonexperimental studies reviewed here,[13] cost emerges with the wrong sign in Opp (1986) and with a very weak effect in Whiteley (1995). Furthermore, Whiteley does not test explicitly whether the P term as such adds much to the explanation or whether the interactive specification provides a better fit than the additive one. It should also be noted that the indicator of P is sim-ply the perception of personal influence, as in the Finkel, Muller, and Opp study, which is not quite the same as the probability of being *decisive*.

The other issue is whether the other incentives incorporated in the ex-tended rational choice model are unambiguously rational. In my view, only one of them is, the selective outcome incentive. This taps the amount of political ambition an individual possesses. Whiteley shows that those who think about a political career are more likely to be active. The fact that this variable has a strong effect is quite consistent with a rational choice perspec-tive.

The situation is more ambiguous in the case of the two other selective incentives considered by Whiteley. Those who think getting involved provides an opportunity to meet interesting people and to learn about politics tend to be more active. This is not surprising: the more interesting party activity is perceived to be, the greater the involvement. If this is a rational calculus, anything is rational. The same verdict applies to the ideological incentive. It seems that the more right-wing one perceives oneself to be, the more one tends to be active. Again, it is not clear at all why this should count as rational.

These criticisms should not be overstated. In my judgment, Whiteley's study does provide some support for the rational choice model, perhaps more so than any other nonexperimental study. The free-rider problem, in particular, seems less acute in the case of parties. A number of party activists may expect to get some personal reward, in terms of political career in particular, which may be sufficient to outweigh the cost of participation.

What do we learn from these nonexperimental studies of group involvement? It appears that people do calculate, in gross terms, the benefits and the costs, but not exactly along the lines predicted by the rational choice model. It is clear that the importance attached to the collective good, the B term, is crucial. The more concerned one is with the environment, the more likely she is to get involved in an environmental group.

But the distinctiveness of rational choice theory lies in the P and C terms. The results concerning C are disappointing. In Opp's study it seems to trigger participation, in Whiteley's it has a very small effect. I think this stems mostly from weaknesses in the indicators of C. We need better studies to determine how much perceptions of cost really matter in the decision to participate or not in a group.

With respect to P, the results are ambiguous. There is some evidence that people overestimate the probability that their own involvement will be decisive in the success or failure of the group. It also appears that the perception that one can have some personal influence does have some impact on the propensity to participate. What seems to matter, however, is a general sense of personal efficacy, and not the perception that one can be decisive as such. Furthermore, it remains to be seen whether a multiplicative specification is superior to a simple additive one, as rational choice would predict.

Finally, these studies indicate that moral considerations, more specifically, the belief that one ought to get involved if one is deeply concerned with a problem, come into play, in the same way as they do in the case of voting. The same studies suggest, however, that these considerations are not as powerful here as they are in the decision of whether to vote or abstain.

Conclusion

In experiments as well as in real-life situations, people do free ride because they perceive that their contribution is unlikely to be decisive in the success of group action. But they do not free ride all the time. In experiments, when they have the choice, as in Andreoni's experiments, they typically split their total investment more or less equally between collective and individual action, torn as they are between listening to their intelligence, which tells them their interest lies in free riding, and heeding their heart, which tells them one should be concerned about the public good.

When it comes to joining a movement, it would seem that B is the overriding factor. Most of those who are extremely concerned with an issue get involved: they do not ponder whether their own contribution may be decisive, nor do they pay much attention to the opportunity costs. The decision is a more difficult, and more calculated, one for those with less intense feelings. They get involved if they feel personally efficacious, if the group has some chance of being successful, and if some of their friends are also involved. But if any of these conditions is not met, the temptation to free ride may be irresistible.

The rational choice model, therefore, faces the very same limits identified in previous chapters when it attempts to explain why people become active or not in groups, movements, or parties. There are two major limits. The first is that people do not just calculate benefits and costs. They are also striving to follow their conscience to do what they believe is right and to avoid doing what they construe to be wrong.

The second limit concerns P. People do take into account the likelihood that their action will be successful; they are inclined to stay home when they believe the group has no chance of achieving its goal. This is quite consistent with the rational choice model. But P does not come into play in the precise manner assumed by the model. First, many people are prone to overestimate their potential influence. Second, many do not think hard about how to assess their influence. They do not ask themselves, as rational citizens should, whether their being involved or not will change anything; they merely rely on vague feelings of personal efficacy. Third, they pay greater attention to B than to P, contrary to the model's assumptions.

If the model faces the same limits in all these domains, must we conclude that it does not explain why people participate or not in groups any better than it can account for the decision to vote or not to vote? This would be a wrong conclusion, in my judgment. Even if the limits are similar in these two domains, they do not have the same weight.

In the case of voting, I have argued that rational considerations are basically irrelevant for close to half of the electorate and have only marginal influence for the remainder. In the case of experiments, I would say that rational factors are crucial for about half the subjects and irrelevant for very few. I cannot suggest equivalent figures in the case of real groups, but I suspect the numbers would not be too different from those observed in experiments. Even if the problems of rational choice are the same in all domains, they are much less severe in situations where the stakes are higher. The bottom line is that the rational choice model, even if it is not quite satisfactory, does a better job of explaining why people participate in groups than of accounting for why they vote. The norm of civic duty is exceptionally powerful in an election.

CONCLUSION

Rational Choice and Voting

I started my inquiry with the observation that the rational choice model of voting, in its simplest formulation, does not appear to work. An individual who takes into account the tiny probability that her vote could be decisive should rationally abstain. Yet most people vote in national elections, and most of them vote regularly. Voting seems to be a paradox.

One may adopt either of the following positions with regard to this paradox. The first is to argue that the rational choice model is basically flawed and should be discarded. The second is to assert that it is possible to come up with a more complex interpretation within the same framework. The third is to propose that rational choice provides a valid, though very partial, explanation of turnout.

I support the third position. Rational choice can contribute to understanding why people vote or abstain but its contribution is quite limited. It is limited in three ways. First, for about half of the electorate, which possesses a strong sense of duty, the model has simply no explanatory power. These people vote out of a sense of moral obligation, because they believe it would be wrong not to vote; they do not calculate benefits and costs.

Second, even among those with a relatively weak sense of duty, rational choice's contribution is very partial. It is true that for these people, the propensity to vote increases with B and P and decreases with C, but these factors affect the vote much less than the model would lead us to believe.

Yes, turnout increases with the perceived importance of the election, but the fact remains that in countries where the president has very little power, such as Austria, Iceland, and Ireland, median turnout in presidential elections is only two points lower than in the more crucial legislative elections. Yes, turnout is higher when the race is closer, but a gap of ten points between the leading and the second parties seems to reduce electoral participation by only one point. Yes, people are less likely to vote when it is more costly, but rain has no impact at all on those with a strong sense of duty and a very small effect among others (Knack 1994).

Third, rational choice is only partly right with respect to its most original component, the P term. It is true that people are more likely to vote when they feel that their vote can make a difference, and turnout increases when the race is close. According to the model, however, people should think about the probability that their vote will be decisive, that it will decide who wins the election. People's reasoning appears to be much more fuzzy. They do not really think about the possibility that the election could be decided by one single vote. What seems to matter (at the margin, for those with a weak sense of duty) is the vague impression that the outcome is not a foregone conclusion, that there is a race of some sort, that their vote may "count."

Moreover, people do not multiply B by P, they simply add them. The fact that the model is additive rather than multiplicative may appear to be a trivial technical consideration, but it has important substantive implications. In the standard rational choice model it is *expected* benefits that matter, that is, the utility a citizen derives from a party being elected *times* the probability that her vote will decide whether that party will be elected or not. Because P is bound to be infinitesimal, B^*P is practically nil, and the rational citizen decides to abstain.

Minimax regret tried to solve the problem by getting rid of P entirely. I have shown that minimax regret is neither theoretically satisfactory nor empirically supported. The analyses presented in this book suggest that P, not in the strict sense defined by the model but the vague feeling that one's vote may count, matters (a little, among a fraction of the electorate).

In a nutshell, people do not calculate *expected* benefits. They grossly estimate the benefits derived from their party or candidate being elected and they take into account the closeness of the race. But these are separate, not intertwined, considerations.

The upshot is that the expected utility model does not fit with the facts. The limits of expected utility have been known for a long time (see, especially, Allais 1953), and my study has illustrated them. We have seen that many voters overestimate P. And, perhaps even more important, what seems to matter is the perception not that one single vote might be decisive, as it should be in theory, but rather that the outcome may be close.

This suggests that there is some *illusion* at work. As Quattrone and Tversky (1988, 733) argue, many people fail to distinguish between causal and diagnostic contingencies: "some people may reason that if they decide to vote, that decision would imply that others with similar political attitudes will also abstain . . . that is each citizen may regard his or her single vote as diagnostic of millions of votes, which would substantially inflate the subjective probability of one's vote making a difference."

Such reasoning is irrational. Quattrone and Tversky present experimental evidence that demonstrates that many people think in those terms. And I have shown in chapter 3 that responses to the statement that "my vote may not count much, but if all people who think like me vote, it could make a big difference" are related to turnout, even controlling for B, C, and D.

People, then, don't have it quite right. The half of the electorate who thinks about benefits and costs makes very rough estimates and fails to focus on the causal impact of their own personal behavior. Their (loose) decision rule seems to be that since the cost of voting is low, they should vote unless they perceive practically no difference between the parties and candidates. They are also slightly more likely to vote if they think the race is close.

P matters, but the way it matters is different from what rational choice would predict. On the one hand, P is just one marginal consideration that does not interact with B. As a consequence, perceiving P to be nil slightly decreases the propensity to vote; it does not, as in the standard rational choice model, necessarily lead to abstention. On the other hand, what affects the voting decision is not, as the model assumes, the strict probability that the individual could cast a decisive vote, but rather the probability that the outcome could be decided by a relatively small number of votes.

On empirical grounds, then, the rational choice model is only very partially confirmed. The model has considerable limitations. It would be tempting to conclude that the model should be discarded entirely. This is not the conclusion I have reached. I believe the model has some utility.

The fact remains that rational choice is more theoretically satisfactory than any of the alternative explanations. Take the resource and mobilization models. They tell us that people vote if they have the resources to overcome the cost of voting or if they are asked to. The problem is that these models take benefits for granted; they assume that everyone would like to vote if it were easy. Rational choice proposes a more complete picture, in which people consider both the advantages and disadvantages of voting.

It does not suffice, of course, for a model to be theoretically elegant. It must fit with the facts. But the rational choice model does fit partially with the facts. I have shown in chapter 5 that among those with a weak sense of civic duty, B, P, and C each has an independent impact on the propensity to vote. The elements of the calculus of voting play only at the margin, and only among a fraction of the electorate, but they do have an effect.

Furthermore, there are good theoretical reasons why rational choice does not perform as well in the case of voting. The reason is simply that whether the individual makes the "right" or the "wrong" decision when she votes or abstains has minimal consequences in her life. Because voting is a low-stake decision, people can easily afford to make "irrational" decisions; they pay hardly any price for making the "wrong" choice. We should expect rational choice to offer less satisfactory explanations for these kinds of decisions, and this is precisely what we find. As I have indicated in chapter 6, rational choice faces some of the same problems when it comes to understanding why people decide to join or not to join groups, but the problems are less severe and the model does a better job. Voting is a tough test for rational choice. This has to be taken into account in assessing the model.

I have argued that the major motivation that leads most people to vote is the feeling that if one truly believes in democracy one has a moral obligation to vote. Oddly enough, rational choice may have facilitated the due recognition of this quintessentially irrational factor.

Rational choice did not invent the notion of duty. It has always been part of the voting literature. *The American Voter* (Campbell, Converse, Miller, and Stokes, 1960), for instance, identifies five factors affecting turnout, and sense of citizen duty is one of these five. The four others are partisan preference, interest in the campaign, concern over the election outcome, and sense of political efficacy. Likewise, Milbrath and Goel (1977) list a whole litany of attitudes and beliefs that are related to electoral participation, among which sense of civic obligation appears.

Even though sense of duty is mentioned by these authors, it does not have any predominant status. In contrast, when it appears in rational choice models, it is usually acknowledged as a key factor. The first rational choice authors to do so were, of course, Riker and Ordeshook (1968). In their model, D is one of the three basic components of the calculus of voting, alongside $B*P$ and C.

Indeed, once it is acknowledged that it is irrational, in the strict sense of the term, to vote, it becomes imperative to look for other factors that make most people vote. It is in part because I was interested in the rational choice model, both in its merits and its limits, that I felt the need to explore other kinds of motivations such as sense of duty. And I would argue that the import of such feelings has been underestimated in the literature because there have been too few empirically minded researchers who were taking rational choice seriously.

The bottom line is that I cannot personally make sense of why people vote without taking into account the rational choice model. Those who are not fascinated by the fact that most people vote even if it is not in their best personal interest to do so miss something important, and only rational choice can nourish such fascination.

A few years ago, Green and Shapiro (1994) published a devastating critique of rational choice theory. How does my verdict square with theirs? Our evaluations converge when it comes to assessing the empirical foundations of the model. Green and Shapiro argue that "despite its enormous and growing prestige in the discipline, rational choice theory has yet to deliver on its promise to advance the empirical study of politics" (7), and conclude their chapter on the paradox of voter turnout by saying that "readers interested in the determinants of voter turnout, in sum, derive little insight from the empirical work in the rational choice tradition" (68).

My own evaluation is slightly more sanguine. In my view, the model makes a real contribution to understanding of why people vote though that contribution is quite limited.

I would argue, contrary to Green and Shapiro, that the model provides a small but useful contribution to the explanation of voting for the following two reasons. First, rational choice has forced us to give as much thought to reasons for voting as to reasons for not voting. Before rational choice, the dominant paradigm was the alienationalist school (see Dennis 1991), according to which nonvoting represents the absence of integration into the political system. From such a perspective, voting is the norm—the kind of thing people who have learned to deal with the system do—and what needs to be explained is why some do not adhere to this norm. Rational choice, of course, reverses the perspective, as voting appears irrational. It is useful for political scientists to be reminded that there may be very good reasons not to vote. And, as I have indicated, it is easier to appreciate the crucial importance of motivations such as sense of duty once it is recognized that voting, from a pure self-interest perspective, is irrational.

I disagree with Green and Shapiro on another important matter. Green and Shapiro dismiss too easily, in my view, the argument that rational choice is particularly ill-suited to explaining voter turnout because turnout is associated with low costs and low benefits, and that its poor performance in accounting for why people vote is not a sufficient reason for questioning its overall validity.

Green and Shapiro call this arbitrary domain restriction. They question whether turnout is indeed a low-cost activity by referring to "Latin American elections, in which voters spend hours in polling lines, sometimes amid threat of violences" and to "the more than 100,000 African-Americans who persevered through the intimidation and poll taxes of the Jim Crow South" (58). This is a cheap argument. What the rational choice literature has been dealing with is why people vote in a democracy; the theory is not supposed to explain behavior in situations where the democratic process is not functioning properly.

Green and Shapiro add that "there is nothing in rational choice theory that specifies the level at which costs or benefits are sufficiently small to render the theory applicable." According to them, rational choice advocates have been looking at turnout for a long time, thus implicitly acknowledging that the theory could be applied to this kind of behavior, and it is just an easy, post-hoc excuse that is used "once it became apparent that no satisfying solution could be worked out" (58).

It is indeed not entirely clear at what precise level of costs and benefits the theory is or is not applicable. But should we expect such a degree of precision in a theory? Is it not sufficient to assume that the greater the stakes, the more relevant the theory, and, conversely, the lower the stakes, the less useful it is? This is at least what I would claim, and this does not strike me as a more imprecise proposition than those provided by other theories.

Green and Shapiro say that it is too easy to argue that a theory does not apply to a domain in which it does not seem to work. And, indeed, rational choice people would have been more convincing if they had made that point up front, before undertaking to solve the paradox of voting, rather than ex post. Still, the point is not whether it is an excuse or not but rather whether the argument makes sense. It does. It does because it is entirely consistent with the logic of rational choice theory. The rational person should allow more time, resources, and attention to those decisions that have greater implications on her well-being than to those with marginal consequences. While the argument may be suspect, given the context in which it has been advanced, it is nevertheless a valid one.

In short, Green and Shapiro seem to believe that the contribution of rational choice to an understanding of why people vote is tiny and close to nil. My own verdict is that its contribution is quite small but still useful, and that there are good reasons why the model performs poorly in low-stakes situations.

I feel compelled to end this book on a personal note. Over the last few years, I have been reflecting on the reasons that lead people to vote or not to vote. I have looked at turnout rates around the world for all kinds of elections, I have done surveys, semi-structured interviews, and an experiment with university students. I have also talked informally with many people, obsessed as I was to grasp their B, P, C, D, or other motivations.

During the same period, I have had to decide whether I should vote or not. This was no easy decision, especially as I like to think of myself as a rational person and as, like most of my fellow citizens, I have tended to vote in most elections in the past. Is it rational for me, or for anyone for that matter, to vote?

I have been and I am still struggling with this question. I have tried to formulate a general guideline that I am willing to recommend. At this stage, the reader will not be surprised to learn that my decision to vote or to abstain depends on my perceptions of B, P, C, and D.

The very first question to address concerns D: Do I have a moral obligation to vote? My answer is: Yes . . . to a certain extent. My reasoning is quite similar to that of those I have described as voting out of a sense of duty. I strongly believe in democracy; I am convinced that the democratic form of government, while not a panacea for all human problems, contributes to the quality of life in a country, and I am looking forward to an era where all the governments of the world will be selected through free and fair elections.

This, of course, is not a sufficient reason to vote. Should not the rational individual reason that whether she votes or not will not salvage or jeopardize democracy in her country? My only response is that, like many of my fellow citizens, I feel that I must act in accordance with the principles I believe in. As I think of myself as a democrat, it would be incongruous not to vote. I vote, then, because I want to be consistent with my principles. Yes, I would feel somewhat guilty not to vote.

The obligation to vote is not absolute, however. Most important, I do not feel compelled to vote if I have reached the conclusion that it does not matter who wins the election (B is nil) or if I think that none of the parties or candidates deserves to be supported. In other words, I do not feel obliged to vote if I have no good reasons to vote for anyone.

What about P? Is the obligation to vote less compelling if the race is not close, or if my preferred candidate has no chance of winning? Here again much depends on B. If I have strong views about which party is the best, I feel I should vote. If I have only slight preferences, then I might decide that it is not worth voting if the outcome is a foregone conclusion.

Am I not deluding myself when I decide to vote partly because the race is close? I hope not. I start with the initial position that I should normally vote but I am willing to reconsider this position if B is nil or if B is small and P is nil.

What about C? In my view, the cost of voting is extremely small and does not vary much from one election to another. As a consequence, C does not have much impact on my decision, except in an indirect fashion; the fact that C is low makes it easier to vote.

According to this account, I vote most of the time but not necessarily all the time. My most important reason for voting has nothing to do with rational considerations, although I do pay some attention to these, first and foremost to B but also to P and C. Even though I would not claim to be a typical citizen (especially with respect to my level of political interest and to the amount of time I devote to whether I should vote or not), the same message applies: rational choice provides a small but useful insight into my reasons for voting.

My last word will be a plea for more research. In my view, further research is needed along three lines. First, we need more qualitative studies to deepen our understanding of the sense of civic duty. I hope to have thrown some light on what goes through people's minds when they feel they have a moral obligation to vote. But how strong and stable are such feelings? How are they correlated to other attitudes and ideologies? When are they formed? And how do people define the limits of obligation, that is under which circumstances does the citizen feel free not to vote? These are crucial questions that deserve in-depth analyses.

Second, we need cross-national comparative analyses of why people vote. Rational choice advocates have traditionally relied on secondary data that were often of aggregate nature or that had been assembled for different purposes. It is time to design studies with specific measures of B, P, and C. Robert Young and I have done precisely that in a number of studies, the findings of which have been reported here. This is, of course, not enough. We need similar surveys in different countries to determine whether the patterns we have established can be generalized. A particularly intriguing question is whether P is perceived and plays differently in PR systems. Strictly speaking, the probability of casting the decisive vote is the same in all kinds of electoral systems but I would formulate the hypothesis that the perceived probability is greater in PR systems.

Third, we need panel studies to grasp how individuals approach the decision to vote over time. As I have shown in chapter 2, age is closely associated with voting: people are more likely to vote as they grow older. Why? I have demonstrated in chapter 5 that this is partly because sense of duty increases with age, but we need to understand what people learn over time that makes them feel a greater obligation to vote. Panel studies should also help us to determine whether habit is an important factor in the decision to vote. My own analyses have little to say about this.

Further research may lead me to revisit my verdict. For the time being, I conclude that voting is mostly irrational but that rational choice contributes slightly to understanding why so many people decide to vote in most elections.

APPENDIX A

Democratic Elections, 1972–95, and Participation Rate

Country and Election Date	Partici- pation (%)	Country and Election Date	Partici- pation (%)	Country and Election Date	Partici- pation (%)
EUROPE		Denmark		Greece	
Andorra		12/73	88.7	11/74	79.5
12/93	80.9	01/75	88.2	11/77	81.1
Austria		02/77	88.0	10/81	81.5
10/75	92.9	10/79	85.6	06/85	83.8
05/79	92.2	12/81	83.2	06/89	84.5
04/83	92.6	01/84	88.4	10/93	79.2
11/86	90.5	09/87	86.7	Hungary	
10/90	86.1	05/88	85.7	04/90	65.1
10/94	81.9	12/90	82.8	05/94	68.9
12/95	86.0	09/94	84.3	Iceland	
Belgium		Finland		06/74	91.4
03/74	90.3	01/72	81.4	06/78	90.3
04/77	95.1	09/75	73.8	12/79	89.3
12/78	94.8	03/79	75.3	04/83	88.6
11/81	94.6	03/83	75.7	04/87	90.1
10/85	93.6	03/87	72.1	04/91	87.5
12/87	93.4	03/91	68.3	04/95	87.4
11/91	92.7	03/95	68.0	Ireland	
05/95	91.2	France		02/73	76.6
Bulgaria		03/73	81.3	06/77	76.3
10/91	83.9	03/78	83.2	06/81	76.2
12/94	75.2	06/81	70.9	02/82	73.8
Czechoslovakia		03/86	78.5	11/82	72.8
06/90	96.3	06/88	66.2	02/87	73.3
06/92	84.7	03/93	67.5	06/89	65.5
		Germany		11/92	68.5
		11/72	91.1		
		10/76	90.7		
		10/80	88.6		
		03/83	88.4		
		01/87	84.3		
		12/90	77.8		
		10/94	78.9		

(continued)

Country and Election Date	Partici- pation (%)	Country and Election Date	Partici- pation (%)	Country and Election Date	Partici- pation (%)
Italy		Poland		United Kingdom	
05/72	93.2	10/91	43.2	02/74	78.9
06/76	93.4	09/93	52.8	10/74	72.9
06/79	91.1	Portugal		05/79	76.3
06/83	89.0	04/76	83.3	06/83	72.8
06/87	90.5	12/79	87.5	06/87	75.4
04/92	87.3	10/80	85.4	04/92	77.0
03/94	86.1	04/83	78.6		
Liechtenstein		10/85	75.4	SOUTH AMERICA	
03/89	90.9	07/87	72.6	Argentina	
10/93	85.3	10/91	67.8	11/85	82.2
Lithuania		10/95	67.2	09/87	83.6
11/92	75.2	San Marino		05/89	84.2
Luxembourg		05/78	79.0	12/91	89.7
05/74	90.1	05/83	79.5	10/93	79.7
06/79	88.9	05/88	81.1	05/95	80.9
06/84	88.8	05/93	80.3	Bolivia	
06/89	87.3	Slovakia		07/85	82.0
06/94	86.6	09/94	75.7	05/89	73.7
Malta		Slovenia		Brazil	
09/76	95.0	12/92	85.9	11/86	85.0
12/81	94.6	Spain		10/94	82.2
05/87	96.1	03/79	68.1	Chile	
02/92	96.0	10/82	79.8	03/73	81.2
Monaco		06/86	70.6	12/93	91.3
01/93	73.2	10/89	69.9	Columbia	
Netherlands		06/93	77.1	04/74	57.1
11/72	83.5	Sweden		02/78	33.0
05/77	88.0	09/73	90.8	03/82	41.0
05/81	87.0	09/76	91.8	03/86	43.6
09/82	81.0	09/79	90.7	10/91	31.9
05/86	85.8	09/82	91.4	Ecuador	
09/89	80.1	09/85	89.9	01/84	71.2
05/94	78.3	09/88	86.0	06/86	74.0
Norway		09/91	86.7	01/88	77.7
09/73	80.2	09/94	86.8	06/90	67.7
09/77	82.9	Switzerland		05/92	73.0
09/81	82.0	10/75	52.4	Guyana	
09/85	84.0	10/79	48.1	07/73	82.9
09/89	83.2	10/83	48.9	Peru	
09/93	75.8	10/87	46.1	05/80	80.1
		10/91	46.0	04/85	80.5
		10/95	42.2		

(continued)

Country and Election Date	Partici-pation (%)	Country and Election Date	Partici-pation (%)	Country and Election Date	Partici-pation (%)
Surinam		Samoa		Sao Tome and Principe	
10/77	77.8	04/91	78.0	01/91	76.7
Uruguay		Solomon Islands		10/94	52.1
11/89	88.7	02/89	64.9	South Africa	
11/94	91.4	05/93	63.6	04/94	86.9
Venezuela		Vanuatu		Zambia	
12/73	96.5	11/83	98.7	10/91	45.5
12/78	87.5	11/87	83.0		
12/83	87.8			ASIA	
12/88	81.7	AFRICA		Bangladesh	
		Benin		03/73	57.0
OCEANIA		02/91	51.7	02/91	52.0
Australia		Botswana		Cyprus	
12/72	95.4	10/74	33.0	05/81	95.8
05/74	95.4	10/79	58.0	12/85	94.6
12/75	95.4	09/84	76.0	05/91	93.0
12/77	95.0	10/89	68.2	India	
10/80	94.4	12/94	76.6	03/77	60.5
03/83	94.6	Burkina Faso		01/80	56.8
12/84	94.2	04/78	40.2	12/84	63.5
07/87	93.8	Cape Verde		11/89	58.0
03/90	95.5	01/91	75.3	Israel	
03/93	95.7	Gambia		12/73	78.6
Fiji		03/72	79.5	05/77	79.2
05/72	99.3	04/77	82.0	06/81	78.5
07/82	86.0	04/92	55.8	07/84	78.8
Kiribati		Madagascar		11/88	79.7
01/83	75.9	06/93	60.0	06/92	77.4
03/87	84.0	Malawi		Japan	
Nauru		05/94	80.0	12/72	71.7
01/87	92.7	Mali		12/76	73.4
New Zealand		03/92	21.3	10/79	68.0
11/72	89.1	Mauritius		06/80	74.6
11/75	82.5	12/76	91.0	12/83	67.9
11/78	83.7	06/82	90.0	07/86	71.4
11/81	89.0	08/87	85.0	02/90	73.3
07/84	91.7	09/91	84.5	07/93	67.0
08/87	87.2	Namibia		Lebanon	
10/90	85.2	12/94	76.1	04/72	39.0
11/93	85.2	Nigeria		Nepal	
Papua New Guinea		08/83	38.9	05/91	65.0
06/82	96.5				

(continued)

Country and Election Date	Partici- pation (%)	Country and Election Date	Partici- pation (%)	Country and Election Date	Partici- pation (%)
Philippines		Costa Rica		Panama	
05/87	90.0	02/74	79.9	05/94	73.7
South Korea		02/78	81.2	St. Kitts and Nevis	
04/88	75.7	02/82	78.6	06/84	77.7
03/92	71.9	02/86	81.8	03/89	66.4
Turkey		02/90	81.8	11/93	66.4
06/77	70.0	02/94	81.1	St. Lucia	
11/87	93.3	Dominica		07/79	68.0
10/91	83.9	07/80	80.2	05/82	65.8
		07/85	74.6	04/87	60.7
NORTH AMERICA		05/90	66.6	04/87	64.7
Antigua and Barbuda		Dominican Republic		04/92	62.8
05/84	61.1	05/78	72.5	St. Vincent and	
03/89	60.7	05/82	73.9	Grenadines	
Bahamas		05/86	69.5	12/79	63.9
07/77	89.9	05/90	59.4	07/84	88.8
06/82	89.8	El Salvador		05/89	72.4
06/87	87.9	03/72	56.7	02/94	65.6
Barbados		03/85	43.3	Trinidad and Tobago	
09/76	74.1	Grenada		09/76	55.8
06/81	71.6	12/76	65.3	11/81	56.4
05/86	76.7	03/90	68.4	12/86	65.5
01/91	63.7	06/95	61.8	12/91	65.8
09/94	60.3	Honduras			
Belize		11/85	84.0		
12/84	75.0	11/89	76.0		
09/89	72.6	Jamaica			
Canada		02/72	78.9		
10/72	77.2	12/76	85.2		
07/74	71.0	10/80	86.1		
05/79	75.7	09/89	78.4		
02/80	69.3	03/93	60.0		
09/84	75.7				
11/88	75.5				
10/93	69.7				

Note: Democratic elections excluded from the analysis because of missing participation data: Andorra 04/92, Bahamas 08/92, Belize 06/93, Benin 03/95, Bolivia 06/93, Brazil 10/90, Dominica 06/95, El Salvador 03/74, Ecuador 05/94, Fiji 04/77, Kiribati 05/91 and 07/94, Liechtenstein 02/93, Micronesia 03/91, 03/93, and 03/95, Nauru 12/76, 11/77, 12/80, 12/83, 12/89, and 11/92, Papua New Guinea 06/77, 06/87, and 06/92, Solomon Islands 08/80 and 10/84, Sri Lanka 07/77, Tuvalu 09/81, 09/85, 09/89, and 09/93, and Vanuatu 12/91.

Jamaica 12/83 excluded because of boycott (participation rate: 2.7%)

APPENDIX B

Variables, Indicators, and Sources

Variables	Indicators	Sources
Turnout	Percentage of those registered on the electoral list who cast a vote	Inter-Parliamentary Union, *Chronique des élections et de evolution parlementaires;* Mackie and Rose (1991); *European Journal of Political Research* (various years); *Electoral Studies* (various years); IFES, *Elections Today* (various years); *Keesings Record of World Events* (various years); Nohlen and Dieter (1993); Marc P. Jones (South America, personal information); Mozaffar, Shaheen (Africa, personal information)
North America	A dummy variable which equals 1 when the election was held in North America	UNESCO, *Statistical Yearbook*
South America	A dummy variable which equals 1 when the election was held in South America	UNESCO, *Statistical Yearbook*
Africa	A dummy variable which equals 1 when the election was held in Africa	UNESCO, *Statistical Yearbook*
Asia	A dummy variable which equals 1 when the election was held in Asia	UNESCO, *Statistical Yearbook*
Oceania	A dummy variable which equals 1 when the election was held in Oceania	UNESCO, *Statistical Yearbook*
Average life expectancy	Average life expectancy (number of years)	World Bank, *World Tables*
Density	The number of people by squared kilometers of territory	World Bank, *World Tables*; UNESCO, *Statistical Yearbook*

(continued)

Variables	Indicators	Sources
GNP per capita (log)	GNP per capita in constant U.S. dollars measured as GNP per capita in current U.S. dollars divided by corresponding U.S. GDP deflator	World Bank, *World Tables*
Growth of GNP	Annual percentage increase or decrease in GNP per capita in the election year compared to the previous year (based on GNP indicator expressed in local currency)	World Bank, *World Tables*
Illiteracy rate (squared)	The proportion of adult illiterate population	UNESCO, *Statistical Yearbook*
Size of population (log)	Total population	World Bank, *World Tables*
Switzerland	A dummy variable which equals 1 when the election was held in Switzerland	
Compulsory voting	A dummy variable which equals 1 when voting is compulsory	Inter-Parliamentary Union, *Chronique des élections et de l'évolution parlementaires*[a]
Degree of democracy	A dummy variable which equals 1 when the election was held in the country which obtained a score of 1 on political rights	Freedom House
Voting age	A variable which ranges from 16 to 21, corresponding to the voting age requirement	Inter-Parliamentary Union, *Chronique des élections et de l'évolution parlementaires*[a]
Decisiveness	Scale from 0 to 1, depending on the presence and the timing of subnational elections in federations, upper house direct elections in bicameral countries, and presidential direct elections: 1 = no such elections or other elections (subnational, upper house, or presidential) are held simultaneously; 5 = one other election (subnational, upper house, or presidential) held nonsimultaneously; 0 = two other elections (subnational, upper house, or presidential) held nonsimultaneously	Inter-Parliamentary Union, *Chronique des élections et de l'évolution parlementaires; Keesing's Record of World Events*

(continued)

Variables	Indicators	Sources
Plurality	A dummy variable which equals 1 when the election was held under the plurality rule	Same as for turnout[a]
Majority	A dummy variable which equals 1 when the election was held under the majority rule	Same as for turnout[a]
Mixed 1	A dummy variable which equals 1 when the election was held under the mixed rule	Same as for turnout[a]
Mixed 2	A dummy variable which equals 1 when the election was held under the mixed rule, excluding mixed corrective systems	Same as for turnout[a]
PR	A dummy variable which equals 1 when the election was held under the proportional representation rule, including corrective mixed systems	Same as for turnout[a]
Dispropor-tionality	The sum of absolute values of vote-seat share differences, divided by 2	Same as for turnout
Dispropor-tionality × PR		Same as for turnout
Number of parties (log)	The number of parties running in the election which obtained at least 1% of votes	Same as for turnout
One-Party Majority Government	A dummy variable which equals 1 when the election produced a one-party majority government	Same as for turnout
Closeness	The difference in vote shares between the leading and the second parties	Same as for turnout

[a]We had access to the electoral laws of the following countries: Australia, Austria, Belgium, Benin, Canada, Cape Verde, France, Germany, Greece, Hungary, Italy, Nepal, Portugal, South Africa, Spain, Switzerland, and the United Kingdom.

We also consulted the following sources: Andrenkow and Andrenkowa 1995; Blaustein and Flanz (various years); Dimitras 1994; Diskin 1992; Gonzales 1991; Grzybowski 1994; Jones 1995; Juberìas 1994; Mathur 1991; Morriss 1993; Mozaffar 1995; Simon 1995; Sisk 1994; Soltész 1994.

APPENDIX C

1993 Study of Electoral Participation among University Students:
Research Design

This study was conducted before and after the 1993 Canadian federal election, among students at the Université de Montréal and the University of Western Ontario. It involved three waves of questionnaires: two pre-election and one post-election. It also included an experimental format. There were five panel groups in which all three questionnaires were administered. Two of these were treatment groups in which students were subjected to a short lecture about the paradox of voting, and three were control groups. There were five additional groups in which only the post-election questionnaire was administered; four of these were control groups and one was a treatment group.

Montreal

Group	1	2	3	4	5
Course	Socio	Politics	Econo	Econo	Politics
Design:					
Questionnaire 1 (early campaign)	O_1 (155)	O_1 (121)			
Presentation		X		X	
Questionnaire 2 (late campaign)	O_2 (142)	O_2 (97)			
Questionnaire 3 (post-election)	O_3 (134)	O_3 (67)	O_3 (50)	O_3 (35)	O_3 (46)
Panel	(99)	(51)			

Western

Group	6	7	8	9	10
Course	Politics	Politics	Politics	Econo	Econo
Design:					
Questionnaire 1 (early campaign)	O_1 (280)	O_1 (220)		O_1 (67)	
Presentation	X				
Questionnaire 2 (late campaign)	O_2 (224)	O_2 (192)		O_2 (70)	
Questionnaire 3	O_3 (189)	O_3 (156)	O_3 (118)	O_3 (49)	O_3 (145)
Panel	(113)	(94)		(38)	

Note: The numbers in parentheses indicate the number of students who answered the questionnaire. Panel numbers show how many respondents in each class answered all three questionnaires.

APPENDIX D

1993 Study of Electoral Participation among University Students:
Question Wording

Most of the questions were repeated across the three questionnaires (with obvious change to verb tense made to correspond to the pre- and post-election contexts). Questions relating to socioeconomic data were asked either on the first question-naire (for those respondents participating in the panel) or on the third questionnaire (for those respondents participating only in the third wave). Most of the analyses presented in this book have been based on the post-election questionnaire, the wording of which is presented below. One additional question used in the analyses was asked only on the second-wave questionnaire. The wording of that question can be found immediately following the post-election questionnaire.

Post-election Questionnaire
Note: Items marked with an asterisk were asked on the first-wave questionnaire for those participating in the panel design.

Q1*. In general, would you say that politics interests you:
    Very much
    Somewhat
    Not much
    Not at all

Q2. Were you registered to vote in the recent federal election?
    Yes
    No

Q3. In what riding were you registered?
    Please write in the name of the riding: _____
    I was not registered

Q4. Did you vote in the election?
    Yes _____ [please go to Q5]
    No _____ [please go to Q4]

Q5. Why did you *not* vote in the federal election?
    Because I chose not to
    Because it was too difficult to go to vote
    Because it was impossible for me to vote

Q6. What party did you vote for?

Progressive Conservative	Bloc Québécois
Liberal	Other (please specify: _____)
NDP	I spoiled my ballot
Reform party	I did not vote

Q7. How satisfied are you with the outcome of the election *in your riding*?
> Very satisfied
> Satisfied
> Dissatisfied
> Very dissatisfied

Q8. How satisfied are you with the outcome of the election *in Canada as a whole*?
> Very satisfied
> Satisfied
> Dissatisfied
> Very dissatisfied

Q9. How interested are you in the election campaign?
> Very much
> Somewhat
> Not much
> Not at all

Q10. During the election campaign, did you think much about whether or not to vote?
> Very much
> Somewhat
> Not much
> Not at all

Q11. Considering Canada as a whole, how close did you think the election would be?
> Very close
> Rather close
> Not very close
> Not close at all

Q12. In your own riding, how close did you think the election would be?
> Very close
> Rather close
> Not very close
> Not close at all

Q13. How important was it to you, personally, which *candidate* was going to win the election in your *riding*? Please indicate how important this was to you, on a scale of 0 to 10, where 10 means that who was going to win the election in your riding made a *very great difference* to you, and 0 means that it made *no difference at all.*

    0. who was going to win made no difference at all to me

    1.

    2.

    3.

    4.

    5. who was going to win made some difference to me

    6.

    7.

    8.

    9.

    10. who was going to win made a very great difference to me

Q14. Again, how important was it to you, personally, which *party* was going to win the election in *Canada as a whole*? Please indicate how important this was to you, on a scale of 0 to 10, where 0 means that which party was going to win the election in Canada as a whole made a *very great difference* to you, and 0 means that it made *no difference at all.*

    0. which party was going to win made no difference at all to me

    1.

    2.

    3.

    4.

    5. which party was going to win made some difference to me

    6.

    7.

    8.

    9.

    10. which party was going to win made a very great difference to me

Q15. What do you think the chances were, roughly, that *your vote* would determine which candidate would win the election in your riding?

1 chance in 10	1 chance in 100,000
1 chance in 100	1 chance in 1,000,000
1 chance in 1,000	1 chance in 10,000,000
1 chance in 10,000	1 chance in 100,000,000

Q16. Again, what do you think the chances were that *your vote* would determine which candidate would win the election in Canada as a whole?

1 chance in 10	1 chance in 100,000
1 chance in 100	1 chance in 1,000,000
1 chance in 1,000	1 chance in 10,000,000
1 chance in 10,000	1 chance in 100,000,000

Q17. For each of the following statements, please indicate whether you *agree strongly, agree, disagree,* or *disagree strongly.*

> a. It is so easy to vote that I don't see any reason not to.
> b. People who don't vote have no right to criticize the government.
> c. It is important to vote, even if my party or candidate has no chance of winning.
> d. It is interesting to go to the polls and vote.
> e. Whoever wins the election, nothing will change.
> f. If I did not vote, my family would think badly of me.
> g. If I did not vote, my friends would think badly of me.
> h. If people like me don't vote, special interests would come to control the government.
> i. It is the duty of every citizen to vote.
> j. In order to preserve democracy, it is essential that the great majority of citizens vote.
> k. So many people vote that my vote means hardly anything.
> l. If I did not vote, I would feel guilty.
> m. My own vote may not count for much, but if all the people who think like me vote, it could make a big difference.
> n. Politicians are willing to say anything to get elected.
> o. I would feel really terrible if I didn't vote and my candidate lost by one vote.

Q18*. In some countries like Australia, citizens are obliged by law to vote. Do you think compulsory voting in Canada would be:

> A very good idea
> A good idea
> A bad idea
> A very bad idea

Q19*. In federal politics, do you usually think of yourself as being closer to one or to another political party?

> Yes
> No

Q20*. What party do you usually think of yourself as being closest to?

> Progressive Conservative   Bloc Québécois
> Liberal   Other (please specify: _____)
> NDP   I spoiled my ballot
> Reform party   I did not vote

Q21*. Were you eligible to vote in the federal election of 1988?

> Yes
> No

Q22*. Did you vote in that election?

> Yes
> No

Q23*. Were you eligible to vote in the last provincial election?
  Yes
  No

Q24*. Did you vote in that election?
  Yes
  No

Q25*. Were you eligible to vote in the referendum on the constitution in 1992?
  Yes
  No

Q26*. Did you vote in that referendum?
  Yes
  No

Q27*. In what year were you born?
  _____ (Please write the year)

Q28*. What is your gender?
  Female
  Male

Q29*. What is your religion?
  Catholic   Orthodox
  Hindu   Protestant
  Jewish   Other
  Muslim   None

Q30*. How important is religion, to you personally?
  Very important
  Important
  Of little importance
  Not important at all

Q31*. And money: how important is having money, to you personally?
  Very important
  Important
  Of little importance
  Not important at all

Q32*. What is the first language you learned and still understand?
  English
  French
  Other

Q33*. Can you carry on a conversation in French? [*Note:* wording on French questionnaire was: "Can you carry on a conversation in English?"]
  Yes
  No

Q34*. What is your opinion on Quebec sovereignty—that is that Quebec is no longer a part of Canada?

> Are you:
> Very favorable
> Favorable
> Opposed
> Very opposed

Q35. In which faculty are you registered?

> Arts   Engineering
> Social science   Kinesiology
> Science   Other:_____

Q36. How many political science courses have you taken, or are you taking presently, at the university level?

> None   Two and one-half
> One   Three
> One and one-half   More than three
> Two

Q37. How many economics courses have you taken, or are you taking presently, at the university level?

> None   Two and one-half
> One   Three
> One and one-half   More than three
> Two

Q38. How many sociology courses have you taken, or are you taking presently, at the university level?

> None   Two and one-half
> One   Three
> One and one-half   More than three
> Two

Question taken from second-wave questionnaire:

Q1. How difficult do you think it would be for you to go and cast your vote?

> Very easy
> Easy
> Difficult
> Very difficult

APPENDIX E

CSES Data, 1996–2000: Description of Variables

The CSES data set used in the present analysis is the first collection of microlevel data from the Comparative Study of Electoral Systems processed and merged by the Center for Political Studies at the University of Michigan. National post-electoral sample surveys were conducted during 1996–98 in several countries: Australia, Czech Republic, Great Britain, Israel, Lithuania, Romania, Poland, Spain, Taiwan, Ukraine, and the United States. I excluded Lithuania because of the missing data concerning the dependent variable and Ukraine because of its low rating on political rights.

Variables	Indicators
Vote	A dummy variable that equals 1 for those who cast a ballot in the most recent election and 0 otherwise.
Education	The variable indicates, on a scale from 0 to 1, the level of educational attainment with 0 corresponding to the lowest level of educational attainment and 1 to the highest level.
Age	The variable is the age of the respondent from 18 to 96.
Religiosity	The variable corresponds to respondent's score on a scale from 0 to 1. The scale was made of two questions about frequency of attendance at religious services and subjective degree of religiosity.
Income	The variable indicates, on a scale from 0 to 1, the household income with 0 corresponding to the lowest category of income and 1 to the highest category.
Married	A dummy variable that equals 1 for married respondents and 0 otherwise.
Union	A dummy variable that equals 1 if the respondent is a member of a union, 0 otherwise.
Student	A dummy variable that equals 1 if the respondent is a student, 0 otherwise.
Woman	A dummy variable that equals 1 if the respondent is female, 0 otherwise.
Unemployed	A dummy variable that equals 1 if the respondent is unemployed, 0 otherwise.
Housewife	A dummy variable that equals 1 if the respondent is a housewife, 0 otherwise.
Retired	A dummy variable that equals 1 if the respondent is retired, 0 otherwise.

Note: Poland, Australia, United States, Taiwan, Spain, Czech Republic, Israel, and Romania are dummy variables that take the value of 1 for respondents of each country respectively.

APPENDIX F

1995 Study by Thalheimer on the Importance of P in the Decision
to Turn Out: Question Wording

This study attempts to gauge the importance of the probability of casting the decisive
ballot in the decision to vote. The study was conducted in February and March 1995,
at a time when a referendum on Quebec sovereignty was expected to be held in the
same year. Thalheimer interviewed 125 students found frequenting the cafeterias,
lunch counters, and pub at the Université de Montréal. Respondents were first asked
to estimate P and then questioned on whether they would vote if P were nil.

Q1. Generally speaking, would you say that you are interested in politics:

A lot	A little
Somewhat	Not at all

Q2. Did you vote in the 1993 federal election?

Yes
No

Q3. Did you vote in the 1994 provincial election?

Yes
No

Q4. Have you ever thought of the possibility that if you didn't vote your candidate
would lose by one vote?

Yes
No

Q5. Now, let's talk about the present referendum campaign. Would you say that it
interests you:

A lot	A little
Somewhat	Not at all

Q6. In the province as a whole, how close do you think the referendum will be:

Very close	Not very close
Rather close	Not close at all

Q7. On a scale of 0 to 10, *where 10 means that it is certain you will vote and 0 means it is
certain you will not vote,* what are the chances that you will vote in the next referendum?

0. certain that I will vote	4.	8.
1.	5. one in two chances	9.
2.	6.	10. certain that I will not vote
3.	7.	

Q8a. What do you think the chances are, roughly, that your vote will decide if it is the yes side or the no side that wins the referendum? One chance in _____

Q8b. (If "don't know," probe.) Approximately, one chance in how many?

Q9. In your opinion is this chance . . .

Very likely (go to Q11)   Don't know (go to Q11)
Somewhat likely (go to Q11)   Refuse (go to Q11)
Somewhat unlikely (go to Q10)

Q10. Is this chance practically nil? (For those who answered "somewhat" or "very unlikely")
Yes
No

Q11. If you were certain that there would be absolutely no chance that your vote decides the result of referendum, would you vote?
Yes
No

Q12. (If "yes"). Why?

Q13. (If "no"). Why?

Q14. What year were you born in?

Q15. (The gender of the respondent).
Male
Female

Q16. What is your religion?
Catholic   Orthodox
Hindu   Protestant
Jewish   Other
Muslim   None

Q17. What is the level of the last year of schooling you have completed?
None
Elementary (incomplete)
Elementary (complete)
High school (incomplete)
High school (complete)
Technical training, CEGEP, college (incomplete)
Technical training, CEGEP, college (complete)
University (incomplete)
University bachelor
Graduate studies

Q18. What is the first language you learned and still understand?
French
English
Other

APPENDIX G

1995 Quebec Referendum Study: Question Wording

The survey was conducted by the Léger and Léger polling firm, during the last week of the 1995 Quebec referendum campaign on sovereignty. The response rate was 59 percent. A total of 1,004 electors were interviewed during the last week of the campaign and 926 of them were briefly reinterviewed immediately after the referendum.

Prereferendum Wave

Q1. As you probably know, there will be a referendum on sovereignty on October 30. Is it certain that you will vote, very likely, somewhat likely, somewhat unlikely, or very unlikely?

Certain to vote	Somewhat unlikely
Very likely	Very unlikely
Somewhat likely	Certain that will not vote

Q2. How much time do you think it would take you to go to the poll, vote and return. It is about a quarter of an hour, half an hour, three quarters of an hour, an hour, or more than an hour?

Quarter of an hour	An hour
Half an hour	More than an hour
Three quarters of an hour	

Q3. For you personally, it is very easy, somewhat easy, somewhat difficult, or very difficult to *go* to vote?

Very easy	Somewhat difficult
Somewhat easy	Very difficult

Q4. And do you find it very easy, somewhat easy, somewhat difficult, or very difficult to get information to decide how to vote?

Very easy	Somewhat difficult
Somewhat easy	Very difficult

Q5a. Do you strongly agree, somewhat agree, somewhat disagree, or strongly disagree with the following statements:
It is the duty of every citizen to vote.

Strongly agree	Somewhat disagree
Somewhat agree	Strongly disagree

Q5b. In order to preserve democracy, it is essential that the great majority of citizens vote.

Strongly agree	Somewhat disagree
Somewhat agree	Strongly disagree

Q6. In the referendum, what is the risk, in your opinion, that a majority of people will not vote? Would you say there is a large risk, a small risk, or there is no risk at all?

Large risk
Small risk
No risk at all

Q7. In your opinion, if Quebec became a sovereign country, would this change things enormously, a lot, a little, or not at all?

Enormously	A little
A lot	Not at all

Q8. For you personally, does it make much difference whether the *yes* or the *no* side wins? Does it make an enormous difference, a great difference, a small difference, or no difference?

Enormous	Small
Great	No difference

Q9. Do you expect the result of the referendum to be very close, somewhat close, not very close, or not close at all?

Very close	Not very close
Somewhat close	Not close at all

Q10. Have you ever thought of the possibility that the *yes* or the *no* side would win by a *single vote,* and that it would be *your* vote that decides which side wins?

Yes, I have thought about it
No, I havent thought about it

Q11. In your opinion, what are the chances of the *yes* or the *no* side winning by a single vote: very high, somewhat high, somewhat low, or very low?

Very high	Somewhat low
Somewhat high	Very low

Q12. Would you say that the chances of the *yes* or the *no* side winning by a single vote are absolutely zero, almost zero, or just low?

Absolutely zero
Almost zero
Just low

Q13. If you were absolutely sure there is no chance that your vote could decide which side wins, would you still vote?

Yes, I would vote
No, I would not vote

Q14. If you did not vote, would you feel that you had neglected your duty as a citizen enormously, a lot, a little, or not at all?

Enormously   A little

A lot   Not at all

Q15. If you did not vote, would you feel very guilty, somewhat guilty, not very guilty, or not guilty at all?

Very guilty   Not very guilty

Somewhat guilty   Not guilty at all

Q16. If you did not vote, do you think that your friends and family would disapprove very much, disapprove somewhat, approve somewhat, approve very much, or do you think they would not care at all?

Disapprove very much   Approve very much

Disapprove somewhat   Not care at all

Approve somewhat

Q17. In general, would you say you are very interested in politics, somewhat interested, not very interested, or not interested at all?

Very interested   Not very interested

Somewhat interested   Not interested at all

Q18. Are you registered on the voters list?

Yes

No

Q19. In the last three years, there have been three elections, the provincial election in '94, the federal election in '93, and the referendum in the Charlottetown Accord in '92. Did you vote all three times, twice out of the three, once or in none?

Voted three times   Voted once

Voted twice   Voted in none

Q20. In order to classify data, we would need more statistical information. Can you tell me in what year you were born?

Q21. What is the level of the last year of schooling you have completed?

Elementary

High school, general or professional

College pre-university, technical training, certificate (CEP), accreditation (ASP) or proficiency diploma (DEP) (13-15 years)

University certificates and diplomas

University Bachelor

University Masters

University Doctorate

Q22. What is your current main occupation?

Upper management	Blue-collar/Manual worker
Middle management	Homemaker
Professional	Student
Small business owner	Retired
White-collar/Office worker	Unemployed

Q23. What language do you speak most often at home?
French
English
Other

Q24. What is the language you first learned at home and that you still understand?
French
English
Other

Q25. Are you presently married, living with a partner, divorced, separated, widowed or have you ever been married?

Married	Separated
Living with a partner	Widowed
Divorced	Never been married

Q26. In what category is the total income, in 1994, before income tax, of all the members of your household, is it . . . ?
less than $20,000
between $20,000 and $39,000
between $40,000 and $59,000
between $60,000 and $79,000
or $80,000 or more

Post-referendum wave

Q1. Did you vote in the referendum of October 30th?
Yes
No

APPENDIX H

1996 British Columbia Election Study: Question Wording

The survey was conducted by the Léger and Léger polling firm among a sample of 804 electors during the last week of the 1996 British Columbia provincial election. The response rate was 54 percent.

Q1. As you probably know, there will be a provincial election on May 28. This short survey seeks to study why people vote or don't vote. We will not ask you for which party you intend to vote. To begin with, is it certain that you will vote, very likely, somewhat likely, somewhat unlikely, or very unlikely?

Certain to vote	Somewhat unlikely
Very likely	Very unlikely
Somewhat likely	Certain that will not vote

Q2. How much time do you think it would take you to go to the poll, vote, and return? Is it about a quarter of an hour, half an hour, three-quarters of an hour, or more than an hour?

Quarter of an hour	An hour
Half an hour	More than an hour
Three quarters of an hour	

Q3. For you personally, it is very easy, somewhat easy, somewhat difficult, or very difficult to *go* to vote?

Very easy	Somewhat difficult
Somewhat easy	Very difficult

Q4. And do you find it very easy, somewhat easy, somewhat difficult, or very difficult to get information to decide how to vote?

Very easy	Somewhat difficult
Somewhat easy	Very difficult

Q5a. Do you strongly agree, somewhat agree, somewhat disagree, or strongly disagree with the following statements:
. . . It is the duty of every citizen to vote.

Strongly agree	Somewhat disagree
Somewhat agree	Strongly disagree

Q5b. . . . In order to preserve democracy, it is essential that the great majority of citizens vote.

Strongly agree	Somewhat disagree
Somewhat agree	Strongly disagree

Q6. For you personally, does it make much difference who wins the election in the province as a whole? Does it make an enormous difference, a great difference, a small difference, or no difference?

Enormous difference	Small difference
Great difference	No difference

Q7. For you personally, does it make much difference who wins the election in your riding? Does it make an enormous difference, a great difference, a small difference, or no difference?

Enormous difference	Small difference
Great difference	No difference

Q8. Do you expect the result of the election in the province as a whole to be very close, somewhat close, not very close, or not close at all?

Very close	Not very close
Somewhat close	Not close at all

Q9. Do you expect the result of the election in your riding to be very close, somewhat close, not very close, or not close at all?

Very close	Not very close
Somewhat close	Not close at all

Q10. Have you ever thought of the possibility that the election in your riding could be decided by a *single* vote, and that it would be *your* vote that decides who wins?

Yes, I have thought about it

No, I haven't thought about it

Q11. In your opinion, what are the chances that the election in your riding will be decided by a single vote: very high, somewhat high, somewhat low, or very low?

Very high	Somewhat low
Somewhat high	Very low

Q12. Would you say that the chances of the election in your riding being decided by a single vote are absolutely zero, almost zero, or just low?

Absolutely zero

Almost zero

Just low

Q13. If you were absolutely sure there is no chance at all your vote could decide who wins, would you still vote?

Yes, I would vote

No, I would not vote

Q14. If you did not vote, would you feel that you had neglected your duty as a citizen enormously, a lot, a little, or not at all?

Enormously	A little
A lot	Not at all

Q15. If you did not vote, would you feel very guilty, somewhat guilty, not very guilty, or not guilty at all?

Very guilty	Not very guilty
Somewhat guilty	Not guilty at all

Q16. If you did not vote, do you think that your friends and family would disapprove very much, disapprove somewhat, approve somewhat, approve very much, or do you think they would not care at all?

Disapprove very much	Approve very much
Disapprove somewhat	Not care at all
Approve somewhat	

Q17. In general, would you say you are very interested in politics, somewhat interested, not very interested, or not interested at all?

Very interested	Not very interesed
Somewhat interested	Not interested at all

Q18. Did you vote in the last federal election in 1993?

Yes
No

[Note: Questions tapping socioeconomic characteristics were the same as in appendix G, Q20–Q26.]

APPENDIX I

1996 Blais and Thalheimer Study on Reasons for Voting: Question Wording

This study aims to understand the reasons that motivate people to vote. We drew a random sample of 321 telephone numbers in the greater Montreal area; 306 numbers proved to be in service. Of the 306 individuals contacted, 148 (48 percent) accepted to answer the questionnaire. As our study dealt with regular voters, we asked each individual if she/he had voted in the last two referenda (held in 1992 and 1995) and in the last federal (1993) and provincial (1994) elections. All those who reported having voted in each instance (108 out of 148) were administered the questionnaire. It is composed of close-ended questions on each potential reason for voting along with probes and open-ended questions where respondents were free to explain, in their own words, why they vote.

Q1. a. Would you say that you are interested in politics: a lot, somewhat, a little, or not at all?
        b. Do you watch television news regularly?
        c. Do you listen to radio news regularly?
        d. Do you read the newspaper regularly?
        e. Do you read the articles on politics regularly?

Q2. a. Have you ever not voted in a provincial election?
        b. Why?

Q3. a. Have you ever not voted in a federal election?
        b. Why?

Q4. If you were to explain in your own words the main reasons why you vote, what would you say?

Q5. a. Have you ever thought of not voting?
        b. Why?
        c. What made you finally decide to go and vote?

Q6. In general, do you think it changes things a lot, somewhat, or not at all that one party is elected instead of another?

Q7. a. Have you ever thought at an election, that it would change absolutely nothing if one party won instead of another?
        b. Did you vote anyway?
        c. Why?

Q8. a. Are you more inclined to vote when an election is close?
  b. Why?
  c. Would you say that it is not worth voting when you are certain beforehand who will win?

Q9. a. Have you ever thought that an election was so close that your vote could decide who won the election?
  b. When?

Q10. And at the last referendum held in October, did you think of the possibility that the YES side or the NO side could win by a single vote, and that your vote would decide which side won?

Q11. Do you think that it could happen one day that an election is won by one single vote and that your vote decides who wins the election?

Q12. a. If you were certain that there would be absolutely no chance that your vote decides who won the election, would you vote?
  b. Why?

Q13. a. In general, how much time does it take for you to go and vote and return?
  b. Would you vote if it took one hour?
  c. Two hours?

Q14. a. In general, how do you get information to decide for which party to vote?
  b. And how much time does it take for you to get that information?
    (If they question: Where do you get information to decide which party or
      which candidate is the best?)
  c. If you didn't go to vote, you would save about _____ (of time).
  Do you think that you could do something enjoyable or useful instead?

Q15. a. Would you say that for you personally, it is a duty to vote?
  b. Is it a duty that is very important, somewhat important, not very
      important or not important at all?
  c. Is it a duty to vote in each election?
  d. In your opinion, do those who do not vote fail to fulfill their duty?

Q16. a. If you were not to vote, would you feel that you failed to fulfill your duty as a citizen?
  b. Do you think that if one believes in democracy, one absolutely has to
      vote?
  c. If you did not vote, would you feel guilty?
  d. Some people say that those who don't vote don't have the right to criticize
      government. What do you think?

Q17 a. (For those living with a spouse). Does your spouse vote?

b. Always?

c. Has it ever happened that one of you has gone to vote while the other hasn't?

d. Has it ever happened that you did not feel like going to vote and that your spouse has made you decide to go?

e. Did you go to make your spouse happy?

f. Has it ever happened that your spouse did not feel like voting and that you have made him/her decide to vote?

g. Did your spouse do it to make you happy?

Q18 a. (For those not living with a spouse). Has it ever happened that you voted even if you didn't feel like it, to make someone else happy?

b. Do you think that someone else has voted to make you happy?

Q19. If you did not vote, do you think it would be frowned upon by your friends and family?

Q20. Certain people vote out of habit, without really having a reason to vote. Is this the case for you, a lot, somewhat or not at all?

Q21 a. Do you vote in municipal and school board elections?

b. Always? (For those answering Yes, proceed to Q23).

c. Why do you not vote in these elections?

Q22 a. When you do not vote in a municipal or school board election, do you feel as though you have failed in your civic duty?

b. Why?

Q23. Finally, I would like to ask you a few questions to verify whether our sample is representative. Firstly, what year were you born in?

Q24. What is the highest level of education you completed?

Q25. Your marital status?

Q26. Your religion?

Q27. And what is the importance of religion in your life? Is it very important, somewhat important, a little important or not important at all?

Q28. The last two questions : To sum up what we have talked about, what is the main reason why you vote?

Q29 a. And would you say that it is certain that you will vote in the next federal elections?

b. In the next provincial elections?

c. In the next municipal elections?

d. In the next school board elections?

NOTES

Introduction

1. Strictly speaking, she has one chance out of two to have the decisive vote since if she does not vote there is a tie and there is a 50 percent probability that her preferred candidate wins (through the toss of a coin or in a second ballot). If the expected number of voters (besides herself) is odd, her vote will be decisive if her preferred candidate loses by one vote and her own vote creates a tie. Here again, though, her vote will be decisive only if it creates a tie and her candidate wins on the toss of a coin or in a second ballot.

2. It could salvage it if citizens are assumed to be extremely risk-averse. See below.

3. As one rational choice author put it: "The consumption motive (the voting act has utility per se) tells us nothing. He votes because he likes to would be an equivalent theory. . . . We have to make a strong behavioral assumption to get any empirical content or predictions" (Peters 1998, 194).

4. For a thorough empirical test of Uhlaner's model see Lapp (1999). Lapp's overall conclusion is that the model is not supported by the data.

5. Barry's position is more radical than Aldrich's. For Barry, the rational choice model simply does not hold for voting; for Aldrich, it just performs less well, as people do not carefully calculate and make many errors.

6. They point out that there are three potential answers to why people do not take part in politics: because they can't, because they do not want to, or because nobody asked. The first explanation is in terms of resources, the second refers to psychological engagement, and the third to mobilization. They acknowledge that a comprehensive theory should encompass all these dimensions but argue that a resource model offers a more powerful starting point.

7. The resource model looks more compelling for acts other than voting. On the one hand, voting is relatively easy and it is not clear that civic skills are that important in performing the act (except, perhaps, in the United States where citizens have to register). On the other hand, Brady, Verba, and Schlozman (1995, 283) note that voting is driven more by political interest (psychological engagement) than by resources.

8. This is also acknowledged by Brady et al. (1995, 290).

9. Strictly speaking, the test is whether each of $B^\star P$ and C has an independent impact. The issue of whether B and P have additive or multiplicative effects is taken on in chapters 3 and 5.

1. When and Where Are People More Likely to Vote?

1. My presentation focuses on Powell (1982). The first study (Powell 1980) includes Lebanon, which is dropped in subsequent work. His last piece is confined to 21 "industrialized" democracies.

2. He examines presidential elections in what he calls strong presidential systems (Chile and the United States).

3. In his 1986 piece he resorts to dummy variables for Switzerland and the United States. The United States is considered a special case because of its more demanding registration conditions.

4. More specifically, they replicate Powell (1986). In his first piece (1980) Powell found no correlation between PR and turnout. In his book (1982), he distinguishes three types of districts: single-member majority at one end, multimember PR at the other end, and, in between, Germany, Ireland, and Japan, with two to four representatives per district. That variable proved to have only an indirect impact on turnout. In the 1986 article, which deals only with industrialized democracies, he resorts to four categories (national election, large district PR, small district PR, and single-member districts) and comes up with a significant direct effect.

5. The starting date for each country is the first election that was widely contested by national parties.

6. They find a relationship in the post-1945 period but not in the whole sample. The same pattern holds for unicameralism.

7. As in Blais and Carty (1990), the United States is excluded.

8. The coefficients, however, have the expected signs.

9. The findings are presented and discussed in Blais and Dobrzynska (1998). The results presented here are slightly different from those reported in that piece because data on turnout in five elections held in 1994 and 1995 have been subsequently revised. Differences are very minor, however, and do not affect any of the conclusion.

10. Jackman, however, is careful to test for that possibility.

11. Black (1991) also examines industrial democracies. As for Blais and Carty, their data base includes the elections covered by Mackie and Rose (1982, 1991). The countries included are 24 industrialized ones having competitive elections regularly since the end of the Second World War. The starting point for each country is the first election in which most seats were contested and most candidates fought under common party labels. The problem with this approach is that it is not clear that all elections could be deemed to be truly democratic (many were not held under universal suffrage).

12. There was a total of 359 elections. I was not able to obtain data on turnout in 34 cases and I excluded one case where the election was boycotted.

13. For all socioeconomic variables, I use data pertaining to the year of the election if the election is held in July or later. If the election is held in the first six months, I use data pertaining to the previous year.

14. Radcliff (1992) suggests that economic downturns depress turnout only at intermediate levels of welfare spending, and that the impact is reversed at high and low levels of spending. Some of the results obtained by Radcliff (especially the fact that average turnout in the two previous elections is not statistically significant), however, are perplexing. Furthermore, Jackman and Miller (1995, appendix 3, n. 3) failed to replicate his findings for industrialized countries.

15. Verba, Nie, and Kim find the relationship to be weaker for voting than for community activity. It remains that the median net gap between rural and urban turnout is five points.

16. Powell (1982) also reports a negative relationship, which is however not

statistically significant, perhaps because it is based on a smaller number of observations.

17. The correlation between the two variables (-.52) is not overwhelming. The implication, of course, is that some of the impact of economic development is mediated through a higher literacy rate. If illiteracy is dropped from the equation in table 1.1, the coefficient of GNP per capita increases to 3.80.

18. There is no instance of three other nonsimultaneous elections.

19. Thirteen percent of PR elections have a deviation index of 10 or more. The average deviation index in PR systems is 5.7.

20. This is of course more likely to be the case in single-member districts. On the importance of measuring competitiveness at the district level, see Cox (1997).

21. I have also run regressions with effective number of electoral and legislative parties but we obtain slightly better results with the simple measure of the number of parties. In my view, this simple measure corresponds more closely to the kind of information that is most easily available to most electors.

22. The missing cases are those that were the first democratic elections in a country or that were the first to be held during the period studied here.

23. To the extent that one is interested in contextual factors that may lead to an increase or decrease in turnout in a given election, the analysis should be in dynamic terms, which entails either measuring the dependent variable in terms of changes in turnout from one election to the other or keeping turnout as the dependent variable and including turnout at the previous election as a control variable. Arcelus and Meltzer's results also indicate the presence of autocorrelation, which was not corrected.

24. The missing cases are: Barbados, Costa Rica, Israel, Jamaica, Japan, Malta, Nauru, and Trinidad and Tobago.

25. The regression analysis (see table 1.4) pertains to 195 cases as annual increase in per capita GDP was not available for the first election held in 1960 or 1961 in Australia, Belgium, Denmark, Japan, New Zealand, and Sweden.

26. Both variables are first-order differences: change in per capita GDP over the previous year and change in the vote gap between the first two parties over the previous election. In the latter case, the variable was transformed in the following way: I gave the value of +1 if the gap had been reduced by at least 5 percentage points, of -1 if it had been increased by at least 5 points, and of 0 otherwise. It would seem that minimal changes in closeness do not matter; only when they reach a certain level do they appear to make some difference.

27. The variable corresponds to the number of years the voting age was reduced.

28. The 1986 election was given a score of +1 and the 1988 election a score of -1.

29. Mackie and Rose (1991, 123) indicate that among electors resident in Finland turnout declined by only 1.7 percentage points.

30. The variable took the value of +1 in 1962, 1981, and 1988, and of -1 in the following elections of 1967, 1986, and 1993.

31. Not too much should be made of the fact that the relationship is not statistically significant, as this involves only one case. The findings of the cross-sectional and longitudinal analyses converge: PR slightly increases turnout.

32. I focus on these two polar types because both types can be found in all countries and they best illustrate situations with large and small electorates.

33. I exclude Sweden because local elections are held concurrently with national elections.

34. I would argue that people's perceptions of the impact the different levels of government have on their lives are the best indicators of the relative importance of various governments. Some people may vote in national but not in local elections because they feel the latter are less important. This almost amounts to a tautology, however. The more interesting proposition that I am interested in is whether people are less likely to vote in local elections because they believe local governments have smaller effects on their lives.

35. This is consistent with what Richardson (1973) observed in Japan.

36. If that interpretation is correct, it should follow that turnout in local elections is higher when they all take place at the same time, as they are more likely to attract media attention.

37. I consider only those countries that remained democratic (a score of 1 or 2 on political rights) throughout a given decade. For those countries that have remained democratic since 1972, I assume that they had been democratic in the 1960s.

38. The analysis is restricted to countries that have had referenda in at least two decades.

2. Who Votes?

1. Sometimes researchers use panel data, sometimes they use recall data for the previous election.

2. This procedure was first utilized in the British election studies; see Butler and Stokes 1969 and Sarlvik and Crewe 1983. For a detailed description of the procedure, see Johnston, Blais, Brady, Gidengil, and Nevitte 1996, appendix A.

3. Since half of irregular voters vote (on average), mean turnout is 75 percent, and regular voters account for 63/75 (84 percent) of that turnout. This of course applies only to those who are eligible to vote in both elections and excludes the entering and leaving electorates.

4. This applies only to national legislative elections. As we have seen, turnout in local elections is much lower.

5. Reported turnout in our sample was 74 percent. The overall turnout in the election was 70 percent.

6. Their multivariate analysis, however, is based on a subsample of 8,334 respondents.

7. Wolfinger and Rosenstone also report that turnout is lower in the South, even after controlling for all other variables, but they show that this difference is eroding as the gap is extremely small among young people.

8. I have excluded Ukraine, which did not have a score of 1 or 2 on political rights during that period, and Lithuania, because the survey did not ask whether the respondent had voted in the election.

9. Schmitt and Mannheimer (1991) show that, in European elections, voting and intention to vote do not always yield similar relationships with other variables.

10. I share the view of Brady, Verba, and Schlozman (1995, 292), who write, "[T]he evidence we have reviewed is consistent with the notion that social desirability bias is a general human trait that is uncorrelated with specific characteristics of the respondents. This means that it would not bias our results at all (except for the intercept of our regressions because of overall overreporting)." For similar verdicts see Cassel (1998) and Baughman (1998).

11. I have selected Great Britain as the reference point.

12. And both exceptions are not statistically significant.

3. Do People Believe that Their Vote Could Be Decisive?

1. Green and Shapiro (1994, 55; see also Schwartz 1986, 108) argue that this "merely transforms the paradox of not voting into the paradox of foolish voters." In my view, this is an overstatement. Citizens could be depicted as relatively reasonable if they only slightly overestimate P and/or if the most readily available information is to the effect that P is not minuscule.

2. Size always refers to the size of the electorate. Closeness is measured in different ways but usually refers to the margin of victory of the winner, that margin being expressed in vote percentages. Cox (1988) argues that it is preferable to use the raw margin when the units being compared are of about equal size. That, however, is not the case for most of the studies being considered here. Most studies use the margin of victory in the election but some resort to the margin in the previous election.

3. All these studies are also based on aggregate data. Matsusaka and Palda (1993) report that the relationship between closeness and turnout that they observe at the aggregate level in the 1979 and 1980 elections does not hold at the individual level when they use survey data, and thus suggest that the relationship is an ecological fallacy. It should be pointed out, however, that the Canadian Election Study that they use includes respondents from only 96 constituencies out of 262 (LeDuc, Clarke, Jenson, and Pammett 1974) and does not allow, therefore, a full test of the hypothesis.

4. They divide the sample into three groups according to D and two according to B, thus yielding six subgroups for each of the three elections. In fifteen out of eighteen instances, turnout is higher among those who think the election will be close; the median difference is 5 percentage points.

5. In 1972 perceptions of national closeness are not significant, but perceptions of state closeness are. In 1964 closeness is correlated with validated vote, not with reported vote. Altogether, in Aldrich's data, closeness has a significant impact in the elections of 1956, 1960, 1964, and 1972. The effect is nonsignificant, but of the correct sign, in 1952.

6. It is appropriate to control for the general level of political interest, which, as I have argued in the introduction, may reflect some taste for politics and is likely to be formed before a campaign starts, but not for interest in the *campaign* as such.

7. In the post-election questionnaire, the question asked what the chances *were* that their vote *would determine* who *would* win.

8. The approach followed here is similar to that of Gelman, King, and Boscardin (1998), who estimate that the probability of a single vote being decisive in a close American presidential election to be about one in 10 million.

9. That is, if electors knew in advance that the margin of victory in their riding was less than 100, all those supporting the winning candidate would have reasoned that their chance of casting the decisive vote was one chance out of 100. This assumes that all margins, from 0 to 99, are equally probable, an assumption that appears quite plausible.

10. I focus on perceptions of P at the constituency level, but the same pattern

holds for perceptions of P at the national level. If there are 295 constituencies, the probability of the two leading parties having the same number of elected members in the other 294 constituencies is slightly higher than one chance in 294, let us say around one chance in 100. The median response for the national P is appropriately 100 times that for P at the constituency level.

11. Note, however, that the question invited them to give a rough estimate.

12. Among panel respondents, the correlations between perceptions of P and perceptions of closeness at the riding level were .08 in the first questionnaire, .04 in the second, and .04 in the third.

13. The lectures were presented by Robert Young at Western and myself at the Université de Montréal; the lectures were identical in all classes.

14. The estimates were transformed to a 0 to 1 scale, 0 corresponding to one chance in 100,000,000 and 1 to one chance in 10.

15. The results refer to perceptions of P at the riding level, as measured after the election. The initial impact (right after the presentation, two weeks before the election) was even stronger (-.13) but slightly receded afterwards. The impact with respect to perceptions of P at the national level is also significant, though somewhat smaller (see Blais and Young 1996, table 4).

16. The most frequent answer ($n = 24$) was one chance out of the total number of voters (five million); thirteen respondents said there was no chance at all.

17. As the result of the referendum proved to be extremely close, the probability of casting the decisive vote was perhaps closer to one chance in 100,000. At the time of the survey, however, the No side was clearly ahead in the polls, so much so that some sovereignists were urging the premier of the province to postpone the referendum.

18. It should be kept in mind that in the case of the Quebec referendum the figure represents those who thought their vote could decide which side wins province-wide, whereas in British Columbia it corresponds to those who felt that P was not practically nil in their own constituency.

19. Again, it should be kept in mind that we are dealing with the probability of casting a decisive vote province-wide in the Quebec referendum and in one's constituency in British Columbia. It is truly amazing that the percentage is almost as high in the former than in the latter. In both studies, there is a moderate correlation between having thought about the possibility and believing that the chances of casting a decisive vote were not almost zero.

20. Regular voters were defined as those who had voted in each of the last two referenda (on sovereignty in 1995 and on the Charlottetown Accord in 1992) and in the last federal (1993) and provincial (1994) elections. For further details on the study, see appendix I.

21. It would seem that the experience of filling out questionnaires about elections sensitizes respondents to politics and increases their propensity to vote (for similar findings, see Clausen 1968 and Granberg and Holmberg 1992). Turnout was lower at Western than at Montreal, because of the electoral list. Outside of the province of Quebec, the electoral list had been compiled one year earlier for the referendum on the Charlottetown Accord; as a consequence, students not on that list because of age or change of residence had to make the effort to register. I also performed analyses in which I included participation in previous elections. Those who had voted in previous elections seemed more likely to vote in the 1993 election, thus suggesting

that there might be a habitual component in turnout. I have decided not to include that variable in my final analyses as it is not clear that participation in previous elections is truly exogenous. I should add that including past vote, in this study as well as in the others reported below, does not substantially affect any of my conclusions.

22. According to equation 4, the probability of voting for an individual who is at the maximum value of 1 on both B_n and P_c is 26 percentage points greater than for an individual who is at the minimum value of 0 on both variables. The same difference is 19 percentage points when we rely on the interactive term as specified in equation 1. The additive impact of B_n and P_c is thus greater than the multiplicative impact of B_c and P_c.

23. It could be argued that the stakes were higher in 1995 than in 1980. In 1980 the populace was asked to give the government a mandate to negotiate sovereignty-association and the government was committed to holding a second referendum to ratify any new agreement with the rest of Canada. In 1995 the government was asking for a mandate to declare sovereignty (as well as to negotiate a new partnership with the rest of Canada). This can hardly account for the 15-point difference in turnout, however.

24. It is significant at the .10 level with a one-tailed test.

25. The variable takes the following values: 0 = Certain not to vote; .2 = Very unlikely to vote; .4 = Somewhat unlikely to vote; .6 = Somewhat likely to vote; .8 = Very likely to vote; 1 = Certain to vote. Respondents in British Columbia were not reinterviewed after the election, and we thus examine intention to vote or to abstain rather than reported behavior. In the Quebec referendum we observed a strong correlation between vote intention (measured in the last week of the campaign) and reported behavior, and relationships remain basically the same whether vote intention or reported vote is the dependent variable.

26. At least one rational choice author has proposed a model along those lines: "Although less sophisticated than the probabilistic model, the margin of victory model is more intuitive and more likely to be the model some voters will use" (Peters 1998, 191).

27. This section is drawn from Blais, Young, Fleury, and Lapp (1995).

28. One of the questions was whether respondents agreed with the statement, "I sometimes don't vote when the outcome of the election is not going to be close." It cannot be assumed that disagreeing with the statement entails operating with a minimax regret calculus.

29. Thalheimer (1995), however, found that 22 percent of the students overestimated P six months before the Quebec referendum, at a time when the outcome was not perceived to be very close.

4. What Is the Cost of Voting?

1. For the computation, I have put those who said more than an hour at an hour and a half.

2. On the problems of accurately measuring how people spend their time, see Szalai (1972).

3. More specifically, 75 percent (in Quebec) and 82 percent (in British Columbia) of those who expect it will take only one quarter of an hour to vote find it very easy

to vote. What is perhaps more surprising is that among those who think it will take an hour or more, only 19 percent in Quebec and 16 percent in British Columbia say it is difficult to vote, and as many as 49 percent in Quebec and 41 percent in British Columbia say it is very easy.

4. We know only that they had not voted in each of the previous three ballots, but they are very likely to have never voted, as most of them were very young.

5. The overall degree of difficulty is about the same in the two cases. Two contradictory factors are probably at work. On the one hand, the referendum dealt with a single issue, whereas in an election electors may wish to obtain information on a number of different issues. On the other hand, in the referendum, Quebeckers had to decide whether it was desirable to form a new country, a decision with potentially huge consequences, many of them difficult to predict with any degree of certainty (see Nadeau, Martin, and Blais 1999).

6. It should be kept in mind that we interviewed only regular voters. The pattern could be different among irregular voters.

7. The simulation works in the following fashion. In a first step, I compute each individual's predicted probability of voting, given her score on each of the independent variables. I then estimate, on the basis of these individual probabilities, the average predicted probability of voting for the whole sample (.77). In a second step, using the same equation, I estimate each individual's as well as the total sample's average predicted probability of voting, changing individuals' scores on one variable (cost) while maintaining their scores on all other variables. In this particular case, I have tested the scenario in which all individuals with a score of 0 on cost (strongly agreeing with the statement that "it is so easy to vote that I don't see any reason not to") were to have a score of .33 instead (which amounts to "merely" agreeing with the statement). Average predicted probability of voting under this scenario is .75, that is, two points lower than the initial average predicted probability. All the simulations presented in chapters 4 and 5 follow the same logic.

5. Is It a Duty to Vote?

1. For an argument in favor of compulsory voting, see Lijphart 1997.

2. In the Roman Catholic faith, sins are construed as being either venial or mortal in nature. A *mortal* sin represents a serious fault against God's commandments, a fault sufficient to make one go to hell. A *venial* sin represents a more benign fault, that can be expurgated in purgatory before going to heaven.

3. This is not old history. In a document issued during the Canadian 1997 election, the Canadian Conference of Catholic Bishops "emphasize each Christian's moral obligation to exercise this democratic right and to participate fully in building the reign of God through active and thoughtful involvement in society" (*Montreal Gazette,* May 15, 1997, p. A17).

4. She would not feel guilty if she had not voted because of illness or exceptional circumstances that made it very difficult to vote. As for any sin, the bottom line is the intention, and proper consideration must be given to circumstantial factors. As Jasso and Opp (1997) note, "[A]lthough norms are often formulated unconditionally in everyday life, they actually hold only in certain types of situations, and the actors seem to be aware of this."

5. For instance, 71 percent of Canadians said that if we stopped having elections

in Canada, things would be worse, and only 4 percent said things would be better (Blais and Gidengil 1993, 548).

6. Almond and Verba (1965) report that more people feel obliged to participate in their local community in the United States than in the United Kingdom, Germany, Italy, and Mexico, but there was no direct question as such on the obligation to vote.

7. Stoetzel does not indicate the exact question. The question would seem to be: "When voting, do you feel you are carrying out a duty or exercising a right?" Among men, 55 percent chose duty and 28 percent right; among women the respective percentages were 64 percent and 19 percent.

8. For evidence that these statements form an underlying factor, see Blais and Young (1996, table 7).

9. Equation A also indicates that sense of duty is greater at the University of Montreal than at Western. In the same vein, it can be noted that the sense of duty is more widespread in Quebec than in British Columbia (see Blais, Young, and Lapp forthcoming). This could be so because there is greater attachment to the collectivity in Quebec, and/or religion has had a greater impact on people's values. Both interpretations would be consistent with my general perspective.

10. In fact, many students privately checked whether indicating more than DM 200 would suffice to exclude them from any risk of selling their voting right; the experimenters confirmed that it would.

11. It could be objected that we obtain such results because duty is more precisely measured than pressures since we have more questions on the former than on the latter. We reran equations, however, in which duty was measured through a single question, and the results were basically the same.

12. A few respondents indicated they feel a duty to vote in federal and provincial elections but not at the municipal or school-board level. These respondents were considered to have a sense of duty for "significant" levels of government. For a more elaborate discussion, see Blais and Thalheimer (1997).

13. The questions used to measure tax duty in these studies are very similar to those utilized in my analyses. They had questions about whether respondents feel a moral obligation to be completely honest in filling out tax returns and about whether they would feel guilty if they understated their income.

14. There is no difference between the first and the last three.

6. Do People Free Ride?

1. It is a form of free riding for all those whose B is greater than C. If someone believes that it does not make any difference who wins the election, she abstains but does not free ride. One free rides when she does not vote despite the fact that it matters to her who wins the election.

2. Again, this has to be qualified. Voting entails the rejection of the free-ride option only if the person perceives P to be extremely small and if she does not perceive C to be pratically nil.

3. This does not mean that Olson's argument with respect to size is compelling. On the contrary, the evidence shows that "there is not one simple relationship between group size and collective action" (Udehn 1993, 242).

4. And Olson may be right in insisting on the role of coercion when it comes to explaining the rise of labor unions.

5. This was the standard situation. There were some variants, to which I return below.

6. The propensity to free ride does not seem to depend on whether the required number of contributions is three or five.

7. Of course, offering an equal split just because one anticipates being punished if she proposes an unequal split is entirely consistent with rational choice. But declining an unequal split, and losing money in doing so, is not a rational move. Therefore, those who fear being punished assume that the other players are not rational, in the strict sense of the term. From either perspective, the outcome is, in the final analysis, inconsistent with rational choice.

8. See also Muller and Opp (1986) and Opp (1989).

9. Opp (1989, 236) argues that people come to believe they can be influential in order to reduce cognitive dissonance costs. The argument is as follows. Suppose an individual has a strong attachment to political protest but realizes she has no influence on the provision of the public good. In order to reduce cognitive dissonance, she has three options: to enhance her influence, to reduce her involvement, or to overestimate her perceived influence. The first option is close to impossible, the second is very costly since she has strong feelings about the public good; the third—self-illusion—is the least costly. In this way, people "rationally" come to believe that they are influential. This does not work. First, this does not explain why people come to participate in the first place. Second, and most important, this illustrates the pitfalls of a "soft" theory of rational choice which were discussed in the introduction. People must have reasons to overestimate P. If any reason can count as rational, the theory amounts to saying that people choose A rather than B because they believe they will get greater satisfaction from A than from B. At this point, the theory becomes tautological.

10. The same verdict would apply to Opp's analysis of participation in the East German revolution of 1989. See Opp, Voss, and Gern 1995.

11. Whiteley (1995) repeats to some extent but slightly amends Whiteley, Seyd, Richardson, and Bissel (1994). I refer to the most recent piece and thus only to Whiteley.

12. In Whiteley et al. (1994), C is even nonsignificant. There may be a problem with the operationalization of cost. Perceptions of cost were tapped through reactions to statements like "Party activity often takes away from one's family." It may well be that those who attend more meetings (and are more active) are more prone to agree with such statements. As in the case of voting, it is the opportunity costs that matter. From that perspective, the approach used by Verba, Schlozman, and Brady (1995), who look at the amount of free time available to an individual, appears more interesting. These authors do find free time to affect the propensity to get involved in time-based acts.

13. Finkel, Muller, and Opp (1989) do not have a measure of C.

REFERENCES

Abramson, Paul R., John H. Aldrich, Phil Paolino, and David W. Rohde. 1992. "'Sophisticated' Voting in the 1988 Presidential Primaries." *American Political Science Review* 86:55–69.

Ackaert, Johan, Lieven de Winter, Anne-Marie Aish, and André-Paul Frognier. 1992. "L'abstentionisme électoral et vote blanc et nul en Belgique." *Res Publica* 34:209–26.

Aldrich, John H. 1976. "Some Problems in Testing Two Rational Models of Participation." *American Journal of Political Science* 20:713–34.

———. 1993. "Rational Choice and Turnout." *American Journal of Political Science* 37:246–78.

Alford, Robert R., and Eugene C. Lee. 1968. "Voting Turnout in American Cities." *American Political Science Review* 62:796–813.

Allais, Maurice. 1953. "Le comportement de l'homme rationnel devant le risque: Critique des postulats de l'école américaine." *Econometrica* 21:503–46.

Almond, Gabriel A., and Sidney Verba. 1965. *The Civic Culture: Political Attitudes and Democracy in Five Nations*. Boston: Little, Brown.

Alvarez, R. Michael, and Jonathan Nagler. 2000. "A New Approach for Modeling Strategic Voting in Multiparty Elections." *British Journal of Political Science* 30:57–75.

Anderson, Barbara A., and Brian D. Silver. 1986. "Measurement and Mismeasurement of the Validity of the Self-Reported Vote." *American Journal of Political Science* 30:771–85.

Andrenkov, Vladimir, and Anna Andrenkova. 1995. "Different Ways to Democracy: A Comparative Analysis of the Electoral Systems of Russia, Ukraine, Lithuania, Latvia, and Estonia." Paper presented at the Conference on Comparative Democratic Elections, Cambridge, Mass.

Andreoni, James. 1995. "Cooperation in Public-Goods Experiments: Kindness or Confusion?" *American Economic Review* 85:891–904.

Arcelus, Francisco J., and Allan H. Meltzer. 1975. "The Effect of Aggregate Economic Variables on Congressional Elections." *American Political Science Review* 69:1232–65.

Ashenfelter, Orley, and Stanley Kelley Jr. 1975. "Determinants of Participation in Presidential Elections." *Journal of Law and Economics* 18:695–733.

Barnes, Samuel H., and Max Kaase. 1979. *Political Action: Mass Participation in Five Western Democracies*. Beverly Hills, Calif.: Sage.

Barry, Brian. 1978. *Sociologists, Economists, and Democracy*. Chicago: University of Chicago Press.

Barzel, Yoram, and Eugene Silberberg. 1973. "Is the Act of Voting Rational?" *Public Choice* 16:51–58.

Baughman, John. 1998. "Deciding to Vote, Deciding to Tell: A Bivariate Probit Model of Overreported Vote." Paper presented at the annual meeting of the Midwest Political Science Association, Chicago.

Beck, Nathaniel. 1975. "The Paradox of Minimax Regret." *American Political Science Review* 69:918.

Berch, Neil. 1993. "Another Look at Closeness and Turnout: The Case of the 1979 and 1980 Canadian National Elections." *Political Research Quarterly* 46:421–32.

Bjorklund, Tor. 1988. "The 1987 Norwegian Local Elections: A Protest Election with a Swing to the Right." *Scandinavian Political Studies* 11:211–30.

Black, Jerome. 1978. "The Multicandidate Calculus of Voting: Application to Canadian Federal Elections." *American Journal of Political Science* 22:609–38.

———. 1991. "Reforming the Context of the Voting Process in Canada: Lessons from Other Democracies." Pp. 61–176 in *Voter Turnout in Canada,* edited by Herman Bakvis. Toronto: Dundurn Press.

Blais, André. 1982. "Le Public Choice et la croissance de l'état." *Revue canadienne de science politique* 15:783–807.

———. 1986. *A Political Sociology of Public Aid to Industry.* Toronto: University of Toronto Press.

Blais, André, and Kenneth Carty. 1990. "Does Proportional Representation Foster Voter Turnout?" *European Journal of Political Research* 18:167–81.

———. 1991. "The Psychological Impact of Electoral Laws: Measuring Duverger's Elusive Factor." *British Journal of Political Science* 21:79–93.

Blais, André, and Agnieszka Dobrzynska. 1998. "Turnout in Electoral Democracies." *European Journal of Political Research* 33:239–61.

Blais, André, and Elisabeth Gidengil. 1993. "Things Are Not Always What They Seem: French-English Differences and the Problem of Measurement Equivalence." *Canadian Journal of Political Science* 26:541–56.

Blais, André, and Louis Massicotte. 1996. "Electoral Systems." In *Comparing Democracies: Elections and Voting in Global Perspective,* edited by Lawrence Leduc, Richard G. Niemi, and Pippa Norris. Thousand Oaks, Calif.: Sage.

Blais, André, and Richard Nadeau. 1996. "Measuring Strategic Voting: A Two-Step Procedure." *Electoral Studies* 15:39–52.

Blais, André, and Kim Thalheimer. 1997. "Understanding Reasons for Voting." Montreal: Typescript in author's files.

Blais, André, and Robert Young. 1996. "Why Do People Vote? An Experiment in Rationality." Political Economy Research Group, University of Western Ontario.

———. 1999. "Why Do People Vote? An Experiment in Rationality." *Public Choice* 99:39–55.

Blais, André, Robert Young, Christopher Fleury, and Miriam Lapp. 1995. "Do People Vote on the Basis of Minimax Regret?" *Political Research Quarterly* 48:827–36.

Blais, André, Robert Young, and Miriam Lapp. Forthcoming. "The Calculus of Voting: An Empirical Test." *European Journal of Political Research.*

Blaustein, Albert P., and Gisbert P. Flanz. 1971–95. *Constitutions of the Countries of the World.* Dobbs Ferry, N.Y.: Oceana Publications.

Bollen, Kenneth A. 1993. "Liberal Democracy: Validity and Source Biases in Cross-National Measures." *American Journal of Political Science* 37:1207–30.

Booth, William James, Patrick James, and Hudson Meadwell, eds. 1993. *Politics and Rationality.* Cambridge: Cambridge University Press.

Brady, Henry E., Sydney Verba, and Kay Lehman Schlozman. 1995. "Beyond SES: A Resource Model of Political Participation." *American Political Science Review* 89:271–95.

Brians, Craig Leonard. 1997. "Residential Mobility, Voter Registration, and Electoral Participation in Canada." *Political Research Quarterly* 50:215–27.

Brunk, Gregory G. 1980. "The Impact of Rational Participation Models on Voting Attitudes." *Public Choice* 35:549–64.

Burkhart, Ross E., and Michael Lewis-Beck. 1994. "Comparative Democracy: The Economic Development Thesis." *American Political Science Review* 88:903–10.

Butler, David, and Austin Ranney, eds. 1994. *Referendums Around the World: The Growing Use of Direct Democracy*. Washington, D.C.: AEI Press.

Butler, David, and Donald Stokes. 1969. *Political Change in Britain*. London: Macmillan.

Cain, Bruce E. 1978. "Strategic Voting in Britain." *American Journal of Political Science* 22:639–55.

Caldeira, Gregory A. and Samuel C. Patterson. 1982. "Contextual Influences on Participation in U.S. State Legislative Elections." *Legislative Studies Quarterly* 7:359–81.

Campbell, Angus, Philip E. Converse, Warren E. Miller, and Donald E. Stokes. 1960. *The American Voter*. New York: Wiley.

Capron, Henri, and Jean-Louis Kruseman. 1988. "Is Political Rivalry an Incentive to Vote?" *Public Choice* 56:31–43.

Cassel, Carol A. 1998. "Overreports of Voting and Theories of Turnout: The Nonvoting Voter Revisited." Paper presented at the annual meeting of the Midwest Political Science Association, Chicago.

Chapman, R. G., and K. S. Palda. 1983. "Electoral Turnout in Rational Voting and Consumption Perspectives." *Journal of Consumer Research* 9:337–46.

Clarke, Harold D., Jane Jenson, Lawrence LeDuc, and Jon H. Pammett. 1979. *Political Choice*. Toronto: McGraw-Hill Ryerson.

Clausen, Aage R. 1968. "Response Validity in Surveys." *Public Opinion Quarterly* 32:588–606.

Converse, Philip E. "Of Time and Partisan Stability." *Comparative Political Studies* 11:139–71.

Cox, Gary W. 1988. "Closeness and Turnout: A Methodological Note." *Journal of Politics* 50:768–75.

———. 1997. *Making Votes Count: Strategic Coordination in the World's Electoral Systems*. New York: Cambridge University Press.

Cox, Gary W., and Michael C. Munger. 1989. "Closeness, Expenditures, and Turnout in the 1988 U.S. House Elections." *American Political Science Review* 83:217–31.

Cox, Gary W., Frances M. Rosenbluth, and Michael F. Thies. 1995. "Closeness, Strategic Elites, and Turnout: Evidence from Japan." Typescript. University of California at La Jolla.

Crain, W. Mark, and T. H. Deaton. 1977. "A Note on Political Participation as Consumption Behavior." *Public Choice* 32:131–35.

Crain, W. Mark, Donald R. Leaven, and Lynn Abbott. 1987. "Voting and Not Voting at the Same Time." *Public Choice* 53:221–29.

Crewe, Ivor. 1981. "Electoral Participation." Pp. 216–63 in *Democracy at the Polls: A Comparative Study of Competitive National Elections,* edited by David Butler,

Howard R. Penniman, and Austin Ranney. Washington, D.C.: American Enterprise Institute.

Dahl, Robert, and Edward Tufte. 1973. *Size and Democracy*. Stanford, Calif.: Stanford University Press.

Dalton, Russell J., and Martin P. Wattenberg. 1993. "The Not So Simple Act of Voting." In *Political Science: The State of the Discipline II*, edited by Ada W. Finifter. Washington, D.C.: American Political Science Association.

Darvish, Tikva, and Jacob Rosenberg. 1988. "The Economic Model of Voter Participation: A Further Test." *Public Choice* 56:185–92.

Dawes, Robyn M., John M. Orbell, Randy T. Simmons, and Alphons J. C. Van de Kragt. 1986. "Organizing Groups for Collective Action." *American Political Science Review* 80:1171–85.

Dennis, Jack. 1970. "Support for the Institution of Elections by the Mass Public." *American Political Science Review* 64:819–35.

———. 1991. "Theories of Turnout: An Empirical Comparison of Alienationist and Rationalist Perspectives." In *Political Participation and American Democracy*, edited by William Crotty. New York: Greenwood Press.

Denver, David, and Gordon Hands. 1985. "Marginality and Turn-out in General Elections in the 1970s." *British Journal of Political Science* 15:381–98.

Dimitris, Panayote E. 1994. "The Greek Parliamentary Election of October 1993." *Electoral Studies* 13:235–39.

Diskin, Abraham. 1992. "The Israeli General Election of 1992." *Electoral Studies* 11:356–61.

Downs, Anthony. 1957. *An Economic Theory of Democracy*. New York: Harper and Row.

Eagles, Munroe. 1991. "La participation et l'abstentionisme aux élections fédérales canadiennes: une analyse écologique." Pp. 3–37 in *La participation électorale au Canada*, edited by Herman Bakvis. Toronto: Dundurn.

Eagles, Munroe, and Stephen Erfle. 1989. "Community Cohesion and Voter Turnout in English Parliamentary Constituencies—Research Note." *British Journal of Political Science* 19:115–25.

Eckel, Catherine C., and Philip J. Grossman. 1996. "Altruism in Anonymous Dictator Games." *Games and Economic Behavior* 16:181–91.

Eijk, Cees Van Der, and Erik Oppenhuis. 1990. "Turnout and Second-Order Effects in the European Elections of June 1989: Evidence from the Netherlands." *Acta Politica* 25:67–94.

Ferejohn, John A., and Morris P. Fiorina. 1974. "The Paradox of Not Voting: A Decision Theoretic Analysis." *American Political Science Review* 68:525–46.

———. 1975. "Closeness Counts Only in Horseshoes and Dancing." *American Political Science Review* 69:920–25.

Filer, John E., Lawrence W. Kenny, and Rebecca B. Morton. 1993. "Redistribution, Income and Voting." *American Journal of Political Science* 37:63–87.

Finkel, Steven E., Edward N. Muller, and Karl-Dieter Opp. 1989. "Personal Influence, Collective Rationality, and Mass Political Action." *American Political Science Review* 83:885–903.

Fireman, Bruce, and William A. Gamson. 1979. "Utilitarian Logic in the Resource Mobilization Perspective." Pp. 8–44 in *The Dynamics of Social Movements*, edited by Mayer N. Zald and John D. McCarthy. Cambridge: Winthrop.

Fisher, Stephen L. 1973. "The Wasted Vote Thesis: West German Evidence." *Comparative Politics* 7:293–99.

Fishkin, James S. 1982. *The Limits of Obligation*. New Haven: Yale University Press.

Forsythe, Robert, Joel L. Horowitz, N. E. Savin, and Martin Sefton. 1994. "Fairness Is Simple Bargaining Games." *Games and Economic Behavior* 6:347–69.

Foster, Caroll B. 1984. "The Performance of Rational Voter Models in Recent Presidential Elections." *American Political Science Review* 78:678–90.

Frank, Robert H. 1996. "What Price the Moral High Ground?" *Southern Economic Journal* 63:1–17.

Franklin, Mark N. 1996. "Electoral Participation." Pp. 216–35 in *Comparing Democracies: Elections and Voting in Global Perspective*, edited by Lawrence LeDuc, Richard G. Niemi, and Pippa Norris. Thousand Oaks, Calif.: Sage.

Frohlich, Norman, Joe A. Oppenheimer, Jeffrey Smith, and Oran R. Young. 1978. "A Test of Downsian Voter Rationality." *American Political Science Review* 72:178–97.

Gastil, Raymond D. 1979. *Freedom in the World: Political Rights and Civil Liberties*. New York: Freedom House.

Gelman, Andrew, Gary King, and John Boscardin. 1998. "Estimating the Probability of Events That Have Never Occurred: When Is Your Vote Decisive?" *Journal of the American Statistical Association* 441:1–9.

Gonzales, Luis E. 1991. *Political Structures and Democracy in Uruguay*. Notre Dame, Ind.: University of Notre Dame Press.

Granberg, Donald, and Soren Holmberg. 1992. "The Hawthorne Effect in Election Studies: The Impact of Survey Participation on Voting." *British Journal of Political Science* 22:240–48.

Gray, Virginia. 1976. "A Note on Competition and Turnout in the American States." *Journal of Politics* 38:153–58.

Green, Donald P., and Ian Shapiro. 1994. *Pathologies of Rational Choice Theory: A Critique of Applications in Political Science*. New Haven: Yale University Press.

Grofman, Bernard. 1993. "Is Turnout the Paradox that Ate Rational Choice Theory?" Pp. 93–103 in *Information, Participation, and Choice: An Economic Theory of Democracy in Perspective*, edited by Bernard Grofman. Ann Arbor: University of Michigan Press.

Grzybowski, Marian T. 1994. "Parliamentary Elections in Czech and Slovak Republics and in Poland, 1991–1993." Paper presented at the XVIth International Political Science Association World Congress, Berlin.

Guth, Werner, and Hannelore Weck-Hanneman. 1997. "Do People Care about Democracy? An Experiment Exploring the Value of Voting Rights." *Public Choice* 91:27–47.

Hansen, Stephen, Thomas R. Palfrey, and Howard Rosenthal. 1987. "The Downsian Model of Electoral Participation: Formal Theory and Empirical Analyses of the Constituency Effect." *Public Choice* 52:15–33.

Harsanyi, John C. 1969. "Rational Choice Models of Political Behavior vs Functionalist and Conformist Theories." *World Politics* 21:513–39.

Helliwell, John F. 1994. "Empirical Linkage between Democracy and Economic Growth." *British Journal of Political Science* 24:225–48.

Hirczy, Wolfgang. 1995. "Explaining Near-Universal Turnout: The Case of Malta." *European Journal of Political Research* 27:255–72.

Hoffman, Elisabeth, Kevin McCabe, Keith Schachat, and Vernon Smith. 1994. "Preferences, Property Rights, and Anonymity in Bargaining Games." *Games and Economic Behavior* 7:346–80.

Hoffmann-Martinot, Vincent. 1992. "La participation aux élections municipales dans les villes françaises." *Revue française de science politique* 42:3–35.

Hoffmann-Martinot, Vincent, Colin Rallings, and Michael Thrasher. 1996. "Comparing Local Electoral Turnout in Great Britain and France: More Similarities than Differences?" *European Journal of Political Research* 30:241–57.

Ito, Takatoshi. 1990. "Foreign Exchange Rate Expectations: Micro Survey Data." *American Economic Review* 80:434–50.

Jackman, Robert. 1987. "Political Institutions and Voter Turnout in the Industrial Democracies." *American Political Science Review* 81:405–23.

Jackman, Robert, and Ross A. Miller. 1995. "Voter Turnout in the Industrial Democracies During the 1980s." *Comparative Political Studies* 27:467–92.

Jackson, Robert A. 1996. "The Mobilization of Congressional Electorates." *Legislative Studies Quarterly* 21:425–45.

Jasso, Guillermina, and Karl-Dieter Opp. 1997. "Probing the Character of Norms: A Factorial Survey Analysis of the Norms of Political Action." *American Sociological Review* 62:947–64.

Johnston, Richard, André Blais, Henry E. Brady, and Jean Crête. 1992. *Letting the People Decide: Dynamics of a Canadian Election*. Montréal: McGill-Queen's University Press.

Johnston, Richard, André Blais, Henry E. Brady, Elisabeth Gidengil, and Neil Nevitte. 1996. "The 1993 Canadian Election: Realignment, Dealignment, or Something Else?" Paper presented at the annual meeting of the Canadian Political Science Association, San Francisco.

Jones, Mark P. 1995. "A Guide to the Electoral Systems of the Americas." *Electoral Studies* 14:5–21.

Juberias, Carlos Flores. 1994. "Electoral Systems in Eastern Europe: How Are They Changing? Why Are They Changing?" Paper presented at the XVIth International Political Science Association World Congress, Berlin.

Kahneman, Daniel, Paul Slovic, and Amos Tversky. 1982. *Judgment under Uncertainty: Heuristics and Uncertainty*. New York: Cambridge University Press.

Karnig, Albert K., and B. Oliver Walter. 1983. "Decline in Municipal Voter Turnout." *American Politics Quarterly* 11:491–505.

Kau, James B., and Paul H. Rubin. 1976. "The Electoral College and the Rational Vote." *Public Choice* 27:101–7.

Kenney, Patrick J., and Tom W. Rice. 1986. "The Effect of Contextual Forces on Turnout in Congressional Primaries." *Social Science Quarterly* 67:329–36.

———. 1989. "An Empirical Examination of the Minimax Hypothesis." *American Politics Quarterly* 17:153–62.

Kim, Jae-on, John R. Petrocik, and Stephen N. Enokson. 1975. "Voter Turnout among the American States: Systemic and Individual Components." *American Political Science Review* 69:107–23.

King, Gary, Robert O. Keohane, and Sidney Verba. 1994. *Designing Social Inquiry: Scientific Inference in Qualitative Research*. Princeton, N.J.: Princeton University Press.

Kirchgässner, Gebhard, and Jorg Schimmelpfennig. 1992. "Closeness Counts If It Matters for Electoral Victory: Some Empirical Results for the United Kingdom and the Federal Republic of Germany." *Public Choice* 73:283–99.

Knack, Stephen. 1994. "Does Rain Help the Republicans? Theory and Evidence on Turnout and the Vote." *Public Choice* 79:187–209.

―――. 1996. "Does 'Motor Voter' Work? Evidence from State-Level Data." *Journal of Politics* 57:796–811.

Laasko, Markku, and Rein Taagepera. 1979. "Effective Number of Parties: A Measure with Application to West Europe." *Comparative Political Studies* 12:3–27.

Lapp, Miriam. 1999. "Incorporating Groups Into Rational Choice Explanations of Turnout: An Empirical Test." *Public Choice* 98:171–85.

LeDuc, Lawrence, Harold Clarke, Jane Jenson, and Jon Pammett. 1974. "A National Sample Design." *Canadian Journal of Political Science* 7:701–8.

Ledyard, John O. 1984. "The Pure Theory of Large Two-Candidate Elections." *Public Choice* 44:7–41.

―――. 1995. "Public Goods: A Survey of Experimental Research." Pp. 111–94 in *The Handbook of Experimental Economics*, edited by John H. Kagel and Alvin E. Roth. Princeton, N.J.: Princeton University Press.

Lewis-Beck, Michael S., and Brad Lockerbie. 1989. "Economics, Voters, Protests: Western European Cases." *Comparative Political Studies* 22:155–77.

Lijphart, Arend. 1992. "Forms of Democracy: North-South and East-West Contrasts." In *Nord und Sund in Amerika: Gegensatze, Gemeinsamkeiten, Europaischer Hintergrund*, edited by Wolfgang Reinhard and Peter Waldmann. Freiburg: Rombach.

―――. 1997. "Unequal Participation: Democracy's Unresolved Dilemma." *American Political Science Review* 91:1–15.

Lipset, Seymour Martin. 1981. *Political Man: The Social Bases of Politics*. Baltimore: Johns Hopkins University Press.

Mackie, Thomas, and Richard Rose. 1982. *The International Almanac of Electoral History*. 2d ed. London: Macmillan.

―――. 1991. *International Almanac of Electoral History* 3d ed. London: Macmillan.

Marwell, Gerald, and Pamela Oliver. 1993. *The Critical Mass in Collective Action: A Micro-Social Theory*. Cambridge: Cambridge University Press.

Mathur, Hansraj. 1991. *Parliament in Mauritius*. Stanley and Rose-Hill: Editions de l'Océan Indien.

Matsusaka, John G., and Filid Palda. 1993. "The Downsian Voter Meets the Ecological Fallacy." *Public Choice* 77:855–78.

Milbrath, Lester W., and M. L. Goel. 1977. *Political Participation*. Chicago: Rand McNally.

Moon, Bruce E. 1991. *The Political Economy of Basic Human Needs*. Ithaca, N.Y.: Cornell University Press.

Morlan, Robert L. 1984. "Municipal vs. National Election Voter Turnout: Europe and the United States." *Political Science Quarterly* 99:457–70.

Morriss, Peter. 1993. "The South Korean National Assembly Elections 1992." *Representation* 31:60–62.

Morton, Rebecca B. 1991. "Groups in Rational Turnout Models." *American Journal of Political Science* 35:758–76.

Mosteller, Frederick. 1968. "Association and Estimation in Contingency Tables." *Journal of the American Statistical Association* 63:1–28.

Mozaffar, Shaheen. 1995. "The Political Origins and Consequences of Electoral Systems in Africa: A Preliminary Analysis." Paper presented at the Conference on Comparative Democratic Elections, Cambridge, Mass.

Mueller, Dennis C. 1989. *Public Choice II.* Cambridge: Cambridge University Press.

Muller, Edward N., and Karl-Dieter Opp. 1986. "Rational Choice and Rebellious Collective Action." *American Political Science Review* 80:471–89.

Nadeau, Richard, Pierre Martin, and André Blais. 1999. "Attitude Toward Risk Taking and Individual Choice in the Quebec Referendum on Sovereignty." *British Journal of Political Science* 29:523–40.

Nicholson, Stephen P., and Ross A. Miller. 1997. "Prior Beliefs and Voter Turnout in the 1986 and 1988 Congressional Elections." *Political Research Quarterly* 50:199–213.

Niemi, Richard G. 1976. "Costs of Voting and Nonvoting." *Public Choice* 27:115–19.

Niemi, Richard G., Guy Whitten, and Mark N. Franklin. 1992. "Constituency Characteristics, Individual Characteristics, and Tactical Voting in the 1987 British General Election." *British Journal of Political Science* 22:229–54.

Nohlen, Dieter. 1993. *Enciclopedia Electoral Latino-americana y del Caribe.* San José: Instituto Interamericano de Derechos Humanos.

Olson, Mancur. 1965. *The Logic of Collective Action.* Cambridge: Harvard University Press.

Opp, Karl-Dieter. 1986. "Soft Incentives and Collective Action. Participation in the Anti-Nuclear Movement." *British Journal of Political Science* 16:87–112.

———. 1989. *The Rationality of Political Protest: A Comparative Analysis of Rational Choice Theory.* Boulder, Colo.: Westview Press.

Opp, Karl-Dieter, Peter Voss, and Christiane Gern. 1995. *The Origins of a Spontaneous Revolution. East Germany 1989.* Ann Arbor: University of Michigan Press.

Overbye, Einar. 1995. "Making a Case for the Rational Self-Regarding, 'Ethical' Voter . . . and Solving the 'Paradox of Not Voting' in the Process." *European Journal of Political Research* 27:369–96.

Palfrey, Thomas R., and Howard Rosenthal. 1983. "A Strategic Calculus of Voting. " *Public Choice* 41:7–53.

———. 1985. "Voter Participation and Strategic Uncertainty." *American Political Science Review* 79:62–78.

Patterson, Samuel C., and Gregory A. Caldeira. 1983. "Getting Out the Vote: Participation in Gubernatorial Elections." *American Political Science Review* 77:675–89.

Peters, Emory. 1998. "The Rational Voter Paradox Revisited." *Public Choice* 97:179–95.

Powell, G. Bingham. 1980. "Voting Turnout in Thirty Democracies." Pp. 5–34 in *Electoral Participation,* edited by Richard Rose. Beverly Hills, Calif.: Sage.

———. 1982. *Contemporary Democracies: Participation, Stability and Violence.* Cambridge: Harvard University Press.

———. 1986. "American Voter Turnout in Comparative Perspective." *American Political Science Review* 80:17–45.

Quattrone, George A., and Amos Tversky. 1988. "Contrasting Rational and Psychological Analyses of Political Choice." *American Political Science Review* 82:719–37.

Quid? Tout pour toi. 1995. Paris: Editions Robert Laffont.

Radcliff, Benjamin. 1992. "The Welfare State, Turnout, and the Economy: A Comparative Analysis." *American Political Science Review* 86:444–54.

Rallings, Colin, and Michael Thrasher. 1990. "Turnout in English Local Elections: An Aggregate Analysis with Electoral and Contextual Data." *Electoral Studies* 9:79–90.

———. 1993. *Local Elections in Britain: A Statistical Digest*. Plymouth, England: Local Government Chronicle Elections Centre.

Richardson, Bradley M. 1973. "Urbanization and Political Participation: The Case of Japan." *American Political Science Review* 67:433–52.

Riker, William H., and Peter C. Ordeshook. 1968. "A Theory of the Calculus of Voting." *American Political Science Review* 62:25–43.

Rose, Richard, and Harre Mossawir. 1967. "Voting and Elections: A Functional Analysis." *Political Studies* 15:173–201.

Rosenstone, Steven J. 1982. "Economic Adversity and Voter Turnout." *American Journal of Political Science* 26:25–46.

Rosenstone, Steven J., and John Mark Hansen. 1993. *Mobilization, Participation, and Democracy in America*. New York: Macmillan.

Rosenthal, Howard, and Subrata Sen. 1973. "Electoral Participation in the French Fith Republic." *American Political Science Review* 67:29–55.

Sarlvik, Bo, and Ivor Crewe. 1983. *Decade of Dealignment*. Toronto: Methuen.

Schlozman, Kay, Sydney Verba, and Henry E. Brady. 1995. "Participation's Not a Paradox: The Views of American Activists." *British Journal of Political Science* 25:1–36.

Schmitt, Hermann, and Renato Mannheimer. 1991. "About Voting and Non-Voting in the European Elections of 1989." *European Journal of Political Research* 19:31–54.

Scholz, John T., and Mark Lubell. 1998. "Trust and Taxpaying: Testing the Heuristic Approach to Collective Action." *American Journal of Political Science* 42:398–417.

Scholz, John T., and Neil Pinney. 1995. "Duty, Fear and Tax Compliance: The Heuristic Basis of Citizenship Behavior." *American Journal of Political Science* 39:490–512.

Schwartz, Thomas. 1986. *The Logic of Collective Choice*. New York: Columbia University Press.

Seidle, Leslie, and David Miller. 1976. "Turnout, Rational Abstention, and Campaign Effort." *Public Choice* 27:121–26.

Settle, Russell F., and Burton A. Abrams. 1976. "The Determinants of Voter Participation: A More General Model." *Public Choice* 27:81–89.

Sigelman, Lee, Philip W. Roeder, Malcolm E. Jewell, and Michael A. Baer. 1985. "Voting and Nonvoting: A Multi-Election Perspective." *American Journal of Political Science* 29:749–65.

Silberman, Jonathan, and Garey Durden. 1975. "The Rational Theory of Voter Participation: The Evidence from Congressional Elections." *Public Choice* 23:101–8.

Silver, Morris. 1973. "A Demand Analysis of Voting Costs and Voting Participation." *Social Science Research* 2:111–24.

Simon, Herbert A. 1955. "A Behavioral Model of Rational Choice." *Quarterly Journal of Economics* 69:99–118.

Simon, Janos. 1995. "Electoral Systems and Democracy: Comparative Electoral Systems in Central Europe during the Transition." Paper presented at the Conference on Comparative Democratic Elections, Cambridge, Mass.

Sisk, Timothy D. 1994. "Electoral System Choice in South Africa: Implications for Intergroup Moderation." Paper presented at the XVIth International Political Science Association World Congress, Berlin.

Soltész, Erzsébet. 1994. "Democracies in Eastern Europe: Hungary, Poland and Slovakia." Paper presented at the XVIth International Political Science Association World Congress, Berlin.

Stoetzel, Jean. 1955. "Voting Behavior in France." *British Journal of Sociology* 6:104–22.

Stoker, Laura, and M. Kent Jennings. 1995. "Life-Cycle Transitions and Political Participation: The Case of Marriage." *American Political Science Review* 89:421–36.

Strate, John M., Charles J. Parrish, Charles D. Elder, and Coit Ford III. 1989. "Life Span Civic Development and Voting Participation." *American Political Science Review* 83:443–65.

Szalai, Alexander. 1972. *The Use of Time: Daily Activities of Urban and Surburban Populations in Twelve Countries.* La Haye, Netherlands: Mouton.

Thalheimer, Kim. 1995. "The Impact of the Probability Factor on the Decision to Vote." Montreal: Typescript in author's files.

Tollison, Robert, Mark Crain, and Paul Pautler. 1975. "Information and Voting: An Empirical Note." *Public Choice* 24:43–49.

Traugott, Michael W., and John P. Katosh. 1979. "Response Validity in Surveys of Voting Behavior." *Public Opinion Quarterly* 43:359–77.

Tsebelis, George. 1990. *Nested Games: Rational Choice in Comparative Politics.* Berkeley: University of California Press.

Tucker, Harvey J. 1986. "Contextual Models of Participation in U.S. State Legislative Elections." *Western Political Quarterly* 39:67–78.

Udehn, Lars. 1993. "Twenty-five Years with the Logic of Collective Action." *Acta Sociologica* 36:239–61.

Uhlaner, Carole J. 1986. "Political Participation, Rational Actors, and Rationality: A New Approach." *Political Psychology* 7:551–73.

———. 1989a. "Rational Turnout: The Neglected Role of Groups." *American Journal of Political Science* 33:390–422.

———. 1989b. "'Relational Goods' and Participation: Incorporating Sociability into a Theory of Rational Action." *Public Choice* 62:253–85.

———. 1993. "What the Downsian Voter Weighs: A Reassessment of the Costs and Benefits of Action." Pp. 67–79 in *Information, Participation, and Choice: An Economic Theory of Democracy in Perspective,* edited by Bernard Grofman. Ann Arbor: University of Michigan Press.

Uhlaner, Carole Jean, and Bernard Grofman. 1986. "The Race May Be Close but My Horse Is Going to Win: Wish Fulfilment in the 1980 Presidential Election." *Political Behavior* 8:101–28.

Verba, Sidney and Norman H. Nie. 1972. *Participation in America: Political Democracy and Social Equality.* New York: Harper and Row.

Verba, Sidney, Norman H. Nie, and Jae-on Kim. 1978. *Participation and Political Equality: A Seven Nation Comparison.* Cambridge: Cambridge University Press.

Verba, Sidney, Kay Lehman Schlozman, and Henry Brady. 1995. *Voice and Equality: Civic Voluntarism in American Politics.* Cambridge: Harvard University Press.

Verba, Sidney, Kay Lehman Schlozman, Henry Brady, and Norman H. Nie. 1993. "Race, Ethnicity and Political Resources: Participation in the United States." *British Journal of Political Science* 23:453–97.

————. 1993 "Citizen Activity: Who Participates? What Do They Say?" *American Political Science Review* 87:303–18.

Whiteley, Paul F. 1995. "Rational Choice and Political Participation: Evaluating the Debate." *Political Research Quarterly* 48:211–33.

Whiteley, Paul F., Patrick Seyd, Jeremy Richardson, and Paul Bissell. 1994. "Explaining Party Activism: The Case of the British Conservative Party." *British Journal of Political Science* 24:79–94.

Wolfinger, Raymond E. 1994. "The Rational Citizen Faces Election Day or What Rational Choice Theorists Don't Tell You about American Elections." Pp. 71–89 in *Elections at Home and Abroad,* edited by M. Kent Jennings and Thomas E. Mann. Ann Arbor: University of Michigan Press.

Wolfinger, Raymond E., and Steven J. Rosenstone. 1980. *Who Votes?* New Haven: Yale University Press.

INDEX

Abrams, Burton A., 33
absentee voting, 44
abstaining, 11, 45, 47, 116
African-Americans, 9, 141
age, 144; sense of duty and, 97; and
    voter turnout, 26, 27, 36, 49–50, 51,
    52
Aldrich, John H., 7, 9, 45, 61, 62, 79
alienationist school, 141
Allais, Maurice, 138
Almond, Gabriel A., 37
altruism, 123–24, 127
American Voter, The (Campbell et al.), 140
Andreoni, James, 122–23, 126, 135
antinuclear movement studies, 128–29,
    131
arbitrary domain restriction, 9, 141–42
Arcelus, Francisco J., 33
Australia, 52
Austria, 40, 137

Baer, Michael A., 46
Barry, Brian, 3, 9, 16, 116, 117; on voting
    costs, 84, 89–90
benefits *(B)*, expected, 135, 143;
    collective action and, 117; consump-
    tion, 4, 7–8; *vs.* costs, 2, 7, 8, 9;
    rational choice model and, 1, 2, 3, 4,
    10, 138; resources model and, 12;
    turnout and, 43
benevolence, 123–24. *See also* fairness
Black, Jerome, 21, 23, 30
Blais, André, 20–21; and Thalheimer
    study, 169–71; on turnout, 20–21, 24,
    30, 32; and Young study, 68, 71
Brady, Henry E., 12, 24, 176n10
Britain. *See* Great Britain
British Columbia election (1996), 76–77,
    81, 104; cost of voting in, 85, 86, 88–
    89; decisive vote probability in, 69–

70, 71; questionnaire following, 166–
    68; sense of duty in, 95–96, 102;
    voting determinants in, 100, 102–03
byproduct theory, 117

C. See costs *(C)* of voting
calculus of voting model, 1, 2. *See also*
    rational choice model
Campbell, Angus, 140
Canadian elections: 1988, 46, 47, 78;
    1993, 48, 63–65, 72, 85, 88, 95–96. *See
    also* British Columbia election
Carty, Kenneth, 20–21, 24, 30, 32
Census Bureau (US), 49
Charlottetown Accord, 86
Civic Culture, The (Almond and Verba),
    37
civic duty. *See* duty
civil liberties, 22. *See also* democratic
    rating
closeness, of elections, 2, 177n2; and
    decisive voting, 58, 59–62, 66, 69; and
    turnout, 35, 43, 61–62, 74, 75, 77–78
coalition government, 30
collective action, 116–18, 128, 130
collective action and, 117; consump-
community: and duty, 111; social
    pressure and, 14; and turnout, 24, 26,
    52
Comparative Study of Electoral Systems
    (CSES) survey, 51, 159
competitiveness, 30
compulsory voting, 18, 19, 21, 26
congressional elections, 58–60
constancy, of voters, 45, 48
consumption benefits, 4, 7–8
Converse, Philip E., 140
costs *(C)* of voting, 15, 83–91, 134, 143,
    182n12; in alternative models, 12, 13;
    vs. benefits, 2, 7, 8, 9; in Canada, 84–
    86, 88–89; and cognitive dissonance,

195

DATE DUE

Printed
in USA